TIGERS OF THE DEATH'S HEAD

SS TOTENKOPF DIVISION'S TIGER COMPANY

IAN MICHAEL WOOD

STACKPOLE
BOOKS

Published by
STACKPOLE BOOKS
5067 Ritter Road
Mechanicsburg, PA 17055
www.stackpolebooks.com

Printed in the United States of America

10 9 8 7 6 5 4 3 2 1

Library of Congress Cataloging-in-Publication Data

Wood, Ian Michael.
Tigers of the death's head : SS Totenkopf Division's Tiger Company / Ian Michael Wood.
pages cm.
Includes bibliographical references.
ISBN 978-0-8117-1313-9
1. Waffen-SS. Panzer-Division Totenkopf, 3. Panzer Kompanie, 4 (s). 2. World War, 1939–1945—Regimental histories—Germany. 3. World War, 1939–1945—Tank warfare. 4. Tiger (Tank)—History. 5. World War, 1939–1945—Campaigns—Eastern Front. I. Title.
D757.85.W58 2013
940.54'1343—dc23

2013033742

CONTENTS

INTRODUCTION

SS-Panzer-Regiment 3's 9. Kompanie had an operational life of just over two years, fighting mainly on the Eastern Front and ending World War II in Perg, Austria, on 8 May 1945. The company's personnel then spent a number of years in American or Russian confinement; only a handful managed to escape and make it home.

During the 1950s the Russians started releasing captured German military personnel and allowed them to return home. In 1959 the first veterans meeting took place, and former *9. Kompanie* soldiers spent many hours recounting their experiences. It was from this first meeting that Wolfgang Barth gathered and recorded individual reports and learned the fate of other company members. Barth permitted me to use this huge collection of records as the basis for this book. Other veterans gave me their time for interviews or questionnaires, allowing me to assemble a more coherent picture of the events during March–April 1945. Between 2010 and 2013 I visited the battlegrounds in Poland, Hungary, and Austria, where I found many old people who still remembered their own wartime experiences.

Many of the photographs in this book will already be known to the reader, but there are new ones which have never been published before, along with new details on the former soldiers and officers of *9. Kompanie*. These provide insight into the operational and working life of the unit during World War II. This book is my contribution to the ever-growing field of knowledge of the *Panzerwaffe* from World War II and is meant for novice and aficionado alike. Any mistakes are mine alone.

CHAPTER 1

In the Beginning

The *SS-Totenkopf-Division* was the first *Waffen-SS* division to have tanks in its inventory. In November 1939, *SS-Aufklärungs-Abteilung Totenkopf*, the division's reconnaissance detachment, did not possess a *Panzerspähwagen* (armored car reconnaissance) company, and like the rest of the *Totenkopf*, it was deficient in heavy equipment. *SS-Gruppenführer* Theodor Eicke, the division's commander, used all of his contacts across Germany to try to find any depots that had surplus equipment he could use for his division. In November 1939, he was informed that the Skoda Works in Pilsen (considered property of the *Wehrmacht* during this period) had a surplus of heavy artillery guns, prime movers, and tanks. Eicke had for some time been trying to get authorization to form a *schwere Artillerie-Abteilung* (heavy artillery detachment) for *SS-Artillerie-Regiment Totenkopf*, and when he did manage to get authorization, the *Wehrmacht* refused to supply the much-needed heavy guns. Eicke did manage to get his hands on some of the Skoda tanks.

On 20 November 1939, the divisional command issued an order creating a *Panzerkraftwagen Zug* (armored vehicle platoon) for *SS-Aufklärungs-Abteilung Totenkopf* under the leadership of *SS-Obersturmführer* Hardieck, who commanded the *Kradschützen* (motorcycle) company. Initially, the platoon was to contain three *Pz.Kpfw. 35(t)* or *38(t)* in order to fill in the gap that resulted from the shortage of *Panzerspähwagen*. On the twenty-second, *SS-Obersturmführer* Hardieck took command of the new formation. The crews were provided by *SS-Infanterie-Regiment 2*. The *Panzerkraftwagen* platoon was under the leadership of *SS-Oberscharführer* Werkmeister (who would later serve in the *Panzer* regiment). The personnel drove to Pilsen on the twenty-seventh, returned to Germany during mid-December 1939, and were quartered at Burgholz. On 20 December, second and third platoons were added and organized into three sections consisting of two *Panzers* each, giving a total strength of six *Panzers*. The second section was commanded by *SS-Untersturmführer* Zimmermann, the third by *SS-Untersturmführer* Rohde.

The *Panzerkraftwagen* platoon spent the winter of 1939–40 based in Heilbronn. It first saw action on 21 May 1940 during the campaign in France, near Marcatel, while supporting *SS-Infanterie-Regiment 3*. The six *Panzers* had the following call signs: *Löwe*, *Tiger*, *Panther*, *Geier*, *Sperber*, and *Habicht*. During the fighting, the *Panzerkraftwagen* platoon knocked out three British tanks, but the *Panzer* of *SS-Oberscharführer* Werkmeister was knocked out near Arras, along with *Sperber* and *Habicht*. The platoon suffered four wounded: *SS-Rottenführer* Lamp, *SS-Sturmmann* Unger, *SS-Rottenführer* Theissig, and *SS-Rottenführer* Koppl. In fact, during the course of the day, the platoon suffered five total losses in *Panzers*, with only one *Pz.Kpfw. 10(t)* remaining on strength.

On 23 May 1940, the platoon took over six French tanks (three Hotchkiss H38's and three Souma S35's), which had been captured in Choques by *SS-Infanterie-Regiment 3*. At this time, the three section commanders were *SS-Untersturmführer* Zimmermann, *SS-Scharführer* Spuhler, and *SS-Unterscharführer* Mark. On the twenty-seventh, the platoon, with seven *Panzers*, advanced along the Hinges–Le Cornet Malo road at 0300 hours and provided support to *SS-Infanterie-Regiment 3* during the assault on the La-Basse Canal. The remaining *Pz.Kpfw. 10(t)* was knocked out in Le Cornet Malo. The day's fighting resulted in three killed and four badly wounded, including the platoon commander, *SS-Obersturmführer* Hardieck. The wounded were evacuated along with the wounded infantrymen. On the twenty-ninth, the platoon lost five of its French tanks in the area of Estaines, with only one Hotchkiss H38 tank surviving. This tank remained in service with the *Totenkopf* up to July 1943. The establishment of a *Panzerspähkompanie* was ordered on 3 May 1941, with the issue of eight *Panzerspähwagen*.

SS-Sturmgeschütze-Batterie Totenkopf

The battery was formed on 1 June 1941. Gun commanders, gunners, loaders, and radio operators were all sent from the *SS-Artillerie-Ausbildungs-und-Ersatz-Regiment* (artillery replacement regiment) in Munich to Berlin and quartered at the Lichterfelde Barracks. Here *SS-Hauptsturmführer* Toni Laackmann assumed command of the new *Sturmgeschütze Batterie*. Prior to taking command of the battery, Laackmann had been *11. Kompanie* commander in *SS-Infanterie-Regiment 3*. The platoon leaders were *SS-Obersturmführer* Richter, *SS-Untersturmführer* Altermiller, and *SS-Untersturmführer* Weber. In July 1941, the battery was moved from Berlin to Troop Training Grounds Juterbog-Luckenwalde for continuation training on older-type assault guns.

Training started during the third week of July and ended toward the end of August 1941, when the battery received seven *StuG III* assault guns. The battery was loaded on 21 August 1941 in the town of Luckenwalde, arrived in Russia on the twenty-fifth, unloaded in Dno, and was incorporated into *SS-Artillerie-Regiment Totenkopf*. On the twenty-sixth, the 1st Platoon was attached to *SS-Infanterie-Regiment 1*, and the 2nd Platoon was assigned to *SS-Infanterie-Regiment 3*. The 3rd Platoon remained at the disposal of the divisional command. The battery would see extensive service, and after the last *Sturmgeschütze* had been lost, the battery's personnel fought on as infantry. In August 1942, the battery utilized two captured Russian T-34 tanks until withdrawn from the Eastern Front and returned to France in October 1942. The remaining thirty-six personnel would be integrated with the newly formed *Panzer* regiment and *Sturmgeschütze* detachment. Upon arrival, the personnel in France were quartered at the Chateau de Nof.

Battery Commanders

SS-Hauptsturmführer Laackmann, 1 June–17 October 1941
SS-Obersturmführer Meierdress, 17 October 1941–21 February 1942
SS-Obersturmführer Richter, 21 February–22 October 1942

Sturmgeschütze Losses

8 January 1942—1 *StuG* hit; vehicle was a complete burnt-out wreck
8 February 1942—1 *StuG* abandoned after the engine caught fire
7 March 1942—1 *StuG* blown up by the crew
17 March 1942—4 *StuG's* lost during the fighting around Biakowo

CHAPTER 2

Formation of the Tank Battalion and the *Tiger* Company

SS-Panzer-Regiment 3

On 8 March 1942, the German leadership ordered the establishment of a *Panzer-Abteilung* (tank battalion) for the *Totenkopf* Division. The order was back-dated to 5 March 1942 on an order calling for the establishment of a separate *Panzer-Abteilung* for the *Das Reich* Division. The *Panzer-Abteilung* for the *Totenkopf* was to be organized with a *Stab.u.Stabs Kompanie* (headquarters company), two *leichte Panzer-Kompanien* (light tank companies), one *mittle Panzer-Kompanie* (medium tank company), *Panzer WerkStatt Zug*, and a *leichte Kolonne*. The new *Abteilung* was commanded by *SS-Sturmbannführer* Leiner (Theodor Eicke's son-in-law) and was designated *SS-Panzer-Abteilung III*.

On 1 June 1942, the first recruits reported to the Weimar-Buchenwald Barracks. Other personnel came from the *Polizei* Division and the *SS-Panzer-Jäger-Ersatz-Abteilung*, based in Hilversum. *Panzer* crew training was conducted at the German Army *Panzer Truppen Schule* at Putlos; *Panzer* and vehicle mechanics were to be trained at *Panzer Truppen Wunsdorf*; signals and radio operators were trained in Nuremberg. The first training vehicles were civilian cars and trucks with applied wooden boarding resembling mock *Panzers*; later, some additional captured Allied tanks were provided, supplied from captured stock from the 1940 campaign in France. On 24 June 1942, at Troop Training Grounds Debica, 156 new recruits arrived. *SS-Panzer Abteilung III* was formally placed under *Insp. 6 (Panzer)* of the *SS-FHA* (ordnance supply office).

The crews undergoing training in Putlos were under the command of *SS-Obersturmbannführer* Kanth. The first training sessions involved theory in gunnery and target practice. On 30 August 1942, *SS-Panzer Abteilung III* was transported from Weimar Buchenwald to Suippe via Mailly-le-Camp, near Chalon in France. On 22 September 1942, it was decided that all *SS-Panzer-Abteilungen* should be expanded to *Panzer-Regimenter*; this meant that the *Leibstandarte*, *Das Reich*, and *Totenkopf* would receive *Panzer* regiments of two *Abteilungen* each. The *Totenkopf* Division's leadership had already formed cadres for the new second *Abteilung* as early as July 1942, forming the *Stabs Kompanie* (headquarters company) and *5.* and *6. Kompanie*.

SS-Panzer Abteilung III's first tank delivery occurred on 24 September 1942 when one *Befehlswagen Panzer III*, eleven *Panzer III's* with 5cm gun, three *Panzer III's* with 7.5cm short gun (used to equip the 3rd Platoon), and three *Panzer IV's* arrived. *1. Kompanie* received the *Panzer III's*, and the *Panzer IV's* were used to equip the *II. Zug* of *3. Kompanie*. At the end of September, the *Abteilung* was ordered to be ready for a move to Angouleme. On 12 October 1942, *SS-Panzer-Abteilung III* officially became *SS-I/SS-Panzer-Regiment 3*, and *SS-Sturmbannführer* Leiner became the first commander of the newly formed *Panzer* regiment. *SS-Hauptsturmführer* Meierdress (Knight's Cross holder) assumed command of the *I/SS-Panzer Regiment 3*, formally *SS-Panzer-Abteilung III*. On 14 October 1942, *I/SS-Panzer-Regiment 3* had the following leadership posts:

Commander: *SS-Hauptsturmführer* Meierdress
Adjutant: *SS-Obersturmbannführer* Altermuller
Pz.Aufklär.Zug (armored reconnaissance platoon): *SS-Untersturmführer* Quade
1. Kompanie: *SS-Obersturmbannführer* Mooslechner
2. Kompanie: *SS-Obersturmbannführer* Kanth
3. Kompanie: *SS-Hauptsturmführer* Gross

The *II/SS-Panzer-Regiment 3* was commanded by *SS-Hauptsturmführer* Kunstmann. The company commanders were as follows:

Adjutant: *SS-Untersturmführer* Molleken
Pz.Aufklär.Zug: *SS-Untersturmführer* Kohler
5. Kompanie: *SS-Obersturmbannführer* Riefkogel
6. Kompanie: *SS-Obersturmbannführer* Wenke
7. Kompanie: *SS-Hauptsturmführer* Richter

The *Panzer WerkStatt Kompanie* was commanded by *SS-Obersturmbannführer* Theile. The pioneer company was commanded by *SS-Obersturmbannführer* Kinzler, who assumed the post on 25 January 1943.

On 7 November 1942, *1. Kompanie/SS-Panzer-Regiment 3* was attached to *Kampfgruppe B* (formed around *SS-Regiment Thule*). The *Totenkopf* Division had been tasked with forming three *Kampfgruppen* for *Case Anton*, the occupation of Vichy France. The *Totenkopf* had also formed *Kampfgruppen A* and *C*. *1. Kompanie/SS-Panzer-Regiment 3* was led by *SS-Hauptsturmführer* Mooslechner, and *SS-Sturmbannführer* Leiner used *Befehlswagen Kibitz*. The *Panzer Kompanie* moved from Angouleme to Limoges, along with *II/SS-Regiment Thule*. During the march, three *Panzers III's* fell out due to mechanical trouble.

On 10 November 1942, the *Panzer* company moved through Tulle and Brive. During the march, another *Panzer III* fell out due to engine trouble. Over the next three days, further road marches were conducted, and Aurilac was reached on 12 November. During the night of 17 November, the *Panzer Kompanie* was put on alert in readiness for rail transport to Narbonne. The company moved at 2000 hours and arrived on the nineteenth in Narbonne. It conducted a road march of eighty kilometers to Rivesaltes, which lasted about six hours.

On 22 November, the *Panzer Kompanie* was located in Carcassonne, where the *Kompanie* spent three days until the twenty-fifth, when a return march to Rivesaltes was conducted. The town was reached on the twenty-sixth. The *Panzer Kompanie* remained in southern France until 9 December before entraining in Narbonne back to Angouleme.

At the end of November, a new delivery of *Panzers* arrived in Angouleme, with thirty-nine *Panzer III's* and seven *Panzer IV's* for *3. Kompanie*. The *Panzer III's* were used to equip *2., 5.,* and *6. Kompanien*. *6. Kompanie* would receive its full issue of *Panzer III's* on 1 February 1943. On 12 January, *7. Kompanie* collected ten *Panzer IV's* at *HZA Burg*, Magdeburg, and on the same day, the final delivery of twenty-six *Panzer III's* completed the equipping of *SS-Panzer-Regiment 3*. While the *Panzer-Regiment* was still in Russia, a new *4. Kompanie* and *8. Kompanie* were created on 15 February in Angouleme for pending organizational changes which occurred in May. The following field post numbers were issued: *8. Kompanie*—58505; *4. Kompanie*—57182. On 6 April 1943, nine *Panzer IV Ausf. F*, with a 7.5cm L/24 gun, were issued to *SS-Panzer-Regiment 3*.

SS-Sturmgeschütze-Abteilung 3 was issued twenty-two *StuG III's* on 20 January 1943, and *SS-Panzer-Jäger-Abteilung 3* was issued nine *schwere PaK.Sfl* guns (self-propelled antitank guns) on 18 January 1943.

4(s) Panzer Kompanie Tiger

On 13 November 1942, the *SS-FHA* (SS main operational department) order *Tgb.Nr. 7288/42* called for the establishment of a heavy (*schwere*) *Panzer* company for *SS-Panzer-Regiment 3* based on the *Kstn 1176d*, dated 15 August 1942. The new company was to be formed at Troop Training Grounds Bergen at Fallingbostal. The company was to have establishment strength of nine *Tigers* and ten *Panzer III's*, with support units, a *WerkStatt Zug*, *Instand-Staffel*, and a *Berge-Zug* (tank recovery platoon). On 15 November 1942, *SS-Obersturmbannführer* Kanth was informed that he would assume command of the new company. *SS-Panzer-Regiment 3* ordered that the *Panzer* companies were to release men for the initial cadre. The order was obeyed, but the various companies within the regiment kept their best men behind and released surplus soldiers. The initial training on the *Tiger* was to be carried out under the supervision of the army's *schwere Panzer-Abteilung 502*. The new cadre arrived in Fallingbostal on 26 December 1942 and was designated *4(s) Panzer Kompanie* and issued field post number 48786. On 1 January 1943, ten *Panzer III's* were delivered for the company at Fallingbostal. The first field exercise began on 2 January 1943.

✠

At the end of December 1942, the tank regiment instructed both battalions that the crews from both of the armored reconnaissance platoons were to be released for the *Tiger* company as well. *SS-Untersturmführer* Quade and his crews from *I/SS-Panzer-Regiment 3* left Angouleme on 8 January 1943 by train and arrived at Fallingbostal on the ninth. The armored reconnaissance platoon of *II/SS-Panzer-Regiment 3* left Angouleme on 21 January 1943 under the command of *SS-Untersturmführer* Kohler. Upon arrival the crews from *II/SS-Panzer-Regiment 3* had to undergo a fourteen-day conversion course on the *Tiger* alongside crews from *Panzer-Regiment Großdeutschland*. Previously, they had spent four weeks training on the *Panzer III*.

SS-Untersturmführer Greisinger assumed command of the *WerkStatt Zug*. The company's support units were under the supervision of the company's *Spieß*, Bauer. The field kitchen section was led by *SS-Unterscharführer* Loibold. The tank recovery platoon was under the command of *SS-Unterscharführer* Biermann, who led it until August 1943, when *SS-Oberscharführer* Baumann took over; the weapons section was under the command of *SS-Hauptscharführer* Drabbing. The *Instand-Staffel* (maintenance) was led by *SS-Hauptscharführer* Haderer. On hand was *SS-Oberscharführer* Karl Frank, an engine specialist from Maybach. The *Kompanie Trupp Führer* was *SS-Unterscharführer* Holzner.

The other platoon leaders included *SS-Untersturmführer* Rathsack, who commanded the 3rd Platoon. *SS-Untersturmführer* Rathsack had been assigned to *4(s) Kompanie* as of 23 November, but didn't join the company until after 13 December upon completing a course at *Panzer Truppen Schule Wunsdorf. SS-Untersturmführer* Rathsack had previously served with *SS-Panzer-Abteilung 2 Das Reich* in the *3.Kompanie* as a platoon leader with the rank of *SS-Oberscharführer. SS-Untersturmführer* Rathsack had attended the *SS-Junker Schule Braunschweig* (officer school) from 1 November 1941 to 30 April 1942; he was commissioned on 21 June 1942.

The 1st Platoon was commanded by *SS-Obersturmbannführer* Rinner. The 2nd Platoon was commanded by *SS-Untersturmführer* Quade, the 4th by *SS-Oberscharführer* Berger. The Half (*Halb*) Platoon was led by *SS-Scharführer* Otto Baumann, who would later serve in the *Tiger* company of *SS-Panzer-Regiment 2* and in *schwere-SS-Panzer-Abteilung 102/502* as leader of the Half Platoon in *1. Kompanie*.

On 30 January 1943, the *WerkStatt* platoons for *SS-Panzer-Regiment 1* and *SS-Panzer-Regiment 2* left Fallingbostal for Russia. On the same day, the collection commando was sent to collect nine new *Tigers*, departing from Fallingbostal by rail. The original transportation date for the *WerkStatt* platoon was ordered for 1 February 1943. Upon arrival, it was found that the new *Tigers* still had technical problems. The collection commando returned to Fallingbostal on the seventh.

On 18 February 1943, *4(s) Panzer Kompanie* was organized as follows:

Kompanie Trupp—one *Tiger*, two *Panzer III's*, one VW, and a single motorcycle
1st Platoon—two *Tigers* and two *Panzer III's*
2nd Platoon—two *Tigers* and two *Panzer III's*
3rd Platoon—two *Tigers* and two *Panzer III's*
4th Platoon—two *Tigers* and two *Panzer III's*

Support units
Nachschub (supply) Platoon—fifteen vehicles, including Opel and Mercedes trucks
Field kitchen *Staffel*—three vehicles and kitchens, two ration wagons, one motorcycle with side car
Munitions and weapons *Staffel*—four vehicles and two trailers
Instand-Staffel (maintenance)—seven trucks

WerkStatt Platoon
1. Staffel—six *18t Zgkw** (*Berge-Zug*)
2. Staffel—one *18t Zgkw* with crane, one truck with crane, one Bussing 105, and two trucks
3. Staffel—eleven vehicles
4. Staffel—one VW and one truck (carried out repairs on the company's vehicles)

The manpower strength was 250 officers, NCOs, and other ranks.

On 10 February 1943, *4(s) Panzer Kompanie* was loaded onto four rail transports in Fallingbostal. The transports travelled via Breslau into Kowel, where, on 14 February, the *Tigers* underwent a track change from transport tracks to combat tracks. The first transport arrived in Poltawa on the sixteenth; two other transports, including one transport carrying the *WerkStatt* platoon and the company support sections arrived on the seventeenth, but because of congestion in Poltawa, only one transport could be unloaded. The other transport unloaded on the eighteenth, and on the nineteenth, the final elements of *4(s) Panzer Kompanie* arrived in Poltawa, along with *3. Panzer-Kompanie* of *I/SS-Panzer-Regiment 3*. The transport commander supervising the unloading in Poltawa was *SS-Untersturmführer* Kohler.

The *Tiger* company was quartered in a former Russian army barracks in the town. On 20

*The *Sd.Kfz. 9* half-track, commonly known as the *FAMO*. To tow the heavy *Tiger*, three units were coupled together.

February, the company commander, *SS-Hauptsturmführer* Kanth, was transferred to the *Stabs Kompanie* of *SS-Panzer-Regiment 3*. The *Tiger* company was now taken over by *SS-Hauptsturmführer* Mooslechner, former commander of *1. Kompanie* of *I/SS-Panzer-Regiment 3*. *1. Kompanie* was now commanded by *SS-Obersturmbannführer* Riefkogel, who came from *II/SS-Panzer-Regiment 3*. The *Tigers* of the company underwent a full inspection carried out by *SS-Hauptscharführer* Haderer and his men. On the same day, orders were issued that the *Tigers* were to be ready to move into a new assembly area, Krasnograd, a distance of eighty-two kilometers.

I/SS-Panzer-Regiment 3 left Poltawa with the following inventory:

Stab.u.Stabs Kompanie—eight *Panzer III's* (three *Befehlswagen*)
1. Kompanie—fourteen *Panzer III's* (five with 7.5cm L/24 gun)
2. Kompanie—fourteen *Panzer III's*
3. Kompanie—ten *Panzer IV's*
4 (s) Kompanie—nine *Tigers* and ten *Panzer III's*

4(s) Kompanie reported on its activities from December 1942 to February 1943:

> Fallingbostal, the birthplace of our unit (for those who don't know)—think of an urbanized heath land. It's the place of Herman Lons, who wrote about it in his natural fables. Here we are surrounded by hills and clean air, but something is going on. It's the first day of January 1943. The train station is busy with field-grey-clad soldiers wearing the *Totenkopf* symbol on their collars. There are lines of rail transports carrying more soldiers. The civilians look on with bemusement; the local barracks are filling up. The soldiers think they are forming up for a new medium company, but they are here to train on a new cat, the *Panzer VI Tiger*.

On the following Wednesday, 6 January 1943, the men continue their work regardless of the winter. They work on their vehicles day and night. Also formed is the *WerkStatt* platoon. The commander of the company is *SS-Hauptsturmführer* Kanth. At the same time, the *Leibstandarte* and *Das Reich Panzer* regiments also have *Tiger* companies forming. The guard commander looks at his watch—soon it will be time to wake up the men of the *WerkStatt* platoon and sign over to the next guard shift. Security is a priority. The shrill cries of "wake up" stir the men from the *Werk-Statt* platoon from their sleep. Curses can be heard as they make their way to the cold water wash rooms. Later, after some exercise and hot coffee, they feel better.

Already waiting for them at the *WerkStatt* is the senior mechanic, *SS-Hauptscharführer* Haderer, who is lord of this world and his men. He is always on hand to lend his experience; he is also a modest man. Today along with his foreman, he is checking the current work on the *Tiger*. The men are practicing track repairs and relinking tracks as well. Haderer has a *Volkswagen* and a three-ton Mercedes diesel truck. At the moment he is sharing a driver with the *Spieß*. The man is driving back and forth. Haderer resides in his office, where he keeps a camp bed; his desk is covered with paperwork. Clouds emanate from his cigar. Haderer wants to see the *WerkStatt* perform correctly as the commander, *SS-Untersturmführer* Greisinger, is due to inspect the place. Greisinger wants his men ready for the pitfalls of Russia, with their tanks as combat-ready as possible, because the rumor is that we are heading back to Russia. The men work day and night. On the first of February, the work rate increases. It's now been ordered that the *Tiger* companies of the *Leibstandarte* and *Das Reich* leave and entrain for Russia. Our date of departure is set for 10 February.

The first early sun of spring is starting to shine. Today the *Schirrmeister* has his hands full. The transportation must be loaded. The men wrap themselves up after refuelling and drive toward the station. We have a hastily prepared meal. We shake hands with some comrades as they will leave in a couple days. At 1600 hours, the heavy vehicles' engines howl as they begin readying themselves for loading. Soon we will be leaving Germany and will be facing a very formidable foe. A shrill whistle as the train enters the station—we begin loading, which proceeds through the night. The vehicles are loaded onto rail flat cars, and ammunition is packed into freight cars. Many comrades are looking bleary eyed; others are lost in their own thoughts.

The transport commander is *SS-Untersturmführer* Kohler, who orders that all vehicles be wedged tightly on the transports so they are secure. The company commander arrives around midnight and gives instructions to the men; he wants to know if the vehicles have been protected against the frost. A rail trip to Russia is not a luxury affair—some of the men are packed into cattle cars with basic coal stoves in the middle with wooden benches which fold down. These benches also have parasites hidden in them. The *Berge-Staffel*, with six heavy *18t Zgkw*, has already prepared its vehicles for the long journey ahead.

The train glides through Germany. Some of the men point out their home towns or villages. The next stop is Breslau. Soon the train is on the move again. Picking up speed, we cross into Poland and arrive in Kowel on Sunday, 14 February 1943. After four days on the move, we change tracks on the *Tiger*, from transport to combat tracks. The huge tracks leave little space on the flat car when the *Tigers* are reloaded back onto the transport. This happened during the afternoon when a snow storm blew up in our faces, causing limited vision, but the storm quickly passes, leaving a new layer of snow on the ground. A German rail official passes our train and tells of the news from the front. We notice his nice clean uniform. The news is not good: Stalingrad is in crisis and the south flank is trembling, so the best divisions of the *Waffen-SS* are heading to southeast Russia.

Our train rolls forward, and we leave Kowel. Soon enough we arrive at another station. We are parked just outside as it seems the station is already stuffed with transports. The station is called Poltawa. Nearby there is a huge detonation from an aerial bomb; the shock waves hurt our ears. This was our greeting from the Russians. Also waiting outside the station are two other transports carrying the company and the *WerkStatt* platoon. We rolled into the station in the morning and began unloading. We drove through the town in a long column and took up quarters in an old Russian army barracks. *SS-Untersturmführer* Kohler served as temporary commander. On 16 February, a third transport arrives in Poltawa. On the twentieth, the company's official history begins. On the same day, *SS-Hauptsturmführer* Kanth is transferred to the *Panzer* regiment as the new adjutant. *SS-Hauptsturmführer* Mooslechner takes command of the company.

SS-Hauptscharführer Haderer and his men check the *Tigers* and determine that they do not need any repairs. The other trucks and vehicles are checked to make sure they have the right amount of oil and lubricant for the Russian winter. On the twenty-fourth, we receive notice that we will be on the move soon to a new assembly area. Before the move, all vehicles are given a full parade—i.e., a full check—before departure. Early the next morning, nine *Tigers* roll forward. The *Panzer III's* remain with the vehicle column, but soon the *WerkStatt* has its first job. A vehicle overturns and is soon recovered and towed back through Poltawa. Otherwise, the company rolls forward toward Krasnograd, eighty kilomters away.

Hans Georg van Kerkhom reported:

On 1 October 1942, as part of the year 1924 class, I was sent to the Deutschland-Freimann Artillery Barracks to join the recruits for six weeks of basic training at the field replacement battalion. I joined *3. Kompanie* and trained as a radio operator. Between 16 and 20 November 1942, we were transported by rail to Angouleme via Strasbourg and Paris. Upon disembarkation we were loaded into trucks and driven to a *Panzer* barracks. This was a big surprise to us all. We found that many of the *Panzer* troops were volunteers. We spent about one week at the barracks.

Since we were the new guys, we were split into different companies. As a radio operator, I was posted to the armored reconnaissance platoon commanded by *SS-Untersturmführer* Quade. Under his commanded, we received continuation training on the *Panzer III* for approximately four weeks. We underwent chemical warfare training as well; *SS-Untersturmführer* Quade was a qualified instructor in this type of warfare.

Then came Christmas. We had a great time, with wine and song, chanting out slogans. We also wanted to know if we were going to Africa since parts of the division had already been selected and loaded. The first week of the New Year, we were all examined for suitability for the tropical climate. Our blood types were also taken, but things would turn out differently.

In the East, Stalingrad had been recaptured; the southern front was engulfed and faltering. The division was now going not to Africa but back to Russia. On 8 January 1943, division issued an order that Quade's armored reconnaissance platoon was to be ready to march on the ninth. We boarded the train and headed toward Paris, then Köln, and changed at Bremen for Hamburg. We spent one night there. I went to the *Reeperbahn* [an area notorious for numerous brothels].

The next and final stop was the Troop Training Grounds at Fallingbostal, where we found out we were to be integrated into the new *schwere Kompanie Tiger* for the *Panzer* regiment. Other units of the division had already been loaded and sent to Russia, but we still had to undergo conversion training on the *Tiger*, which lasted fourteen days. I was to be a radio operator in the new tank. The crews were distributed amongst the vehicles, and we had ten *Panzer III's* and ten *Tigers* (actually nine *Tigers* issued). Before long, we were issued with winter clothing. We had a quiet day. The next day, we were loaded onto rail transports and departed for Russia. We arrived in Poltawa and came under the command of the division.

The first recruits in Weimar, June 1942. WAGNER

Another group photograph of the first recruits in Weimar, June 1942. WAGNER

SS-Hauptsturmführer Gross introduces himself to the new recruits, June 1942. Gross has been awarded the Iron Cross, First and Second Classes; the Infantry Assault Badge; and Wound Badge in Silver (three or four wounds). WERDEHAUSEN

SS-Obersturmführer Bahr, in the black *Panzer* uniform, confers with two other officers. WERDEHAUSEN

SS-Hauptsturmführer Gross sizing up the new recruits. WERDEHAUSEN

Block 17, the new home for *1. Kompanie, SS-Panzer-Abteilung III.* WERDEHAUSEN

SS-Untersturmführer Schulz on parade in Weimar. Schulz is standing as the righthand marker.

SS-Untersturmführer Wagner poses next to a *Panzer II Ausf. C* used for training purposes in Weimar. Wagner was later posted to *5. Kompanie, II/SS.Pz.Rgt 3.*

A *Panzer III Ausf. F* used for training purposes, taken in Weimar, summer 1942. WERDEHAUSEN

Recruits on parade come under the eye of *SS-Untersturmführer* Wagner. WAGNER

Group photo taken in Weimar, summer 1942.

Early portrait of Wolfgang Barth, July 1942.

Wolfgang Barth posing with his new black *Panzer* uniform, August 1942.

Group photo taken in Angouleme, autumn 1942. The reed-green drill uniform is being worn (common for recruits).

Wolfgang Barth and a comrade in good humor, Angouleme.

Another view of the barracks in Angouleme.

The barracks in Angouleme housing *I/SS.Pz.Rgt. 3.*

At the end of November 1942, *I/SS.Pz.Rgt. 3* took delivery of fourteen *Panzer III's* and seven *Panzer IV's* in Angouleme. The delivery of new tanks at the end of November also included *Panzers* for the *Pz.Aufklär.Zug, Stabs.Kp., SS-Pz.Rgt.*, and *5. Kompanie, II/SS-Pz.Rgt. 3.* These *Panzer III's* look to be *Ausf. J* or *L*, with the 5.0cm L/60 main gun.

From this new delivery, five *Panzer III's Ausf. L* are issued to the *Panzer-Aufklärungs-Zug, Stabs.Kp., I/SS.Pz.Rgt. 3.*

One of the new *Panzer IV Ausf. G's* issued to *3. Kompanie, I/SS.Pz.Rgt. 3.*

Wolfgang Barth and a comrade try out the new winter fashion, one-piece protective overalls, usually worn over the black tanker uniform.

A parade of *1. Kompanie* is conducted in temporary barracks located in the south of France during *Case Anton*, the occupation of Vichy France.

Personnel of *I/SS.Pz.Rgt. 3* on the beach by the Mediterranean Sea, November 1942. SCHILLING

Group photograph taken on the beach by the Mediterranean Sea, French-Spanish border, November 1942. SCHILLING

1. Kompanie forms up for inspection to be conducted by a Spanish officer in Rivesaltes, with their *Panzer III Ausf. L* and a *Panzer III Ausf. N* (right) mounting the 7.5 cm L/24 main gun. WERDEHAUSEN

Ludwig Lachner posing in his new black *Panzer* uniform.

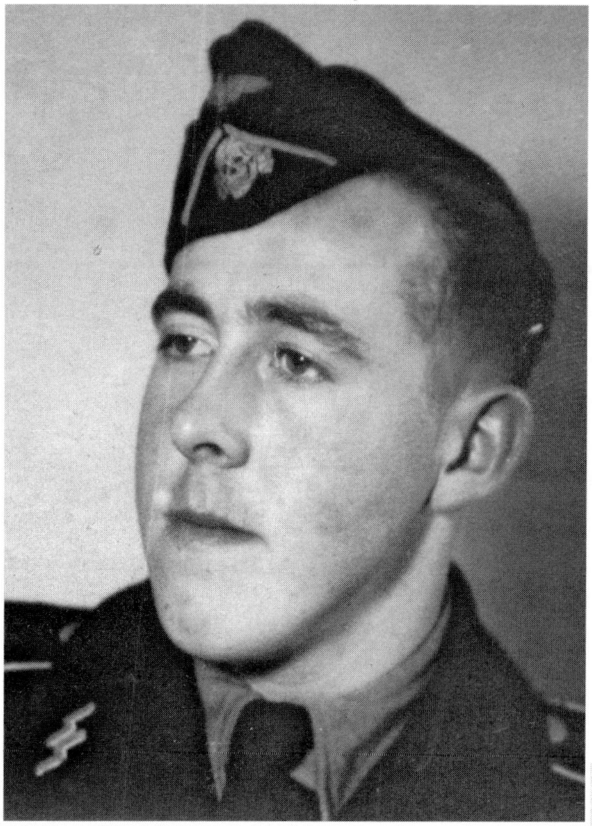

Lachner and other soldiers of *SS-Pz.Abt. III* undergoing training at Troop Training Ground Putlos under the supervision of the German Army. The training tanks are early-model *Panzer IV's*, probably *Ausf. C*.

Two soldiers touring Angouleme during October 1942. *SS-Pz.Abt. III* had been transferred from La Braconne to Angouleme during October 1942, arriving on the twelfth.

Lachner sitting on top of a *Panzer IV* at Putlos Troop Training Grounds.

Lachner and two other soldiers in Lubeck, November 1942.

Lachner on the training field at Putlos, covered with MG link ammunition belts.

Lachner and Hempfinger (in the commander's cupola) pose on a *Panzer IV Ausf. D* at Putlos. Hempfinger was listed as missing in action on 30 July 1943 on the Mius Front.

SS-Rottenführer Kern posing in front of the Guard Block, Angouleme, autumn 1942. Kern had been transferred from the *SS-Polizei-Division* along with Lachner in May 1942.

CHAPTER 3

First Battles

Charkow, February–March 1943

On 20 February 1943, *I/SS-Panzer-Regiment 3*, with *4(s) Panzer-Kompanie*, left Poltawa for Karlovka. The march was conducted in severe winter conditions. The road surface was covered in ice. During the march, six tanks slid off the road, including the *Befehlspanzer* of *SS-Hauptsturmführer* Meierdress; it crashed into a roadside ditch. From *4(s) Panzer-Kompanie*, a single truck overturned but was recovered and towed back to Poltawa for repairs. A total of thirteen tanks were reported damaged from the night's march. *I/SS-Panzer-Regiment 3* arrived in Karlovka during the early morning of the twenty-second. The next objective was to reassemble north of Pereschtschepino. As *I/SS-Panzer-Regiment 3* approached the village, the Russians tried to take the road from the right side. The tanks fanned out across the open terrain, with *1. Kompanie* at point as the first houses came into view.

The Russian attack was beaten back by gunfire from the tanks. The Russians lost several antitank guns. By early evening, Pereschtschepino was captured. It was here that *4(s) Panzer-Kompanie* incurred its first loss: the driver of *SS-Obersturmbannführer* Rinner's *Tiger* drowned. A second *Tiger* also broke through the ice; this *Tiger* was recovered in mid-April 1943. A section from the *Panzer-Pionier-Kompanie* from *SS-Panzer-Regiment 3* was on hand to help with the recovery.

The *4(s) Panzer-Kompanie* reported:

As the *Tiger* of *SS-Untersturmführer* Rinner exited Pereschtschepino, it had to cross a frozen river. The bridge was not wide enough, nor could it take the weight of the *Tiger*. Suddenly, the *Tiger* crashed through the ice and sank up to the turret. The *Werk-Statt* platoon drove in to the village and set up near a wind mill. Shortly thereafter, the *Berge-Staffel* arrived as well. On 27 February, *SS-Untersturmführer* Greisinger ordered the recovery of the *Tiger*. It was deemed that the area was secure enough for such an attempt. *SS-Untersturmführer* Greisinger had inspected the area on the twenty-sixth, the same day that *SS-Obergruppenführer* Eicke, our division commander, was killed. *SS-Brigadeführer* Max Simon took over the command of the division.

The recovery of the *Tiger* involved five *18t Zgkw's*—four at the front and one at the rear. Once out of the river, the *Tiger* was inspected. It was deemed not to be a total loss, which was good news. The *Tiger* had to be towed all the way to Dnepropetrovsk for large-scale repairs. This was the *WerkStatt* platoon's first large-scale recovery. It filled us with satisfaction on a job well done.

During the night of 22–23 February, *I/SS-Panzer-Regiment 3* assembled south of Pereschtschepino and continued the advance in a southerly direction toward Werbki. On the twenty-third, *I/SS-Panzer-Regiment 3* halted to take on a new allocation of fuel and ammunition and continued the advance, with *3. Kompanie* at point. On the twenty-fourth, Wjasowak was attacked and captured by 0930 hours. During the fighting, two Russian antitank guns were knocked out, with the loss of one *Panzer III*. The battalion reassembled north of the road from Popassnoje to Pawlograd. During the night of 24–25 February, the *leichte Kolonne* (column) for *I/SS-Panzer-Regiment 3* reported fighting near the village of Nageshdovka. The column was camped near Kotschereshki.

Between 25 and 26 February, *I/SS-Panzer-Regiment 3* saw action in the areas of Zaredarovka and Strastnoj. The fighting on the twenty-sixth was especially hard because of severe weather. On the twenty-seventh, Zaredarovka was captured. During the day, the battalion reassembled along the railway line near Sacherjewski. A *Panzer III* from *2. Kompanie* fell out because of fuel pump damage. *SS-Obersturmbannführer* Rinner was posted to the *Stabs Kompanie* of *SS-Panzer-Regiment 3* as the new regimental adjutant; he was later killed on 21 March 1943. *SS-Obersturmbannführer* Schroder from the *Stabs Kompanie* of *II/SS-Panzer-Regiment 3* took over his platoon, with *SS-Untersturmführer* Kohler remaining as commander of the Half Platoon. On the twenty-eighth, *SS-Panzer-Regiment 3* assembled along the road leading from Panjutina. On the last day of February, *I/SS-Panzer-Regiment 3* had thirteen *Panzers* in repair.

On the last day of February 1943, the *Werk-Statt* platoon from *4(s) Panzer-Kompanie* was in Orelka. The vehicles of the *WerkStatt* could move only during the morning because in the afternoon the platoon was busy recovering vehicles that had become bogged down in the mud. Along the main road, there were trucks awaiting recovery every 100 meters or so. Some trucks had already been blown up. The company column was spread out over a kilometer. Over the last few days, the *Tigers* and the company's support units had been trying to maintain unit cohesion while on the march. A seven-man work detail in Orelka was tasked with freeing a bogged-down Mercedes truck that had a *Tiger* engine loaded on the back. Luckily, there was a truck nearby with a mounted crane. The majority of the *WerkStatt* platoon set up in Orelka.

At the end of February 1943, Gunther Traupe of *6. Kompanie* of *II/SS-Panzer-Regiment 3* wrote: "The adjutant of the regiment [Rinner] came over to us and said he would get a *Tiger* to tow us but we would have to wait—some nearby engineers just wanted to blow up our *Panzer III*. Anyway, we waited and waited—no *Tiger* showed up, but our radio operator heard an engine noise. A small *Tiger* [a *Panzer IV*] arrived and towed us away."

Between 1 and 2 March, *I/SS-Panzer-Regiment 3* fought in Uljanowka and the area of Jefremowka. On 2 March, a new allocation of *Tiger* engines arrived for the *SS-Panzer-Korps*. On 3 March 1943, the *WerkStatt* platoon spent four days in Nischni Orel. By now the engines on the *Tigers* and *Panzer III's* needed checking, and the running gear was showing signs of damage. Also on 3 March, the *Tiger* company's first action in Russia occurred. It took part in the destruction of a Russian column (regimental strength) moving west from Dmitrowka to Grushino.

Fritz Hitz reported for 3 March 1943:

> We always lead with a *Tiger* up front, with two *Panzer III's* as escorts. I was in the crew of Bieber—the gunner was Hempfinger, the loader was Hitz, the driver was Walter Gansera, and the radio operator was Theo Engels. For a while we drive counter to the front line. Hempfinger and I smoke cigarettes with some anxiety, but not with fear. We watch the fireworks as if watching a magic show, then we hear the command "Make ready, hatches closed." I have antitank shells at the ready, with one round in the gun breech, as the second order is rang out.
>
> T-34 to the front—now we are moving forward with some pace. Our big brother, the *Tiger*, is with us. The Russians come at us with everything they have. We looked at our gun, the 5cm long, wondering if this could cope with the Russian tanks. The gunner reported that he could not traverse the turret. He tried again. Nothing happened. We found that a machine-gun belt had gotten stuck in the turret ring. We drove at the Russians, antitank gun avoiding shells from a lone antitank gun, but the *Tiger* commanded by Konrad Berger took care of this. He also, I think, knocked out two T-34 tanks, but I can't say for sure.
>
> I shouted to the commander to go right, but then things got gloomy as a dog with an explosive pack hit our *Panzer*. The pack detonated, and our track was shredded. The commander reported this to the company commander. Mooslechner ordered that the loader get out and look. I dismounted and inspected the damage. In my tool kit was a hammer and my 08 pistol. Lucky for us, Konrad Berger and his *Tiger* provided covering fire. He was returning fire across the open terrain. I did my best trying to repair the track. It felt as if the whole company was waiting for me.
>
> I managed to repair the track, and we got moving again. Mooslechner later announced, "Well done, *Panzer 424*."

The *4(s) Panzer Kompanie* reported: "A *Hauptscharführer* came to visit us. He had just been in a conversation with the company commander. He told us the commander's opinion of the *Tiger* during its first action: 'It was like a wolf running wild amongst a herd of sheep. The *Tiger* just destroyed everything we fired at,' he said. 'He felt unbeatable.'"

Between 4 and 5 March, *I/SS-Panzer-Regiment 3* and other units of the *Totenkopf* Division assisted the *Das Reich* Division in encircling a Russian tank brigade and in capturing Ochotschaje. On the sixth, the *Totenkopf* was placed as corps reserve for the *SS-Panzer-Korps*. On the seventh, *4(s) Panzer-Kompanie* managed to conduct some much-needed maintenance. On the eighth, the *Totenkopf* was taken out of reserve and sent into the area south of Walki, in the direction of Staryi Mertschik. That same day, the following occurred near Grijekowo, according to the report from *4(s) Panzer-Kompanie*:

> The next move was ordered for the following morning, 8 March 1943. The columns of the company had driven about ten kilometers when we hit our first obstacle. Not more than 300 meters in front of us was one of those treacherous rivers. There was

no bridging equipment or bridges available that can take the weight of the *Tiger*, so *SS-Untersturmführer* Kohler decided to proceed with his *Tiger*. He managed to make some distance when all of a sudden he crashed through the ice. No one suspected how thin the ice was.

The crew could not get out before the *Tiger* went under the snowy cold water. The whole fighting compartment was flooded. The crew, including *SS-Untersturmführer* Kohler, were dripping. We were soaked to the skin. Kohler looked totally dejected. Then *SS-Untersturmführer* Rathsack arrived in his *Tiger* and started to cross as well. His *Tiger* became bogged down as the rear of the hull sank into the embankment. The engine compartment filled up with sludge and ice water, completely flooding his engine compartment. Well, the men of the *WerkStatt* soon set to work on Rathsack's *Tiger*, which had to be pulled out and the engine compartment drained. The *Tiger* of *SS-Untersturmführer* Kohler is a different matter. A large number of nonresidential Russians are grouped together and tasked with constructing a mound that will reach the sunken *Tiger*. This took several days. When the mound was within reach, the *WerkStatt* started putting hose pipes inside the *Tiger* and connected them to pumps. It took a long time to drain the *Tiger*.

The driver of *SS-Untersturmführer* Kohler's *Tiger* recalls this event as the "Bath of Grijekowo":

The exact location and the names of those rivers are no longer in my memory, but it was 8 March 1943. The company lost two *Tigers* while trying to cross a river. A few days ago, a *Tiger* had broken through the ice, and its driver had drowned after he became stuck inside the tank. Now we were confronted by a river which was frozen over. The bridge could take only six tons and looked shaky, but our *Tigers* were needed in the Walki-Charkow area. The first *Tiger* that had broken through the ice had taken days to recover using ropes and pulleys. The crew had to stand on the embankment shivering, and the *Tiger* with the drowned driver could only be recovered at the end of April.

We at this time were the crew of *SS-Untersturmführer* Kohler. The gunner was Motzschnik, the loader was Hans Rex, the radio operator was Grunerth, and I was the driver. I tried the bridge at first, but it couldn't take the weight, so we had to cross the river. We moved to the left of the bridge. Before we moved, I took out my rations—butter, liverwurst, and some bread. I pulled my pistol to my right side as I didn't want to get stuck and I didn't want to drown. As we moved forward, the commander spoke softly. We could hear unpleasant sounds as the ice cracked, and we could see the opposite bank of the river. If we got to the other side, we would drink schnapps, but as we got closer, there was sudden movement. The old crate lurched upward like an elevator. Immediately, I wanted to get out, but freezing water was already coming inside the tank.

The weight of the water on top of my hatch meant I couldn't get out. I tried to move inside the interior of the *Tiger*, but somehow I was blocked by a five-day ration box. I was wearing thick winter clothing, and movement was difficult. I had to move into the turret space. I got past the gun when I got stuck again, and water was coming in fast. I could see a turret hatch open. I clutched my fists and pushed as hard as I could. My life was before me like a film. I was thinking about my mother, sister, and father. I kept pushing, and slowly, I got through the hatch and my head was above water. A comrade tried to reach me, but the water was freezing. He ran off and came back with a ladder, which he stretched out to me. I leaned out to the ladder and grabbed hold of it, and I was dragged to the embankment. I passed out.

When I woke up, I was in a Russian house wrapped in fur. We recovered the crate in mid-April and then towed it to Dnjepropetrowsk for repairs. We gathered our belongings and travelled to Budi. We came back to the company after *SS-Untersturmführer* Kohler was already back at the company. The radio operator had to spend some time in the hospital before he came back to us. Herman, Hans, and I procured some fresh produce as rations in the area of Grijekowo. This was the happiest time for me in Russia.

Fritz Hitz reported on 10 March 1943:

The company was carrying out technical service. We had full ammunition bags, a full tank with ammunition. Some comrades were in a house along with *SS-Unterscharführer* Hackel and gunner Hempfinger, and I keeping busy on the tank. Suddenly, some shots rang out. We saw the muzzle flash coming from a house, and everyone thought the Russians were making a raid. We returned fire and waited to see their response.

More shots rang out, and I saw *SS-Unterscharführer* Hackel stumble. I ran over to him and caught him under his arms as he fell. The shots had hit him in the chest. One comrade climbed into the turret and returned fire with the turret MG. Hempfinger and Theo Engels came back with a captured partisan. A bullet had gone through Hempfinger's trousers and gotten stuck in his cigarette case. A few days later, we were mourning another comrade's death, an *Unterscharführer* who had been crushed to death as a *Tiger* reversed into a house where he was sitting.

On the 10 March 1943, *2. Kompanie* of *I/SS-Panzer-Regiment 3* was attached to *Panzer-Grenadier-Division Das Reich*. The next day, the *Leibstandarte* entered Charkow in a surprise attack. Elements of the *Totenkopf* moved forward toward Chugujev and Rogan and proceeded to cut the road to the southeast. On 12 March, *I/SS-Panzer-Regiment 3* was attached to *Kampfgruppe Baum*. (Baum was commander of *SS-Panzer-Grenadier-Regiment 1 Totenkopf*.) The *Kampfgruppe* moved from the area of Zurkuny in readiness for an attack on Chugujev. During the afternoon, *Kampfgruppe Baum* became involved in fighting for the village of Bolschaja Danilovka. Later, *SS-Obersturmbannführer* Baum wanted to take Chugujev in a night assault, but Russian tanks were reported in the rear area of the *Kampfgruppe*. The night of 12–13 March was spent securing the lines of supply and communications. *I/SS-Panzer-Regiment 3* lost a *Panzer III* on the twelfth as well.

On the thirteenth, *Kampfgruppe Baum* advanced toward Rogan, but the advance was slowed because of severe weather and because *I/SS-Panzer-Regiment 3* had to fight several tank duels with the Russians. On the fourteenth, *Kampfgruppe Baum* was slowed again, this time because it had to wait for fuel to arrive. It remained inactive for the better part of the day. On the fifteenth, *Kampfgruppe Baum* and *I/SS-Panzer-Regiment 3* became involved in fighting in the northern district of Charkow, in Chugujev. This continued into the following day, when *SS-Obersturmbannführer* Riefkogel of *1. Kompanie* of *SS-Panzer-Regiment 3* led two successful counterattacks against combined Russian tank and infantry forces. The Russians lost nine tanks on the sixteenth, while *I/SS-Panzer-Regiment 3* reported the loss of one *Panzer III*.

On 18 March, security for the Chugujev sector was handed over to the German Army's *6. Panzer-Division*. *I/SS-Panzer-Regiment 3* was assigned to *II/SS-Panzer-Grenadier-Regiment 2 Eicke* under the command of *SS-Sturmbannführer* Launer. The advance on Bjelgorod was slowed yet again because of severe weather. That night, *SS-Sturmbannführer* Launer called a halt to any further movement. On the nineteenth, *I/SS-*

Panzer-Regiment 3 and *4(s) Panzer-Kompanie* saw action in Siborowka and proceeded to advance to the heights near Iwanowka, where the company commander, *SS-Hauptsturmführer* Mooslechner, was killed. A faulty fuse detonated a shell inside his *Tiger*. *SS-Hauptsturmführer* Biermeier, the former commander of *6. Kompanie*, took over as the new *Tiger* company commander. On the twenty-first, *SS-Obersturmbannführer* Rinner was seriously wounded near Staritza during a Russian artillery barrage.

On 22 March, the *Tigers* remained in Ternowaya, and the next day, the company conducted maintenance. That same day, Hitler ordered that the *schwere Panzer-Kompanien* from all three *Waffen-SS* tank regiments were to reorganize with fourteen *Tigers* instead of nine. On 24 March, twenty *Tiger* crews were organized for transport to Germany to collect fifteen new *Tigers*. On 26 March, six tank crews departed for Paderborn to await a new allocation of *Tigers*. The following day, *SS-Sturmann* Fritz Hitz was awarded the Iron Cross, Second Class, for his actions on 3 March. The *320. Infanterie-Division* started relieving elements of the *Totenkopf*, which was to be moved into an area south of Bjelgorod for rehabilitation. With the capture of Charkow and Bjelgorod, this was the last significant German victory on the Eastern Front.

Fritz Hiss recorded the following in his diary during this period:

> 21 January The former *Stabs-Kompanie/Panzer-Aufklärungs-Zug* of *II/SS-Panzer-Regiment 3* is to be retrained on the *Tiger*, along with crews from *Panzer-Regiment Großdeutschland*. We move from Angouleme to Fallingbostal in Germany.
>
> 2 February Transport from Fallingbostal to Russia.
>
> 17 February Arrival in Poltawa. We are quartered in a former Russian army barracks.
>
> 3 March First action at Isjum. The attack begins at 1515 hours and finishes at around 1750. It is our baptism of fire. Our tank is hit by a Russian shell, which causes damage to the track, but we have all survived. Radio message from the company commander, *SS-Hauptsturmführer* Mooslechner, giving praise to *Panzer 424*.
>
> 5 March Before we drive, I have to deliver a message which involves my being attacked by the Russians. I later find a bullet hole in my pants.
>
> 10 March Olschani. Our tank falls out. *SS-Unterscharführer* Hackl is killed by Russian partisans.
>
> 20 March Arrived in Charkow after a week. It is minus 38 degrees Celsius.
>
> 26 March Awarding of medals: Iron Cross, First and Second Classes.
>
> 28 March I was awarded the Iron Cross, Second Class. I am the first in the company to hold the Iron Cross. I was very proud of it.
>
> 1 April After a double postal delivery, the next enemy is the snow. Many men get frostbite.
>
> 13 April The company drives to Mikojanowka, but it's still bitterly cold.
>
> 30 April Move to Gurjewski.

April–June 1943: Rest and Reorganization

On 2 April 1943, *I/SS-Panzer-Regiment 3* was sent to Nikolskoje for reorganization. On 3 April, *SS-Panzer-Regiment 3* commander, *SS-Sturmbannführer* Leiner, was removed from his post because of his performance during the Charkow battles. *SS-Sturmbannführer* Kunstmann was given command of the regiment, while *SS-Sturmbannführer* Bochmann became the new commander of *II/SS-Panzer-Regiment 3*. On 22 April, the *4(s) Panzer-Kompanie* was ordered to reorganize along *Kstn 1176e*, dated 5 March 1943; this called for three platoons equipped with four *Tigers* each, with a *Kompanie Trupp* of two *Tigers*. The 4th Platoon was disbanded, and *SS-Oberscharführer* Berger became the new *Spieß* on 1 May after *Spieß* Bauer was sent on home leave. On 24 April, the *Totenkopf* Division was placed in a new assembly area west of Charkow. On 1 May, the following personnel joined the company: Krawatzky, Brieger, Glockl, Leutz, and Wagner.

On the same day, *I/SS-Panzer-Regiment 3* was ordered to reorganize, with two medium tank companies and one light tank company, but in fact, the battalion added a fourth company equipped with *Panzer IV's* (field post number 57182 and, later, after being reorganized in October 1943, 48182). On 3 May 1943, *I/SS-Panzer-Regiment 3* moved into the area of Kosatschek and remained there for six days. On 9 May, *4(s) Panzer-Kompanie* was transferred to the control of *II/SS-Panzer-Regiment 3* and redesignated as *9. Kompanie*. The *Tiger* company's *Panzer III's* were handed over to *3. Kompanie*. The new *4. Kompanie* received a new issue of fourteen *Panzer IV's*, which arrived on 1 June. *4. Kompanie* was commanded by *SS-Obersturmbannführer* Hackl. This delivery was originally meant for *2. Kompanie*. On 9 May, the following personnel joined the *Tiger* company: Lehmkuhl (from *Regiment "Thule"*), Lommer, Keller, Probst, and Schuler. Also arriving that month were Beneke and Herter.

On the 10 May, three *Tigers* that had been repaired in Dnjepropetrowsk were returned to service. The *Tiger* company moved to the new assembly area of Jushy. The move took two days. Joining *II/SS-Panzer-Regiment 3* in May was the newly activated *8. Kompanie*, which received fifteen *Panzer IV's* on 20 May. The same day, *9. Kompanie* marched into the area of Budi.

On 28 June, *9. Kompanie* marched into a new assembly area in readiness for Operation Citadel. Crews were quartered in Blishnitz. *SS-Panzer-Regiment 3* assembled in the area of Strelezoje, Kaszjoje, and Bessonowka. By 3 July, the regiment had moved up to its jump-off point near Rakowo. *SS-Hauptsturmführer* Biermeier was still the company commander. *SS-Obersturmbannführer* Schroder was assigned to the *Kompanie Trupp*. The 1st Platoon was commanded by *SS-Untersturmführer* Kohler, the 2nd Platoon by *SS-Untersturmführer* Quade, and the 3rd Platoon by *SS-Untersturmführer* Rathsack.

SS-Sturmgeschütze-Abteilung 3 was in possession of thirty-five *StuG's*, having received fourteen new replacements on 20 May 1943. *SS-Panzer-Jäger-Abteilung 3* had eleven *schwere PaK Sfl* (self-propelled antitank guns) on strength.

Kursk, July 1943

In the early-morning hours, *SS-Panzer-Regiment 3* advanced from the area of Rakowo at the start of Operation Citadel in the Kursk salient. Almost immediately, the regiment lost a *Panzer III* 1.5 kilometers southeast of Rakowo. *9. Kompanie* was attached to *I/SS-Panzer-Regiment 3*, which was supporting the *I/SS-Panzer-Grenadier-Regiment 5 (gep)* from *SS-Panzer-Grenadier-Regiment Totenkopf*. The fist obstacle was a tank ditch which had to be breached by divisional engineers. The *Tigers* provided covering fire along with the *StuG's* from *SS-Sturmgeschütze-Abteilung 3*. The Russians replied with artillery and antitank fire.

As the ditch was breached, the *Tigers* started to move across and advance toward Hill 216.5. During the afternoon, only six *Tigers* were left in running order for the push toward Gonki. Five had sustained mine damage. Three *StuG's* had also been put out of action by antitank fire, while four *StuG's* fell out because of mine damage. On 6 July, *9. Kompanie* and *I/SS-Panzer-Regiment 3* provided support to *II/SS-Panzer-Grenadier-*

Regiment Totenkopf during the assault on Hill 225.9. The *Luftwaffe* provided close support. Later, *9. Kompanie* and *I/SS-Panzer-Regiment 3* started to move against Ternowka. *Tiger 902* drove over a mine. The crew worked most of the night to repair the track.

On 7 July, *9. Kompanie* saw action near Nepchajewo. Near Ssmorordino, *Tiger 912* was hit by Russian artillery fire, which killed the commander, *SS-Unterscharführer* Richard Muller, and the gunner, Zimmermann. The next day was a dark one for the regiment, whose commander, *SS-Sturmbannführer* Kunstmann, was killed after his command tank was hit twice by antitank gunfire. *II/SS-Panzer-Regiment 3's* commander, *SS-Sturmbannführer* Bochmann, took command of the regiment, and *SS-Hauptsturmführer* Biermeier took command of Bochmann's battalion. *9. Kompanie* was taken over by *SS-Obersturmbannführer* Schroder, who was killed later that day when he was hit by an antitank rifle round. *SS-Untersturmführer* Kohler took command of the company. *SS-Unterscharführer* Gockl was killed on the same day. *9. Kompanie* fought in the area of Hill 209.5. *Tiger 911* had to be sent back for repairs.

On 9 July, *9. Kompanie* fought in the area of Lutschki and Kotschetowka. On the tenth, the *Tiger* of *9. Kompanie's* commander drove over a mine while two other *Tigers* were returned to action after completing repairs. The company saw action near Kljutschi and broke through the Russian defenses after a *Stuka* bombardment. On 11 July, *Tiger 911* again fell out, this time because of technical damage, and had to be repaired. The company participated in defensive

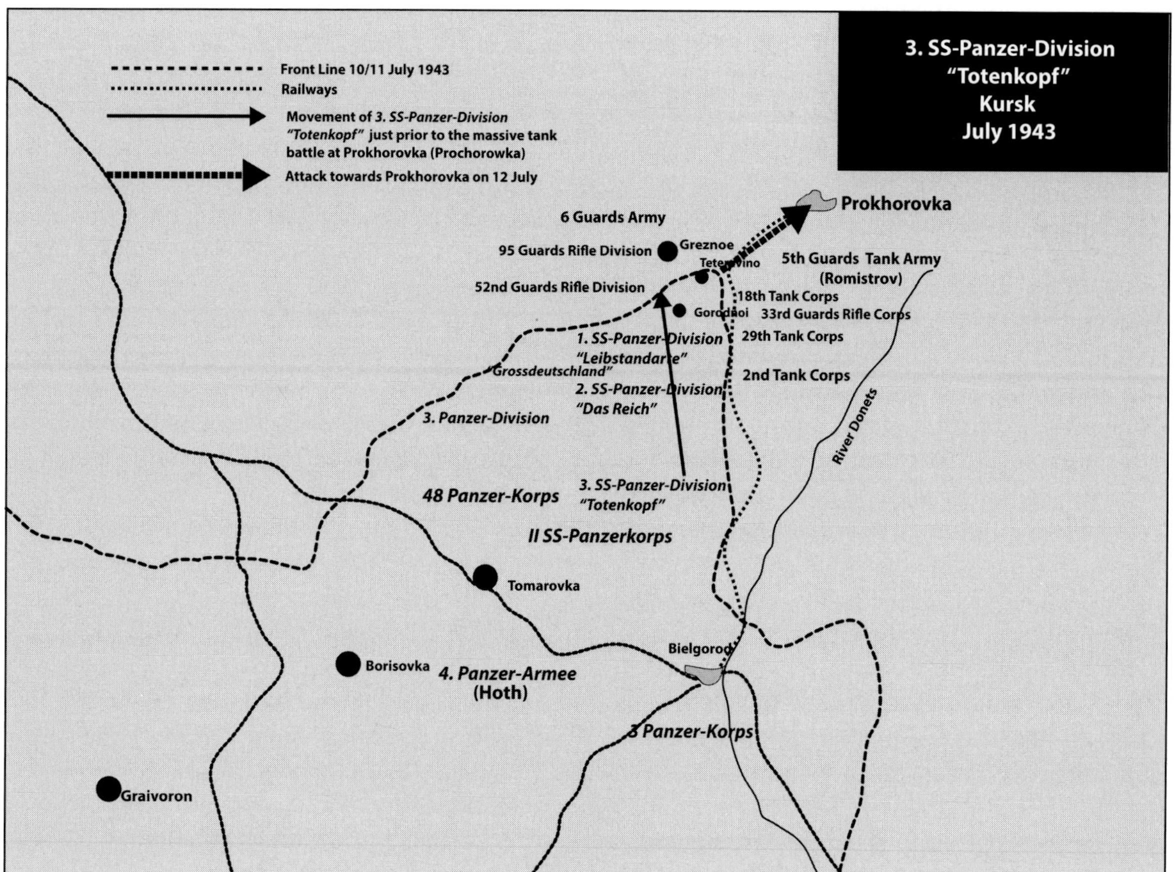

actions near Wassiljewka while providing support to *I/SS-Panzer-Regiment 3*. *9. Kompanie* later had to cross the Psel River on a specially constructed bridge west of Bogorodizkoje for the assault planned for the following day. On 12 July, *9. Kompanie* provided support to *I/SS-Panzer-Regiment 3* during its attack on Andre'evka and along the south bank of the Psel River. The company commander, *SS-Untersturmführer* Kohler, was killed near Kljutschi. *SS-Hauptsturmführer* Richter (Knight's Cross winner) took command of the company. The company had four *Tigers* in repair. Two *Tigers* required four days of work, two had been returned to active service as of 1430 hours, and three others were still being repaired.

On the thirteenth, *SS-Untersturmführer* Schuffler arrived at the company after being posted from the *II/SS-Panzer-Korps's Tiger* battalion. (Schuffler had served with *SS-Kradschutzen-Bataillon 2* between February 1942 and January 1943.) The SS heavy panzer battalion (commanded by *SS-Sturmbannführer* Laackmann) had been transported to the Eastern Front at the beginning of July 1943, unloaded in Ljubotin, and served in the infantry role. *9. Kompanie* started the day with four operational *Tigers*, which saw limited action around Hill 226 and along the Karteschewka road, but by the end of the day, all the remaining *Tigers* were put out of action. All fourteen *Tigers* of the company were in the *WerkStatt* for repairs.

On 15 July, the *Totenkopf* withdrew from the Psel bridgehead and took up new defensive positions along the south bank of the Psel River. On the following day, Hitler suspended Operation Citadel, despite Field Marshal Erich von Manstein's insistence that something could still be salvaged from the attack, which would result in Operation Roland. It was meant to involve units of the *II/SS-Panzer-Korps*, but on 17 July, orders were issued calling for the *Leibstandarte* and *Das Reich* to be regrouped near Bjelgorod.

On the seventeenth, a plane carrying spare parts from Magdeburg for *9. Kompanie* landed at Woltschenka-Charkow. The parts were to be collected from *Panzer-Instandsetzung-Abteilung 545*. On the eighteenth, *9. Kompanie*, along with *I/SS-Panzer-Regiment 3*, supported *167. Infanterie-Division* near Iwanowskij. On the nineteenth, the *Tiger* company was near Lutschki. On the twentieth, orders were issued for *II/SS-Panzer-Korps* for *Das Reich* and *Totenkopf* to redeploy 400 kilometers to the south. The tracked elements of the tank regiment were to load in Bjelgorod and Charkow. During Operation Citadel, *Totenkopf* had lost (total write-offs) two *Panzer III's*, eight *Panzer IV's*, one *Tiger*, and one *StuG*.

On 22 July, *9. Kompanie* drove to Charkow for loading and departed for the Mius front on the twenty-fourth, unloading in the area of Stalino-Rikowo on the twenty-sixth. On the twenty-ninth, *9. Kompanie* collected eight *Tigers* from *SS-Panzer-Regiment 1* in Artemowsk, which was en route to Italy. Also handed over from *SS-Panzer-Regiment 1* were thirty *Panzer IV's* (seventeen to *5. Kompanie* and thirteen to 1st Battalion) and four *Panzer III's*. The *Tiger* company was able to raise the 4th Platoon again, with *SS-Hauptscharführer* Berger in command. The 1st Platoon was commanded by *SS-Untersturmführer* Rathsack, the 2nd by *SS-Untersturmführer* Quade, and the 3rd by *SS-Obersturmbannführer* Schuffler. Each platoon had five *Tigers* while the *Kompanie Trupp* had two *Tigers*. The company support units still had a vehicle inventory of fifty-five wheeled and semitracked vehicles.

Wagner reported:

> The company had moved from Budi and assembled in a wood near Bjelgorod. On 5 July, the *Luftwaffe* flew overhead. Around midday, the company support units fell in behind *I/SS-Panzer-Regiment 3*. A truck from the support units followed the 1st Platoon. Later, another truck driven by Kasimir turned up, but we did lose a Mercedes fuel truck that caught fire and flew into the air due to Russian antitank gunfire.

Two of our *Tigers* got bogged down; others suffered mine damage to the running gear; the commander's *Tiger* sat in a minefield without a track while Probst, the commander, Biermeier, and the driver tried to repair the track. Quade and Rathsack along with the rest of the company moved into a wood.

The next day, the Russian air force attacked our positions. *SS-Sturmbannführer* Kunstmann was killed, and *SS-Sturmbannführer* Bochmann became the new regiment commander. Our company commander, *SS-Hauptsturmführer* Biermeier, is the new commander of *II/SS-Panzer-Regiment 3*. *SS-Obersturmbannführer* Schroder now leads the *Tiger* company, but he lasted only about half a day before he was killed as well. *SS-Untersturmführer* Kohler then took charge. When he was killed, *SS-Hauptsturmführer* Egon Richter, a Knight's Cross winner, took command. I think Lampert was killed also, and Hempfinger was wounded.

Fritz Hitz described the 8 July action at Ternowka (Ternivka):

I was happy to get into a *Tiger* as a loader as I had previous experience. We got the usual command, and off we went. We saw a T-34 next to a windmill which was promptly knocked out. A few minutes later, we hit a second one. We took up a position in a cornfield, and all of a sudden there was a huge cry of *Urrah! Urrah!*. Russian infantry started attacking our *Tiger*. The Russians had been hiding in the field.

SS-Obersturmbannführer Schroder quickly gave the order: "Ludwig, MG fire!" I had to tell the boss we didn't have a turret MG, but instead an extra *Fu 8* radio system because the *Tiger* was a command version. Instead, I yelled at the radio operator to use the hull MG. Next, Schroder looked at me and told me to give him the machine pistol. I looked at him, knowing what was on his mind. He was going to fire on the Russians. I said, "This is madness." He replied, "I gave a direct order."

I found the (MP 40) machine pistol and gave it to him. he put a magazine in the weapon and opened his hatch and started firing. Ludwig and I shook our heads. I was thinking, *God, what am I doing?* when suddenly Schroder fell back inside the turret. His head was in pieces; he had been hit by a round from an antitank rifle. Ludwig quickly told the driver to hit the gas and reverse back and out of danger. The engine roared into life, and we pulled back from the field.

Later, when it was safe, we took Schroder out of the tank and laid him down. Schroder was a real daredevil. During the First World War, he flew planes. We buried Schroder under a tree. In my diary I said it was a great loss. Also killed that day was Gockl. I can remember Ludwig Lachner and Muller, but some other names of the crew escape me.

Karl Kuster wrote in his diary:

1 June Target practise with main gun. Also, parts of the company carried out a limited exercise.

2 June Main gun and MG target practice with elements of the company.

3 June Stand to. The company is brought to full readiness until 1500 hours, then stand down.

4 June Continuation training per company schedule.

5 June Continuation training per company schedule.

6 June Driving practice and mobile exercise with the combat elements.

7 June Training until the afternoon.

8–12 June Continuation training per company schedule.

13 June Continuation training per company schedule. Also, issue of special rations—today it's chocolate.

14–16 June Continuation training per company schedule.

17 June Passed a radio test with grade 8.

18 June Passed a technical exam with grade 7.

19 June Took the position of radio operator in *Tiger 911*, which has just come back from the *WerkStatt* platoon.

20 June Hans Rex's nineteenth birthday today—very nice. About 200 liters of fuel spilled into the fighting compartment of the *Tiger*.

21 June Very quiet day for the company.

22 June Full equipment check.

6 July At 1930 hours, shot a T-34. *Tiger 902* ran over a mine. *Tiger 911* provides limited support.

7 July Sixteen-hour battles east of the main road. *Tiger 912* takes a direct hit from Russian artillery fire. The crew is rescued.

8 July *SS-Obersturmbannführer* Schroder takes over the company, but is killed thirty hours later. *SS-Untersturmführer* Kohler takes over, and he also is killed in *Tiger 911*. *SS-Unterscharführer* Gockl is killed as well.

9 July Repairs at the *WerkStatt* platoon.

10 July Forty-kilometer road march back to the company.

11 July Mine damage—had to be towed for repairs.

12 July In the *WerkStatt* platoon, so far *SS-Obersturmbannführer* Schroder, *SS-Untersturmführer* Kohler, *SS-Oberscharführer* Muller, and Boxleitner [actually Zimmermann] have been killed. *SS-Obersturmbannführer* Schuffler is the new company commander.

Fritz Hiss reported:

20 May The company moves by road to Budi.

27 June Motorized march from Budi to Udi into the next assembly area. We camp in Blischniz.

6 July The attack begins at 0530 in the morning with *Stukas*, rocket fire, and artillery. The Russians fight doggedly using antitank and machine-gun fire.

6 July As we move into the next location, we take Russian prisoners. At the same time, Russian fighter-bombers attack us.

7 July Three *Tigers* are damaged. Commander *SS-Unterscharführer* Muller and loader Zimmermann are both killed.

8 July Under enemy fire. Our *Tigers* are shot at. *SS-Unterscharführer* Gockl is killed; *SS-Obersturmbannführer* Schroder takes command of the company. I assume the post of loader in Schroder's crew. During an attack, Schroder is killed by a round from an antitank rifle. It's tough when someone that we know well is killed.

9 July The company knocks out ten T-34 tanks and a Stalin organ [Soviet multiple rocket launcher]. The Russians start using loud hailers on us.

10 July We change position and are given new assignments. The main enemy locations are Orel-Kursk-Belgorod. During the night, we drive over a mine. Our luck holds again. We are all hoping we survive this hell.

11 July Our asses are out front again during the advance. Three of our *Tigers* fall out due to battle damage from Russian defensive fire.

12 July *SS-Untersturmführer* Kohler is killed. Our company has to use visual and verbal reporting techniques.

16 July I received a letter via the military postal service today, but I'm feeling too lazy to write back home.

17 July We attack through a ravine. We come under strong Russian defensive fire from Stalin organs and suffer high losses, but we manage to recover most of our dead.

18 July We withdraw back through the ravine because we are completely worn out.

19 July Retreat from the area of Orel-Kursk. We are low on ammunition. We move back toward Charkow.

24 July At 1730 hours, we drive from our assembly area toward Charkow for entrainment to God-knows-where. What is waiting for us now?

26 July Arrived near Stalino-Rikowo.

29 July Arrived in a new assembly area. Here we collect some *Tigers* from *SS-Pazner-Regiment 1*, and I also receive the Panzer Assault Badge in Silver [for participation in three armored assaults on three different days].

The Mius Front

On 28 July 1943, the *Totenkopf* Division assembled in the area of Krasnaya. The following day, *SS-Panzer-Regiment 3* set up its command post in Ramovsky. The line of departure was from the area of Ssneshnoje and Krasnaya. On 30 July, *I/SS-Panzer-Regiment 3* was supported by the grenadiers of *SS-Panzer-Grenadier-Regiment Totenkopf* and *9. Kompanie* during its attack on Hill 213.9. Soon the attacking force encountered minefields that took toll of the advancing tanks.

SS-Hauptsturmführer Richter, company commander, reported on the Mius Front:

30 July We drive into no-man's-land and advance toward the Russian defensive positions. Their infantry is dug in in a labyrinth of trenches. They are dug in up to regimental level. The Russian infantry only pull back at the last minute. We see bodies everywhere. We still continue to attack on Hill 213.9 per orders. The enemy positions are heavily defended with mortars and machine guns; all that opposes us is rolled over and crushed as we do on the assault.

The *Tiger* of *SS-Hauptsturmführer* Richter would later drive over a mine. Richter dismounted to inspect the damage when a mortar round exploded nearby, striking him with shrapnel in the stomach. Richter, after receiving treatment in various hospitals, was posted to the *SS-Panzer-Ausbildungs-und-Ersatz-Regiment* in Sennelager from 20 October 1943 to 21 March 1944. He was then posted to *SS-Junkerschule Braunschweig* until April 1944, when he transferred to the school at Bad Tolz. In March 1945, he took command of *II/SS-Panzer-Grenadier-Regiment 95* of the *38. SS-Grenadier-Division Nibelungen*. After Richter, the company was now commanded by *SS-Obersturmbannführer* Schuffler. Slowly, two minefields were cleared, and the attack proceeded. Then the Russians opened fire with artillery and antitank guns. The attack pressed on, with the *Tigers* providing covering fire for the tanks of *I/SS-Panzer-Regiment 3*. Radio operator Gunther Groner was killed during that day as well.

Rolf Stettner of *5. Kompanie* of *II/SS-Panzer-Regiment 3* recalls: "The new metal sheet mines had been developed by the Russians specifically for our *Tigers*. Previously, they had used mines encased in wood, about twenty to thirty centimeters in diameter." For 1 August 1943, he reported: "The *Panzer* regiment had to close formation and push out to the right due to Russian antitank gunfire. Our *Tigers* pushed forward—well, what can you say? I thought they had pushed on, but next to me is a stopped *Tiger*."

SS-Panzer-Regiment 3 was deployed along the road on either side on the approach to Hill 213.9. By the end of the day, the combined *Panzergruppe* of *I/SS-Panzer-Regiment 3* and *9. Kompanie* had reached the northwestern edge of the slopes on Hill 213.9, but eight *Tigers* had to be sent for repairs, mainly to the running gear, tracks, and hull. *SS-Sturmmann* Mathai was killed near Stepanowka. On 31 July, the attack resumed on Hill 213.9. The tanks from *SS-Panzer-Regiment 3* had to fight for every meter. To keep the momentum going, the *Luftwaffe* provided close support with *Stukas*. The *Tigers* of *SS-Oberscharführer* Lampert and *SS-Unterscharführer* Bieber were both knocked out by antitank gunfire. *SS-Oberscharführer* Lampert was killed, but his crew managed to bail out. Also killed during the day's action were Kochesser and Schweitzer.

On 1 August, the attack on Hill 213.9 resumed yet again. The day was almost a repeat of the previous day—minefields, antitank gunfire, and artillery barrages. The tanks from *I/SS-Panzer-Regiment 3* took severe flanking fire from the Russians. Some of the crews who had bailed out fought on as infantry. The *Tiger* of Karl Sandler received a hit to the running gear as well. But *9. Kompanie* suffered another fatality when loader Gunther Schreyer was killed. By the late afternoon, the *Totenkopf* could report to the *II/SS-Panzer-Korps* that Hill 213.9 had been captured, but at great cost.

On 2 August, *9. Kompanie* and other divisional units attacked the Russians across Hill 191.3. It was during this action that *SS-Untersturmführer* Schuffler was badly wounded; he died later the same day from his wounds. The company was then commanded by *SS-Untersturmführer* Quade. *9. Kompanie* also buried Kochesser, Lampert, and Schweitzer.

On the third, the *Panzer* regiment assembled in the area of Stepanowka-Permwomaisk. On the sixth, the *Totenkopf* was informed that it would transfer back to the Charkow sector. On the seventh, *9. Kompanie* was located in Makajewka. A group of *9. Kompanie* personnel drove out to the location where Lampert's and Bieber's *Tigers* were left from 31 July; the radio sets and codes were retrieved and the *Tigers* blown up. The *Totenkopf* manpower losses during the fighting on the Mius Front were horrendous. From 30 July to 2 August, the division lost 1,458 men killed, wounded, or missing. The *Panzer* regiment lost two *Panzer III's* and ten *Panzer IV's*. *SS-Sturmgeschütze-Abteilung* lost one *StuG*; two others were severely damaged.

Charkow, Kremenchug, and the Winter of 1943

On 8 August, *9. Kompanie* assembled in Jasonowodaija for loading. The tracks were changed on the ninth, and the company was loaded onto two separate transports. The first transport had six flat cars. Each transport was commanded by an officer from the company, *SS-Untersturmführer* Quade and *SS-Untersturmführer* Rathsack. The transport travelled to Charkow via Stalino, Barwenkowo, and Krasnograd. The first transport to arrive in Charkow unloaded, and the *Tigers* set out for Walki on a night march. The second transport arrived on the tenth, and the next day, with six *Tigers* under the command of Quade, they moved in the direction of Kolomak and were used on an attack on Tschutowo in the afternoon.

On 12 August, *9. Kompanie* was involved in heavy fighting near Kosliki, which resulted in one *Tiger* being knocked out (*SS-Unterscharführer* Fein's) and four more being immobilized. Only one *Tiger* (Quade's) remained in working order. Fein was killed, along with *SS-Sturmmann* Olitzka and radio operator Blockert; *SS-Rottenführer* Schlaab and *SS-Untersturmführer* Rathsack were wounded.

SS-Oberscharführer Baumann (tank commander) took command of the *Berge-Zug* from *SS-Oberscharführer* Biermann. Baumann had served in *SS-Regiment Deutschland* from October 1936 to August 1941, and he then served in various *Waffen-SS* departments as family and welfare officer in *Ostsee*, *Nordsee*, and *Fulda Werra*. He was posted to the *Totenkopf* on 12 October 1942 and assigned to *4(s) Kompanie* on 15 November 1942. Baumann was transferred to the *schwere Kompanie* from *SS-Panzer-Regiment 2* from 3 October to 29 December 1943. He was posted to *schwere SS-Panzer-Abteilung 102* on 30 December 1943. Later, he served in *1. Kompanie/schwere SS-Panzer-Abteilung* until October 1944, when he attended the fifth *SS-Panzer-Junker-Lehrgang* at Konigsbruck bei Wien from 1 October 1944 to 15 February 1945 (he was promoted to *SS-Hauptscharführer*, *Standarten Oberjunker*, on 1 October 1944) and then attended the *Oberfahnrich-Lehrgang* at the *Oberfahnrich-schule* at *Panzer-Truppen-Schule Wischau* from 20 February to 20 March 1945, when he was posted to the *SS-Panzer-Ausbildungs-und-Ersatz-Regiment* at Paderborn. Baumann was promoted to *SS-Untersturmführer der Reserve* on 20 April 1945. The following day, he was taken prisoner by U.S. forces after finishing the war as a platoon commander in *1. Kompanie/SS-Regiment Meyer* in *SS-Panzer-Brigade Westfalen*.

Rolf Stettner of *5. Kompanie* commented on 19 August 1943: "Over the headphones our regimental commander, Bochmann, orders, '*Tigers* and *Panzer IV's*, free fire at 1,600-meter range. *Panzer III's* move to the right.' The *Tiger* has an 8.8cm gun and the *Panzer IV* has a 7.5cm gun, but our *Panzer III's* have a 5cm gun with a long barrel with an effective range of 600 meters against a T-34. The idea is that the T-34 tanks make a move against our *Panzer III's* from *5. Kompanie*. Then the *Tigers* and *Panzer IV's* can break up the Russian tank attacks from the flank."

Fritz Hiss recorded:

30 July We went over to the attack near Stepanowka. Here comrade Mathai is killed.

31 July The Tiger of *SS-Oberscharführer* Lampert is knocked out, forcing the crew to bail out, but Lampert is killed. We are butchered, the earth trembles.

2 August Today we buried our comrades Lampert, Kochesser, and Schweitzer.

7 August Pulled back to Makajewka. Later, I'm driven in a *3t Zgkw* to recover radio equipment and the codes from two knocked-out tanks.

8 August In Jasonowodaija for loading.

9 August Track change and transport tracks fitted for loading. The company is loaded onto six rail flat cars, each with two *Tigers*, and our flat car carries a field kitchen vehicle.

10 August We arrive in Charkow–Nowo Bavaria, we receive some news that Hitler is in Charkow as well.

11 August From Charkow, we drive back into the front line. In a village our *Tigers* set up a security screen.

12 August During an attack, the *Tiger* of *SS-Unterscharführer* Fein is knocked out and the crew killed, including my best friend, Franz Hofer, near Walki.

13 August Heavy bombardment from Stalin organs. Had a nice birthday and some gifts. Our *Tiger* also had a new engine installed.

18 August A quiet day.

23 August Early on, our *Tiger* suffers engine failure.

24 August Drove around trying to find the company.

26 August Drove into a new assembly area and then moved into the attack.

28 August Nothing special to report.

30 August *SS-Untersturmführer* Quade is killed after the commander's cupola is shot off.

Eric Lehmkuhl wrote in his diary:

In mid-May, I was with *Kradschützen Regiment Thule*, and then I was transferred to the *Tiger* company, which was located in Budi. I was tasked by the company leadership to be a radio operator, but for most of June, I was a company clerk.

Between 6 and 21 July, I was on home leave. On the twenty-seventh, the company was located at the Mius Front. We were ordered to assault Hill 213.9 near Stepanowka, and radio operator Schweizer in Probst's *Tiger* is killed. On 2 August, we loaded in Gorlowka (Horlivka) and unloaded in Merefa.

On 12 August, the attack began west Charkow. As a radio operator in the commander's *Tiger* with *SS-Untersturmführer* Quade, the objective was Kosliki (Kolky). The attacked failed. We had two total losses, and three other *Tigers* were seriously damaged. Our *Tiger* was still operational, but the crew of Fein was killed and his Tiger was completely burned out. *SS-Oberscharführer* Lampert was killed, and *SS-Untersturmführer* Rathsack and *SS-Rottenführer* Schlaab were both seriously wounded.

August 13—further advance with *Panzer-Abteilung Großdeutschland* on Katschalowka. Same again on the fourteenth—heavy losses on both sides. We lost some tanks and so did the Russians.

14 August—fighting in the area of Alexejewka, Murufa, Medjanik, and Ridlo. The total distance was around forty kilometers. On the sixteenth, a further two *Tigers* were returned to service after repairs. Security in the area of Mertschik-Merla.

On the twentieth, thrust toward Kolontajew. *SS-Sturmann* Volger was killed. We linked with the *Grossdeutschland* north of Alexejewka. Strong Russian tanks units were present and they tried a break out in the morning, but they came under strong defensive from our guns. Gunner Lorentz knocked out two Russians tanks.

On the thirtieth, attack with two *Tigers* along the heights south of Kolontajew. The *Tiger* of *SS-Unterscharführer* Privatski sustained a direct hit from an artillery shell, killing the driver, Bachmann; the *Tiger* was a total loss. With infantry support, the heights were taken and secured some time later. During the night, we noticed strong enemy movement, including tanks. *SS-Sturmmann* Winter from the armory and six other men carried out repairs on our main gun, which was defective.

At 0400 in the early-morning hours, the enemy targeted our positions. The *Tiger* of *SS-Untersturmführer* Quade was hit by an antitank rifle shell in the commander's cupola. *SS-Sturmann* Winter was killed, and driver, Hilgart, was wounded; despite his wound, he managed to pull the *Tiger* into cover in the face of heavy Russian antitank gun fire.

Eric Lehmkuhl reported for mid-August 1943:

After the Mius Front, the company was loaded in Jassno-Wadaya and headed north by rail. Near Walki, we unloaded. The *WerkStatt* platoon began work on repairing our *Tigers*. Many of them had battle damage, much of which had to be welded using electrowelding equipment, and afterwards the *Tigers* got a new coat of paint. Those *Tigers* not requiring urgent repairs were put under the command of the regimental commander, *Standartenführer* Bochmann. The company was under the capable leadership of *SS-Untersturmführer* Quade, who has only one eye. The 1st Platoon is commanded by *SS-Untersturmführer* Rathsack.

On 11 August, we moved to a village, ready for deployment. Quade wanted to attack along an east-west axis as the Russians had made some gains along our front line. The situation was serious. We waited until four in the afternoon before we moved. The waiting was unbearable. The column rolled out and we drove toward some heights. As we drove down the other side, we saw the vastness of the Ukraine. Our direction was north. At a distance of 2.5 kilometers, we saw a Russian column on the move with vehicles, tanks, guns, and horse-drawn wagons all being escorted by Russian infantry.

We noticed that the Russian infantry began to fan out in order to protect the column, and before long, the Russians began laying down heavy defensive fire, but overhead we heard the sound of engines, and before long, we spotted a squadron of *He 111* bombers flying over us. They carpet-bombed the Russian column. Following behind this bombardment was our infantry, who followed up with an assault, after a successful attack by the *Luftwaffe*. We receive an order that our tanks are not needed, so we pull back to our original start line, but as we move, we do fire a few rounds at the dispersed Russian column, mainly high-explosive rounds.

The heat is unbearable—it is 30 degrees Celsius. We try to find some shade. Our *Tiger* suffers from gear trouble. The repair is carried out by the indispensable Karl Frank. After an hour, he tells our driver, Franz Hilgart, to try the gears. With a painful grin, Frank smiles as Hilgart crunches his way through the gears. After a peaceful night which is only broken by the sound of ducks, the sun comes up at around five. By eight, the heat is again unbearable. We find some buckets and hose; we use these for a makeshift shower. At noon the company cook, Loibold, has cooked some roast pork, which we eat. Afterward, we all had a brief nap, not knowing that this day would end in tragedy. Quade sweeps into view in his *VW Kübel*. With him is our grinning comrade, Kurt Heinkal.

Quade had just finished an orders group at the regimental headquarters. Our six *Tigers* were to set in motion as quickly as possible. We were to head west at a distance of five kilometers. We formed up in a village, which had been cleared previously by grenadiers from *Regiment Eicke*. They had gone house to house. Then the order came to "close hatches." We moved out and the crews readied themselves for the task ahead. We drove along the road heading towards another village. So far, things had proceeded without incident. As we entered the village, there was no sign of life, only chickens running around. Where was the civilian population? The silence was eerie.

If danger was brewing, we could only guess. Our infantry began moving into the village, and then we saw some brown-clad figures run into the field. We fired some bursts of MG fire, but nothing happened. Were the Russians playing games with us? Quade decided to seize the heights in front of the village. We would attack in a wedge formation. So far, things had been too easy. About one kilometer from the heights, Quade called for a halt. He tasked *SS-Untersturmführer* Rathsack to scout ahead and see if he can observe anything, but shortly before that, there was a flash and a bang. It was hard to describe, but the flash had temporarily blinded our driver as he looked out of the drivers vision block. Also our radio sets were knocked out. I opened the radio set and saw that the fuses had been dislodged. I quickly try to put the fuses back in place. Franz puts the tank in reverse, but he drives carefully and not too fast so that we do not throw a track. After about 200 meters, we find some cover, which means that no more antitank shells came our way. The radios are working again. It is then that we hear the bad news—an *SS-Oberscharführer Tiger* commander reports over the net, "One dead, head shot. *SS-Untersturmführer* Rathsack and his gunner are wounded." We can see our *Tigers* on the right, but what about the 1st Platoon? After a few minutes, we see the flaming *Tiger*—it is *SS-Unterscharführer* Fein in *Tiger 913*. Quade and Hilgart rush over to the burning tank. Our infantry provide covering fire.

So far, we had only advanced 500 meters and saw no sign of the Russians. Those on foot approach Fein's *Tiger* from the side since the 8.8cm ammunition might ignite. Franz Hofer dies from his wounds. Fein is found dead inside the *Tiger*, which had been hit on the front by a 9.2cm antitank shell; this round could penetrate our *Tigers*. Hofer was lying in front us. He was a good-hearted lad, but now the Russians are closing in on us with hand grenades. We remount our *Tiger* and make ready. The balance from the day is heavy: seven dead, three wounded, with one *Tiger* as a total loss; four other *Tigers* are heavily damaged by antitank rounds and need repairing. The company commander's *Tiger* is still in running order; our own *Tiger* had been hit twice. One of them had struck just above the driver's vision block—a little lower would have been deadly.

Not long afterward, the Russians start firing again, putting down a suppressive fire, which causes losses amongst our infantry. The Russian infantry begin to attack our positions, but they pay a heavy price. Quade's *Tiger* fires into the Russian infantry. The attack stalls, and our own infantry launch a counterattack. Now we hear a howling noise from behind us and explosions on the heights: it's our *Nebelwerfer* [multibarreled rocket launcher] firing. Our infantry struggle up the heights. Our contribution is small, with only one *Tiger* in working order. All it can do is provide covering fire. Later in the evening, we roll forward and see the antitank gun positions which had been so devastating. These guns have the same firepower as our 8.8cm; we find eight of these American guns. The *Nebelwerfer* fire had done this damage, totally demoralizing the Russians, who had left their positions.

Now we are standing in a field full of stumps. That night, it's very quiet. If you looked long enough at something, you'd think it moved. In the darkness we can hear the Russians talking very loudly. We talk in a softer voice. Suddenly, a rider comes out of the darkness. We could see his shoulder epaulettes, and we can see he is an officer. During this episode, we were eating sandwiches. Franz, our driver, dropped his, and he tried stammering, "*Rucki Warsch*," and gestured with his hand. The Russian rider suddenly realized the situation he was in. He turned the horse around and bolted, but our infantry fired some shots, which dropped the horse. The rider somehow got up and ran off into the darkness. We ran over to the dead horse and recovered the rider's equipment; the saddle was made of very fine leather.

We give all the leather items to the company shoe maker, who makes some new sport shoes and boots. After some sleep, we awake around three in the morning because of a massive noise of Russian tanks on the move, seemingly all around us, but we quickly realize what is going on: an army *Tiger Abteilung* is moving around us, and we're in the middle. After ten minutes, a tremendous artillery barrage opens, backed by rocket fire, shaking the ground. We move out and form up in a wedge formation just like on a training exercise. We roll forward toward another village. We see the houses on the fire with their thatched roofs, but there seems to be an antitank gun front. A *Tiger* on our right opens fire at a range of 1,000 meters. We do the same. This goes on for fifteen minutes. Soon after we enter the village via the main road, we move off to the right with four *Tigers*. We have some infantry support during the assault. We spend the night in a field again. The Russians suffered heavy losses due to trying to contend with thirty-six *Tigers* (*III/Panzer-Regiment Großdeutschland*). In the evening the comrades from the army leave us, so we have to continue any attack by ourselves with the support of our own grenadiers.

The next objective is another village located on a slope, but we will have to find our way around a swamp, but this is overcome. As we drive up to the village, which is highlighted against the night sky, we come under fire from a Russian Maxim machine gun, which is silenced by our 8.8cm high-explosive shells. The Russians fade away. We move back and refuel and take on a new load of ammunition. We also get something to eat, but before long, we are called forward again.

We move out and find the engineers whom we are meant to support. They are trying to build a bridge across a small ford, but to the north in a wood, the Russians are firing on the engineers. Our task is to assist the infantry in securing the wood and clear the Russians out. Our infantry went forward, and the Russians started firing mortars at us. This turns out to be rather unpleasant, so we change our approach; unfortunately, we get hit by two antitank gun rounds. Quade observes a T-34 at 2,500 meters and fires a shot at the Russian tank. After lunch, we come under heavy artillery fire. The shells are falling all around us, but we remain in our position. In the evening, we pull back to a village. Later, Quade returns from an officer's briefing; he tells us that an attack is to take place at four in the morning on the village called Alexejewka, which is about ten kilometres from us. The attack that Quade outlines could force a decision for the division and *8. Armee* and also encircle large units of the Red Army. Our company has three *Tigers* operational. We move into a field for deployment.

The attack does happen in the morning, but abruptly, the point of attack is changed. It progresses very rapidly, and by the afternoon, we are on the road to Alexejewka. In the night the Russians are trapped. We change our location. The Russians may attempt to break out, and a large portion of the force is inside a wood. We remain inside the *Tiger*; we can't leave, so we try to sleep except while on guard duty. Next to us, the infantry set up an MG 42 heavy machine gun. The night is quiet, but at approximately three, we are abruptly shaken from our sleep by a scream of "Urrah! Urrah!" from the Russian infantry which are coming at us from the woods. The MG 42 opens fire. The first wave of the Russian infantry is cut down under our defensive fire. The roar of the Russian infantry dies down only to be followed by moans of the wounded. Our infantry follow up with the taking of prisoners. We soon get an order to pull back. This was our last action around Alexejewka. This was the division's last success in the East. We are on the move again, this time to Kolontajew, where the division would be involved in a fierce defensive battle.

Eric Lehmkuhl chronicled the period from 24 August to 10 September 1943:

On 24 August 1943, we moved to Kolontajew, which is situated in a swampy area and is a paradise for geese, pigs, and vegetables—all very welcome for our cooking pot. Later, we are committed to action in the daytime. We return at night for some cold soup. If it's possible to get through a Russian artillery barrage, then it's possible to get through our cooking. As a result, we were quite neglected and run down. Our uniforms are smeared in oil. Our underwear is sweat-covered, and the lice make our lives uncomfortable, but we get a two-day quiet period, so we clean and wash extensively, but this happiness lasts only two days.

On the twenty-sixth, we slaughtered a pig. Our specialist, Fritz Lau, took care this. A message from the regiment arrives. We have to immediately leave. We put the pig—it's in two halves—in a box drum. The entrails are in our wash bucket, which is stowed on the engine deck. We also had prepared a tomato salad. After about two kilometers, the heat is unbearable inside the tank, but we had to keep the hatches closed because of Russian artillery fire. We had determined that the temperature was 45 degrees Celsius in the shade. The transmission was hot—you couldn't touch it. We sat there swimming in our own sweat inside the tank. It was impossible to wear our uniforms, which stick to our bodies. The conditions were like a drill instructor who grinds you down. Suddenly, Russian artillery fire falls around our position. We move forward. It was like being chased through a hot shower on the move.

There are heavy thuds and shaking around the tank. Normally, we would sweat from fear. In such moments we do show some fear, but it's something we've been through before. We sweat from the heat. I had my hatch open to let in some air, but to my anxiety, a red-hot splinter comes flying in and hits a coffee jar marked "Unite German Coffee." Even with the hatches closed, the Russian artillery is getting stronger. We can see from our vision block that people are wandering around out of the haze and smoke. Who can survive this barrage? We had our tanks in a field. Certainly, we are shot at, and this is followed up by an infantry attack, but now we started to hear cries and moans. What a miserable sight! The enemy had literally tried to storm our positions with infantry, but a *Rottenführer* comes running over to our tank, screaming for our help. Quade, our company commander, shouts back that we will come. Over the intercom comes the command "Driver march." We set in motion exactly opposite the Russians, whose infantry were attacking our own lines.

The onboard machine gun cuts through the Russian infantry. We hear the cries of "Urrah," but the Russians were trying to break through our lines and fought for every meter. However, the Russian attack was beaten back, but at times, it seemed like a struggle for individual survival, as the Russians would return with new forces to continue the offensive. Although we are aware of the enormous Russian casualties, the thought of victory is already gone because in those days battles like Kolontajew were repeated every day. We had three *Tigers* operational during the current battle. The "Fire Division," as we called ourselves, met several times a day. We fired with all our barrels. We pushed the Russians back, but they always returned. It was a hard experience during those days, coupled with the intense heat inside our tank with the hatches closed, going from one defensive position to another.

The tank was like a sieve. We were hit at every location we went to. After a few days and carrying out at least six attacks, the Russians returned and fired at us. They sent new infantry companies into the jaws of battle. When we fired at them, they just melted away, and the losses were appalling. We were happy in our steel box, but the days at Kolontajew were not yet over. On the following morning at 0400, the Russians opened fire with all barrels in a barrage, trying to finally force a breakthrough, but the attack is aimed right through at the center of our defenses and comes to nothing. At noon, the Russians try again, but we were able to eliminate this attack. We were located on a reverse slope, so we had a distinctive view allowing us to fire round after round. This gives our infantry protection as we are firing shell after shell. Our loader, Ernst Vogler from East Prussia, wanted to open the loaders hatch and discard some empty casings. An antitank shell made of cast steel smashes to pieces inside the interior of the tank, fatally wounding Vogler. However, the fight had to continue. It was like a race against time. We have to survive several salvos from Stalin organs. We have to admire our grenadiers, who are supposed to be fighting a guards rifle division. At the right moment, our on-board MG opens fire into the brown-clad Russian infantry. They reassemble and try again, surging forward. We open fire again. MG cartridges land on my lap. Soon we are able to launch a counterattack. In the heat of the moment, I had forgotten to change the MG ammunition bag. Eventually, our attack comes to a halt. We managed to penetrate about 100 meters. At the end of a very hot day, in the evening we are able to fill up with fuel and take on a full load of new ammunition. The resupply takes several hours.

On another morning the Russians start with a mass artillery barrage. They wanted to put everything in and push us back from the front. The *Totenkopf* had been repelling Russian attacks for over a week, and we had become a thorn in the Russian side. However, they had managed to penetrate our front lines but were pushed back. After we took on new fuel and ammunition in the early-morning hours, in the afternoon we received an alarm and had to respond immediately. The Russians with huge reserves of men and material had taken possession of the heights at the eastern end near Kolontajew. For some reason, this was of importance, and we had to scrape some reserves together, even the sick were involved in the counter attack. We had two *Tigers* and conducted a mobile defense. Never again could we put a full company together. Consequently, we had to fight a serious defensive action. Slowly, we feel that the time of victory is over and that the Eastern Front is bleeding all along the front. There is huge sacrifice in men and material.

The crews of the tanks of Quade and Lachner set off on the march. Meanwhile, at the foot of the heights, something was going on. The infantry could only advance step by step. After the *Nebelwerfer* had intervened, our tanks and *StuG's* fought off the Russian infantry pushing them back across the heights. The Russian infantry looked very demoralized after our *Nebelwerfer* fire, and we pushed ahead, but we could not sing our praises just yet. By evening, the Russians used heavy artillery—17.2cm guns—in a regimental barrage. They fired continuously with a hail of steel, but the "hear and see" moment passes us. We did not see anything move, but to our left we hear Lachner's tank move off, only to get hit after a short time. Lachner reports over the radio that he had been hit by artillery fire and that the engine had been hit. The water temperature was rising.

Quade radioed back, "Do whatever you can to try to remedy the damage." The crew of Lachner, van Kerkhom, Privatski, and the driver Bachmann had to find the problem and repair the engine under heavy fire. As the crew got out and began looking at the engine, a Russian artillery shell went off nearby. Shards killed Bachmann, who was dear to us all and a good comrade. The gunner, Privatski, managed to get the damaged tank going again and drove out of the danger zone and back to the mechanics. Meanwhile, the Russians had eased off with their artillery, but at about 1800 hours, after a short artillery burst from our own guns, we set off. We had six men, including our best weapons technician, Fritz Winter. As our recoil system wasn't working properly, he worked on it until dusk. We saw some Russian infantry come onto view along the heights, but they quickly disappeared. To our left and right were two *schwere Panzerspähwagen* (armored half-tracks) from the *Panzer-Aufklärungs-Abteilung*.

SS-Untersturmführer Rathsack, who had been wounded on the twelfth, remained in the hospital until the thirty-first. By 27 September, he was posted to *schwere SS-Panzer-Abteilung 102*, with which he served in the Normandy campaign as the battalion adjutant and was killed in Trun on 19 August 1944. On the thirteenth, *9. Kompanie* and *III/Panzer-Regiment Großdeutschland* (with thirty-six *Tigers*) attacked Katschalowka and then reassembled for a planned advance on Alexejewka, which took place on the fifteenth.

On the fifteenth, *9. Kompanie* advanced on Konstantinowka. By the afternoon, *9. Kompanie* was on the road to Alexejewka. On the seventeenth, *9. Kompanie* knocked out some forty Russian tanks with six *Tigers* while fighting in the areas of Subebowka and Karaiskasowka. On the twentieth, *9. Kompanie* was involved in an attack on Kolontajew in which elements of the *Totenkopf* Division linked up with *Panzer-Grenadier-Division Großdeutschland* near Parchomowka. On the twenty-second, *9. Kompanie* was involved in counterattacks in the open terrain southeast of Stepanowka, where two *Tigers* were immobilized by antitank gunfire. By the twenty-fifth, both *Großdeutschland* and *Totenkopf* were preparing for withdrawal toward the Dnjepr River. The withdrawal began on the twenty-sixth under extreme Russian pressure. On the thirtieth, while fighting near Kolontajew, the *Tiger* of *SS-Unterscharführer* Privatski was hit by Russian artillery fire. The radio operator, *SS-Sturmmann* Vogler, was killed. On the thirty-first, the *Tiger* company was involved in fighting along the heights south of Kolontajew. The same day, *SS-Untersturmführer* Quade was killed when his *Tiger* was hit and shrapnel struck the commander's cupola. The company was now commanded by *SS-Hauptscharführer* Berger.

On 2 August, *SS-Hauptsturmführer* Saumenicht, commander of *I/SS-Panzer-Regiment 3*, led a small *Kampfgruppe* (one *Tiger*, five *Panzer IV's*, and six *Panzer III's*) and stopped an attempted breakthrough by the Russian XXI Guards Corps that resulted in the destruction of forty-two Russian tanks. For this decisive action, Saumenicht was awarded the Knight's Cross.

On 3 August, *SS-Untersturmführer* Kurt Ebeling arrived and assumed command of *9. Kompanie*. He had been transferred from the heavy tank battalion of *II/SS-Panzer-Korps*. Ebeling had graduated from *SS-Junkerschule Braunschweig* and was assigned to the *Tiger* battalion for the *II/SS-Panzer-Korps* on 1 May 1943. On 3 August as well, the *Tiger* of *SS-Oberscharführer*

Willi Muller was knocked out during the fighting near Kolontajew. As the crew bailed out, Muller was caught by the Russians and beaten to death. The loader, *SS-Sturmmann* Boxleitner, was also killed. On 4 August, an infantry *Kampfgruppe* led by *SS-Hauptsturmführer* Grams, headquarters company commander for *I/SS-Panzer-Regiment 3*, and made up of tankless crews from *I/SS-Panzer-Regiment 3* and *9. Kompanie* saw action during the fighting for some woods. *SS-Scharführer* Rechlin was killed. Herbert Sachse and Fischer were wounded. Franz von Berg was awarded the Iron Cross, Second Class, for his exemplary conduct during the fighting.

9. Kompanie was attached to *I/SS-Panzer-Regiment 3* and conducted defensive operations around Hill 136.5 and Marchailiwka. Between 8 and 9 August, *9. Kompanie* saw action between Kotelewka and Subowka. As the *Totenkopf* pulled back to Poltawa, the rains began, turning the roads into thick muddy mire. On the twenty-first, *I/SS-Panzer-Regiment 3* entrained in Poltawa. The battalion was due to convert and retrain on the *Panther* tank. The battalion returned on 24 July 1944. Fifty percent of the crews from *I/SS-Panzer-Regiment 3* stayed behind with the *Panzer* regiment and acted as replacement crews for *II/SS-Panzer-Regiment 3*.

On the twenty-second, the *Totenkopf* was fighting south and west of Poltawa. On the twenty-seventh, the division had crossed the Dnjepr River near Kremenchug. A collection commando for five new *Tigers*, issued via *Nachschub Ost*, was sent to Dnjepropetrowsk. On 1 October 1943, the *WerkStatt* platoon set up a repair facility in Korristowka, while *9. Kompanie* received a new intake of manpower. The armored reconnaissance battalion for the headquarters company of *SS-Panzer-Regiment 3* was disbanded after seven *Panzer III's* were lost in one action, leaving only one *Befehlspanzer III*.

The following joined the *Tiger* company:

SS-Unterscharführer Achim Nutzenberger, tank commander. (He would later serve in *6. Kompanie* as a platoon leader.)
SS-Oberscharführer Neuner, former *Spieß* of the headquarters company of *SS-Panzer-Regiment 3 Stab*
SS-Rottenführer Eduard Pelzer
SS-Rottenführer Wolfgang Barth
SS-Rottenführer Wolf
SS-Rottenführer Ehlert
SS-Sturmmann Walter Nahm
SS-Oberscharführer Emil Weitner, via the divisional field replacement battalion

Fritz Hiss reported:

2 September Change of position. We are eaten by lice that make a home of us; we are unshaven and covered in filth.

3 September All hell breaks loose—strong Russian artillery bombardment. *SS-Oberscharführer* Muller moves his *Tiger* to the front, but it runs over a mine. Muller is later found dead, and the loader, Boxleitner, is taken prisoner. A *Panzer III* drives up and attacks the Russians and recues Boxleitner. Muller had been beaten to death with shovels.

5 September Back from the front line in the afternoon, we make potato pancakes.

11 September An adjacent tank is on fire, everything around it is in flames

14 September I'm with the *Zgkw* driver, Heinz Mewes; we drove over to the support unit.

17 September The main supply road is quite muddy; vehicles are getting stuck and have to be pulled free by *Zgkw* acting like a tractor.

19 September In Poltawa. We drove into the town like a lame duck.

20 September Had to be towed by *18t Zgkw* due to gear trouble.

24 September Still cannot continue along the road in which we are withdrawing due to constant Russian air attacks.

25 September Take on rations in Kremenchug.

26 September We leave our accommodation in Kremenchug in good spirits and drive toward the bridge, but as we approach, we notice there is total confusion.

28 September Arrived in Alexandria along with the *WerkStatt* platoon. Five new *Tigers* are collected in Dnepropetrovsk; rations are collected.

3 October The company along with the *Tigers* arrive in Protopopowka.

5 October The new *Tigers* are sent to the combat elements via the support unit.

6 October Standing watch on the front line.

9 October During a move on my mother's birthday, a Russian artillery shell hits our *Tiger*.

10 October Withdrawal and building bunkers.

18 October Assembly and move back to the front line. The Russians make a breakthrough near Iwanowka.

21 October *SS-Sturmann* Josef Hodap and Rudi Grabowski are both sent to Vienna on a course.

Eric Lehmkuhl reported:

On 1 September 1943, we return to the *WerkStatt*. The company has no officers; *SS-Hauptscharführer* Berger (*Spieß*) is the company commander. We receive orders to move. The Russians have opened a 700-kilometer breach along the front east of the Dnjepr River. On the Dnjepr River is the Rundstedt Bridge which was built in 1941 and was blown up on 30 August. On 6 October, the Russians have reached the Dnjepr River and start to cross. On the seventh, the company assembles in Usbenskoje; on the eighth, we attack the Kereda Peninsula.

We come across the dead from the infantry, but the peninsula is captured. Again the losses on both sides are heavy. The commander during this operation was *SS-Hauptscharführer* Berger. Until the end of October, we remain on the defensive. We are fighting in the area west of Kremenchug, Protopopowka, Alexandria, Iwanowka, and Nikolajewka. Our *Tiger* has damage. The autumn mud season begins—fighting north of Krivoy Rog.

During the loading of a damaged *Tiger*, two stray T-34 tanks attack the station in Korristowka during the evening; they were knocked out using mines. On the following morning at 0800, some fifty Russian tanks appear. In the station units of the army are unloading; they have just arrived from the Italian Front. The tanks take enemy fire, causing panic on the road, but air support is provided by *Oberst* Rudel's *Stukas*, which are equipped with tank-busting cannons. The Russian tanks have infantry mounted on them. All our tanks fire; the greater part of the attacking Russian tanks are set on fire and the crews bail out. Forty-seven Russian tanks are knocked out.

After several weeks of fighting, the company is worn out. We reassemble in Bobrinez. After reorganizing, we get a new company commander, *SS-Obersturmbannführer* Baedke. Another new officer arrives as well, *SS-Untersturmführer* Neff. Other new arrivals include Knevel, Heimbruch,

SS-Oberscharführer Weitner, and Kriescher. We also receive some new *Tigers*, which have the new commander's cupola similar to the *Tiger II*.

In December, we conduct some limited operations together with some cobbled-together units. The company can still operate at company level despite being worn out. Ever since the retreat from the Dnjepr, we can still fight but with limited strength.

On 3 October, five new *Tigers* arrive in Protopopowka. The Russians were constantly expanding the bridgehead on the Dnjepr River. On 7 October, the *Tiger* company was in Usbenskoje. On the eighth, the remaining operational *Tigers* were part of a *Kampfgruppe* that assaulted the Kolerda Peninsula on the Dnjepr River. One of the *Tigers* suffered an internal explosion which damaged the commander's hatch; luckily, no one was injured. On the ninth, the Russians broke through near Tschikalowka, which was cleared up. On the tenth, some of the damaged *Tigers* were repaired. In Korristowka, the railway station came under attack by two stray T-34s as some damaged *Tigers* were being loaded on to rail transports. The Russian tanks were knocked out with mines. On the following day, more Russian tanks and infantry attacked the station again, but the situation was saved by the intervention of *Ju-87 Stukas* that mounted 3.7cm cannons.

On 15 October, the *Tigers* were involved in a counterattack on Saporoshje (Zaprorizhzhya). On the eighteenth, the *Totenkopf* is placed in reserve under *XI. Armee-Korps* in the area of Pawlych (Pawlych)–Onufrijewka (Onufriivka), but due to the strong rain, the road conditions were dreadful. On the twentieth, the operational *Tigers* were situated west of Iwanowka (Iwanowka). On the twenty-first, the *Tigers* crossed the Ingulez River and assaulted Russian forces near Alexandria and later Iwanowka. The *Totenkopf* is now classified as a full *Panzer-Division* [previously a *Panzer-Grenadier-Division*]. On the twenty-fourth, *9. Kompanie* was instructed to clear a Russian penetration near Dewtschje and establish contact with some engineers. Dewtschje is cleared of Russian forces; near a wood, the *Tigers* come under Russian artillery fire.

Walter Nahm recorded in his diary:

1 October I have been in Snamenka overnight, standing on the platform from 0500 to 0700. I have to wait for a train. Many trains have been marshalled for the front around noon; I manage to get a train to Korristowka for some rest behind the front line. However, according to a station official, I would have to change trains along with some other comrades, as the next train is going in the direction of Pawlisch, the rest area for *SS-Panzer-Regiment 3*. By chance I find out that the regiment is much closer. With all my belongings, I find the headquarters company for *II/SS-Panzer-Regiment 3* in Protopopowka. At the office we meet up with Nutzenberger and Pelzer—great joy on both sides. I'm told that Lasch, Gutmann, and Richards are all wounded; *SS-Untersturmführer* Palm and Westerberg were both badly burnt. Kreuzberger was also wounded; Friedrich and Melz have both been promoted to *Oberscharführer*, and both got the Iron Cross, First Class. *SS-Untersturmführer* Lummitsch was awarded the German Cross in Gold. The tank regiment has only nine tanks available for action in the area of Kremenchug. Since the actions on the Mius Front, many of our tanks need significant repairs and new parts. The *I/SS-Panzer-Regiment 3* was returned to Germany for conversion to the new *Panther* tank. The armored reconnaissance platoon had been disbanded. Nutzenberger, Pelzer, and myself are to be

transferred to the *Tiger* company. Also present was Ehlert. In the evening we manage to get some sleep.

2 October During the afternoon, Nutzenberger is talking to the company commander, an *Untersturmführer*, who tells us if we are both free, he will take us immediately. We go back to our old headquarters company and collect all our things. We look around for new quarters, which we find. We also find out that the house actually has electricity.

4 October Nutzenberger tells us that the transfer to the *Tiger* company is still in progress.

5 October The headquarter's company's *Spieß*, *SS-Unterscharführer* Neuner, tells us informally that we are both a part of the *Tiger* company.

11 October To date, nothing new. *SS-Obersturmbannführer* Beiermeier is promoted to *Hauptsturmführer*. The company *Spieß*, Glashof goes on leave. Usual free time—reading, writing letters, cleaning weapons, and visiting mates. Until yesterday, very pleasant autumn weather, but then the temperature plummets. On the seventh, Nutzenberger, Neuner, Krotzenbischler, and I suddenly turn back to Alexandria. We have to report back to the area commissioner. Nutzenberger comes back and tells us that he will not be joining us at the *Tiger* company but instead will be joining *6. Kompanie* as a platoon leader. In the evening Wolf and I, along with *Spieß* Neuner, are invited to dinner. We have chicken and mashed potatoes with Crimean wine and vodka.

15 October Still pretty quiet. We are quartered in a house with an old woman who makes a lot of potato pancakes. At night there's much air activity. The lame ducks are constantly overhead making a ruckus. Today we take a truck to Kremenchug to clear out the offices for *II/SS-Panzer-Regiment 3* and the *Tiger* company. The Russians are using many artillery barrages. Our infantry are getting bombarded frequently. We search for some poultry, and we catch some chickens and slaughter them. We have a feast back at the company.

16 October The *Spieß* tells us we are both free from duties and we can either go to the *Tiger* company or we can take part in some gunnery training for the *Flak* platoon of the headquarters company. For us it's clear: we want the *Tiger* company and change quarters in the evening.

17 October Since yesterday, last night, it's been raining incessantly. Indeed, it's the beginning of the rainy season. Finally, some post arrives from back home. The Russians have forced a crossing on the Dnjepr near Kremenchug with strong forces. The battalion and the *Tiger* company are put on alert and have to be ready for a counterattack tomorrow morning.

18 October It has become miserably cold. Standing guard at the battalion and the company. Tomorrow we plan to build a sauna.

19 October The Russians, with tanks and infantry, have broken through about thirty kilometers away along the rail line and airfield near Alexandria. Nevertheless, we have a quiet period. We have a uniform check, even on days like this. In the evening we get a visit from Nutzenberger, who would like us back.

20 October Starting today, we are officially with the *Tiger* company. However, we must remain with the headquarters

company. There are no quarters for us at the *Tiger* company. The Russians are using a new type of aircraft, an American fighter-bomber [probably a P-39 Airacobra, which the Soviets used extensively for ground attack]. This type of aircraft buzzed us when we were building a sauna bath. The sound is deafening, but the bath is coming along nicely.

21 October The cold and the rain subside. The roads have almost dried up. Nutzenberger tells me that he has once again requested us back. Wolf is awarded the Iron Cross, First Class.

22 October Overnight the Russians expanded their bridgehead. It is now 150 kilometers long and 20 kilometers wide. Their direction of attack is Odessa. The one exception is Alexandria. All day we can hear the thunder of heavy artillery guns. We have a few tanks available.

On 25 October 1943, the company moved to the area of Snamenka. The following day, some of the *Tigers* received new engines. On the twenty-seventh, the *Totenkopf* assembled in the area of Protopopowka and Alexandria. The *Tigers* from *9. Kompanie* were involved in a local counterattack east of Alexandria with the support of *Ju-87 Stukas*. Later, the *Tigers* took up positions near Golowkowka (Golovny). On the twenty-ninth, operational *Tigers* from *9. Kompanie* traveled to the nearby *Luftwaffe* base just outside Alexandria to meet up with *4. Kompanie (Panther)* from *SS-Panzer-Regiment 2* (from *2. SS-Panzer-Division Das Reich*). *Tigers* and elements of *II/SS-Panzer-Regiment 3* advanced south toward Olimpiadowka and then Malinowka, near Spassowa, where a Russian column was dispersed. On the thirtieth, further attacks were launched on Woltschanka and then toward Nowo Petrowka. On the thirty-first, the *Tigers* moved from the area of Wlassjewka to Graphit.

Walter Nahm described events in his diary:

23 October Guard duty at the battalion command post. Otherwise, the time is spent reading or writing—today we made potato pancakes.

24 October In the morning we have a sauna bath. In the afternoon, alarm—we pack our things, and with *SS-Unterscharführer* Nutzenberger, we drive over to *6. Kompanie*.

25 October At two in the morning, we are at point in the advance party heading toward Snamenka. We have lunch and take up quarters. Our tanks are nearby. We get some sleep. Also with us are Buss and Sklenzky.

26 October At noon, we march to the *Tiger* company. The *Spieß* tells us there are no quarters for us, so we call in on the headquarters company, only to be told that we have to find our own quarters.

27 October In the night at three, tank alarm—Russian tanks have broken through our lines. We pack our things and head off in the direction of the Russian advance. In the early-morning gray, we make out the noise of the Russian engines, so they cannot be far away. Actually, it turns out to be tanks from a *Wehrmacht* tank unit. They had been driving past our positions at midnight. The *Wehrmacht* unit had been changing positions.

28 October In the air, there's much activity. From Italy, the *24. Panzer-Division* has just arrived and has now moved into position next to us.

29 October March orders given at four in the morning. Both the *Tiger* company and the headquarters company move out.

The road leads us through Novo-Praga-Alexandria-Kristinowka and Protopopowka. All the roads are clogged with vehicles of all kinds. We see *Panthers* from *Das Reich*. Also along the way there are many destroyed Russian T-34 tanks and self-propelled artillery. In the evening we reach Protopopowka.

1 November To date, things have been peaceful, but in the distance we can hear the continuous sound of thunder from artillery pieces. After lunch the company *Spieß* comes and tells us that the company commander, Baedke, will launch a counterattack in the early-morning hours, so we go to bed early that night.

2 November *SS-Unterscharführer* Neuner goes on home leave. It's six in the evening, and he leaves the company by truck. The company commander, Baedke, arrives, and Pelzer is assigned to his crew as the gunner. Wolf has to leave the *Tiger* because of a high fever.

3 November During the afternoon, we drive off in a *Maultier* [supply truck with a half-track conversion] on a trip which is about sixty kilometers long. We are consistently on the move. Along the main road, we see several knocked-out T-34 tanks and burnt-out vehicles. Wolf has still not recovered.

4 November We are still in the same location. Wolf feels a bit better but a little tender.

5 November Nothing special to report. Still at the same location. In the morning the commanders of the *8. Armee* and *40. Panzer-Korps* give praise to our division as we leave their commands.

7 November We leave at six in the morning. Our *Tigers* have not arrived. As we move along the road, we slide from the left to right. At around four in the afternoon, we arrive at our new destination.

8 November We get up early in the morning at six in the morning. It has rained all night, and the roads are just mud and slush. All vehicles make continuous efforts to move forward. Only *Maultiers* can move along the road, but the rain doesn't stop.

9 November At midday, thirty men from the company assemble to receive orders from the commander.

11 November No further moves, so we go and watch the film *I Love You*. From the canteen, we get coffee and cake. Two of the men get champagne, so in the evening we have a little booze.

12 November Went to the cinema again in the morning. Today's showing is *Bal Pare*, and it's not a new film. The company took a new delivery of ammunition today.

13 November The day begins with some brisk shooting at around five in the morning. Wolfgang is sent off with the advance party; Rudi and Sablotny left yesterday. On the main road, the regimental commander, Bochmann, is directing traffic himself. We pull back toward Bairak. The village is very busy, and we set up a small tent and build a fire.

14 November Before daybreak, the Russians begin with a huge artillery barrage at six in the morning like a frenzied drum. Our whole front is on fire. This is certainly the intended offensive on Krivoy Rog. We make ready and load everything up on the roadworthy vehicles. We soon approach the front and see infantryman pass us. At ten in the morning, we get orders: the *Tigers* are to seek and skirmish with the

Russians. All day Russian artillery falls in our rear area. The tank regiment knocked out sixty Russian tanks during the day; of these, twenty-eight were destroyed by the *Tiger* company; Wolfgang has to drive forward with a *Zgkw* with the combat elements.

15 November Like yesterday, great artillery fire all day from the Russians. Air activity is brisk—they cause great slaughter just like our *Stukas* used to do. Our *Tigers* expended a great deal of ammunition during the day.

16 November The company commander is with us. *SS-Oberscharführer* Haja is also in our quarters. In the evening we have eggnog. Four *Tigers* return to our location.

17 November Still located in Bairak. Toward evening a massive artillery bombardment followed by mortar fire. Fortunately, we suffer no losses. Biber is now located in our quarters.

18 November We organize some trucks so we can load all our technical equipment and tools, but the truck of the company commander has to be given back. A damaged T-34 is used as a *Berge-Panzer* for towing our *Tigers* from the front line back to Bairak. This is done three or four times during the day. The T-34 stands at the ready on the roadside, but it breaks down. None of us knows how to get it started or repair the engine, but a mechanic from the *Instand-Staffel* knows what to do and gets the engine started. That night we baked and roasted potatoes, because we celebrate that Biber is getting the Iron Cross, First Class. The company cook fries some eggs; Neff plays the fiddle and tells us how beautiful France is. *Feldmarshall* von Manstein sent the division a message: "Bravo, *SS-Totenkopf*, you are fantastic men"—I can add nothing further to this.

20 November At 1400 hours, I wake before Wolf. The company commander had been up since 0500. A new determined attack by the Russians; their artillery is using every known caliber up to 17.5cm. The whole earth shakes; we've never experienced anything like this before. The impacts are shaking the house. Someone yells at me to go to the *Instand-Staffel*, but my route is blocked, and I see Wolf run through the barrage over to the supply section as well. He tells them to pull back. *SS-Oberscharführer* Haja and Wolf try to move the T-34 *Berge-Panzer*, but first they remove the swastika flag off the back of the engine deck. Despite all the shells falling down around us, we manage to pull back from Bairak. We have no idea of the location of the Russian forces. Overhead their air force is busy with fighter-bomber attacks. The civilian population follows behind us, but we wait until dusk when we think it's safe to withdraw back to Boikowka.

Wolfgang Barth recorded in his diary:

21 November Drove with ammunition and fuel to the forward combat elements. This was an easy drive. Ede Pelzer has destroyed eighteen Russian tanks as of yesterday.

22 November Afternoon, we leave along with the support units by heading toward Schewschenkowo (Shevchenkove), where we arrive in the evening. We find some very nice quarters.

23 November Overnight, a frost develops, but soon it rains again. Wolf and I spend the whole day cleaning the house. We can wash all our things and make ourselves clean; we also discovered no lice.

24 November We are both determined to replace a crew as the rains begin again.

Along the main road, the mud is an incredible slush. After many hours, we finally manage to spend a night in a *Tiger* and sleep inside it.

25 November Awake in the *Tiger*. Day passes into another. Finally, it has stopped raining, and now everything is frozen, and it's also incredibly cold.

29 November The commander's crew all received the Iron Cross, First Class, today. After that we had to be towed, but because of the mud and slush, we don't get very far. At a bridge we learn that a *Tiger* has crashed through it. We return later to aid in the recovery.

30 November We are awake. Nothing new in the evening. I nearly shot myself with a flare pistol due to being careless.

1 December Today we had to be towed by four *18t Zgkw* in a drive to Dolinskaja (Dolinskaya). We had rammed fifteen horse carts loaded with T-mines [antitank Teller mines], which gave us a big surprise. When Wolf jumped down off the *Tiger*, he nearly shot his nose off with his MP after it got stuck when he jumped down.

2 December Had to repair our winter clothing and gear. Wolf becomes the gunner to *SS-Unterscharführer* Holzner, and I go to the crew of *SS-Unterscharführer* Heurich.

5 December Second Advent. The first snows fall. The company *Spieß* visits our quarters.

9 December Last few days, I'm not feeling very well, probably due to sinusitis. Wolf reports today at the crew of *SS-Unterscharführer* Holzner.

10 December The Russians have broken through near Kirowograd (Kirowograd). Our company is attached to the infantry. Also very strong air activity over Dolinskaja. My ear has improved and I feel a little better.

11 December My *Tiger* has arrived. After some time spent outdoors, I start to feel ill again, and I'm sent back to my quarters with a 39-degree [Celsius] fever. Wolf helps me pack my things. I reckon now I'm off to hospital.

12 December I feel better today, but I spend the day in bed. The artillery fire is still ongoing and never lets up—it's a wonder no one has been lost to date. At the moment the enemy location is not known. What will becomes of us?

13 December I still have bed rest. Lots of cannon fire in the distance. The situation at the front seems temporary, and things are looking bad—we don't seem to be pulling back and we could be encircled. We have long been ignored.

14 December *SS-Sturmmann* Pavlu arrives at the company. Former town commandant of Cracow, not a bad guy.

24 December The days have passed by fairly quietly. I spent the time in my quarters, but sometimes I have to do guard duty. Otherwise, things are pretty quiet. Orders are issued almost every day, which means the company has to parade almost every day as well. A few days before Christmas we have a severe frost.

On 1 November 1943, the company and the armored group from *II/SS-Panzer-Regiment 3* were positioned at the southern end of Graphit and moved in the direction of Balka Wlassowskaja. Several tanks were knocked out after being fired upon by a strong Russian antitank gun front. The wounded from the armored group had to be collected under the cover of darkness. On the same day, *SS-Obersturmbannführer* Baedke took over command of *9. Kompanie* from *SS-Untersturmführer* Ebeling. New arrivals also included *SS-Standartenjunker (SS-Oberscharführer)* Hans Kriescher (joined the company on the tenth), who had just completed the first special armored course at *Panzer Schule Putlos*, *SS-Untersturmführer* Neff, *SS-Oberscharführer* Weitner, *SS-Oberscharführer* Knevel, and *SS-Oberscharführer* Heimbruch. On the second, the advance on Marijampol starts from Graphit. On the third, the *Tigers* from *9. Kompanie* supported divisional grenadiers during an advance toward the heights southeast of Marijampol, during which the Russian made several counterattacks from the area of Petrowo. On the third, the advance from the area of Marijampol continued; Hill 138.8 was captured. On 4 December, the armored group from *SS-Panzer-Regiment 3* had to form a separate *Kampfgruppe* to repel strong Russian forces near Annowka and Iskrowka. The following day, a counterattack was launched east of Kopany. The rest of the day was spent cleaning weapons and calling roll.

On 7 November, the *Tigers* moved into the area of Losowatka after the *Totenkopf* was relieved by *76. Infanterie-Division*. During the afternoon the *Tigers* reassemble in Bairak. On the eighth, it rained all day, making movement for wheeled vehicles very difficult. Sometimes these vehicles and their drivers had to wait to be towed by tanks. On the tenth, much-needed maintenance was conducted on the *Tigers*. On the twelfth, the first snow fell. On the thirteenth, the *Tigers* redeployed from Bairak into the area of Nowo Gannowka and Batschtina. On the fourteenth, the armored group from *SS-Panzer-Regiment 3*

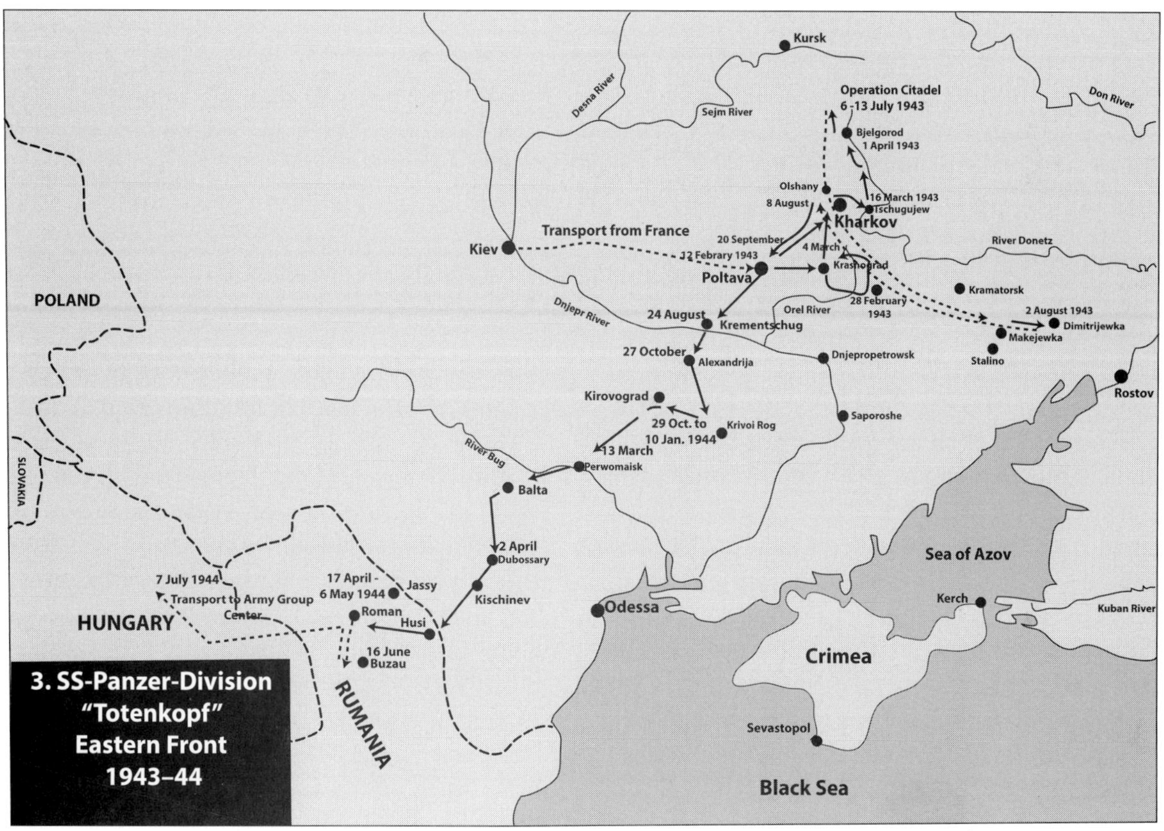

3. SS-Panzer-Division "Totenkopf" Eastern Front 1943–44

launched a counterattack on the Russian 32nd Guards Tank Brigade. The attack started from the area of Batschtina, causing the destruction of sixty Russian tanks; twenty-eight were knocked out by the *Tigers* from *9. Kompanie*. After the engagement, the armored group, under the command of *SS-Hauptsturmführer* Beiermeier, withdrew back to Krassno-Konstantinowka. The *Tigers* took on a new allocation of fuel and ammunition. For his actions, Beiermeier was nominated for the Knight's Cross, which was awarded on 10 December 1943.

The following personnel arrived in Dolinskaja to join *9. Kompanie* during November: Sklenzky, Rettinger, and Sperner. From the *Pionier* company of *SS-Panzer-Regiment 3* came Hoffmann, Birke, Schneider, and Werner (assigned to the *Instand-Staffel*). Probst, Fischer, Loidold, and company *Spieß* Beneke went on home leave. Bernhardt became a gunner.

On the fifteenth, another ten Russian tanks were knocked out by the *Tigers* from *9. Kompanie* during the afternoon north of Bairak. On the sixteenth, another Russian attack is repelled east of Krassno-Konstantinowka. The encampment which quartered the crews from *9. Kompanie* came under mortar and artillery fire on the seventeenth. The armored group launched counterattacks on Hill 168.2 and Hill 173.1. On the eighteenth, two *Tigers* were loaded onto rail transports in readiness for departure to a maintenance facility for long-term repairs, while a captured T-34 tank was used for recovery operations by the *WerkStatt* platoon for the recovery of six *Panzer IV's* stuck in the open terrain forward of the German front lines. Between the nineteenth and twenty-first, a single *Tiger* and a handful of tanks were used for local counterattacks near Krassno-Konstantinowka and defensive actions near Hill 164.9. On the twenty-first, three *Panzer IV's* were knocked out. On the twenty-second, the two entrained *Tigers* commanded by *SS-Unterscharführer* Vollmer and *SS-Oberscharführer* Weitner came under attack by a T-34. Weitner quickly placed himself in the gunner's seat and loaded an antitank round into the main gun breach. He began to turn the turret using the turret handwheel. The T-34 got within a short distance before it slid into a ditch next to the railway embankment. Two men grabbed explosive charges and threw them onto the engine deck of the T-34. Both charges detonated, causing the stricken Russian tank to catch fire. The Russian crew bailed out. The commander surrendered; the second crew member was shot while the driver struggled to exit the burning tank; the fourth crew member remained inside the burning tank. After twenty minutes, the T-34 exploded, sending the turret up into the air. Despite Russian forces being in the area, the rail transport left, reaching Schwetschenkowo on the twenty-fourth.

On the twenty-fourth, a small reserve composed of one *Tiger* and three *StuG's* was kept as a mobile reserve. The next day, a single *Tiger* and two *StuG's* were used to support a small infantry combat team. On the twenty-seventh, a *Tiger* supported *II/Grenadier-Regiment 203* during a counterattack on Owrag Baschtanka. On the twenty-eighth, a *Tiger* broke through a bridge while trying to cross it. The recovery took some time. Another *Tiger* fell out due to engine trouble. On the twenty-ninth, a single *Tiger* was used as an operational reserve covering Nowo Gannowka, Batschtina, and Nowo Petrowka. On the thirtieth, *Grenadier-Regiment 203* and a *Tiger* attacked Hill 151.7.

On 1 December, *SS-Untersturmführer* Friedrich Schinhofen joined *9. Kompanie*. Schinhofen had served with *SS-Infanterie-Regiment 9* during 1941 before serving with *SS-Sturmgeschütze-Batterie Totenkopf* from 8 June to 2 December 1942. He attended the *SS-Junkerschule Braunschweig* and completed two courses, which ended on 1 May 1943. He had been promoted to *SS-Untersturmführer* on 10 March 1943 and served with *9. Kompanie* from 1 December 1943 to 20 March 1944. Later, he would be transferred to *schwere SS-Panzer-Abteilung 102* and served as the adjutant until early August 1944, when he was posted to *3. Kompanie* in *schwere SS-Panzer-Abteilung 102/502*. On 9 November 1944, he was promoted to *SS-Obersturmführer*. He spent the few remaining weeks of the war as the battalion adjutant.

The status of *9. Kompanie* on 1 December 1943 showed only one *Tiger* available for operational use, located near Nowo-Petrowka. Eleven *Tigers* were undergoing repairs in Dolinskaja, and another eleven were undergoing long-term repairs. On the third, the armored group took part in a counterattack against a Russian regiment-size force near Grigorjewka. Another attack on Hill 170.2 failed. On the sixth, the armored group remained in Nowo-Petrowka. On 7 December 1943, the armored group was involved in a counterattack on Dutschny and later took part covering the positions near Tschabanowka, supporting *Grenadier-Regiment 534*. *SS-Oberscharführer* Willy Biber was wounded during the action. On the following day, the armored group was involved in defensive operations in the area of Nowo Praga and near the Lenin Collective Farm. On the tenth, the armored group supported some infantry near Dolinskaja. On the twelfth, seven *Tigers* were transported back to Germany for factory maintenance.

On the fourteenth, *SS-Sturmmann* Rudolf Pavlu joined *9. Kompanie*. Pavlu had joined the SS in 1938, rising to the rank of *SS-Obersturmbannführer* on 9 November 1940 after Germany occupied Poland. Pavlu was posted to the General Government and served on the staff of the Department of Works in the district of Krakow. On 15 September 1941, he became the town commandant for Krakow and served in this position until April 1943, when he requested a transfer to the *Waffen-SS* for frontline duty. Pavlu was quickly promoted to *SS-Hauptscharführer* and commanded his own *Tiger* tank. In June 1944, he attended the third *SS-Panzer-Sonder-Lehrgang* and was promoted to *SS-Untersturmführer der Reserve* on 20 October. In November 1944, he was posted back to *SS-Panzer-Regiment 3*, but he did not rejoin *9. Kompanie*. At the war's end he was taken prisoner and later efforts were made to extradite him to Poland. He escaped twice from captivity but was recaptured both times. He committed suicide in Romlinghoven, near Bonn, during the spring of 1949.

Between 15 and 24 December, *9. Kompanie* spent the time organizing their Christmas function in Dolinskaja. On the twenty-ninth, tank training was conducted while the New Year was ushered in with another party, but on New Year's Eve, *SS-Untersturmführer* Ebeling was severely wounded when he was hit by a bullet that struck him in the upper left arm. This wound kept him in the hospital until the end of the war. While recovering, Ebeling met his future wife at the SS-Hospital in Prague during 1945; she was a nurse on his ward. Also on the thirty-first, *9. Kompanie* received a new allocation of *Tiger* engines.

✠

On 5 January 1944, the Russian offensive against Kirovograd began, and the situation around Zhitomir was critical. The front line of *8. Armee* had been pierced in two places. The armored group of *SS-Panzer-Regiment 3* had been placed under the command of *LII. Armee-Korps* and attached to *13. Panzer-Division*. On the sixth, the armored group, under the command of *SS-Sturmbannführer* Laackmann, moved to Ingulo-Kamenka. On the seventh, the armored group attacked north of Nikolajewka and along the road passing through Ribschina. Three *Tigers* sustained battle damage. On the eighth, the group was involved in defensive actions in the area of Fedorowka and Otradowka along with *13. Panzer-Division*; it also linked up with *Panzer-Grenadier-Division Großdeutschland*. A new allocation of winter clothing was issued to the *Totenkopf*. On the ninth, six new engines for the *Tigers* were flown in and delivered to *9. Kompanie* after being issued by *A.O.K 6*. On the tenth, two *Zgkw 18t* were handed over to the *Totenkopf* for recovery purposes by *Berge-Panzer-Kompanie 3*.

On the eleventh, the *gepanzerte Gruppe* (armored group) rejoined the *Totenkopf Division* and assembled in Bobrinez. On 12 January

1944, the *Tigers* underwent technical maintenance, and on the following day, the *Tigers* arrived in Rownoje. On the fifteenth the *gepanzerte Gruppe* moved into the area of Bolschaja Wyka and conducted several counterattacks near Owsjanikowska along with elements of the *11. Panzer-Division*. The following day, an assault was launched from Petrowka against the area north of Owsjanikowska. The *Tigers* came under heavy antitank gunfire near Hill 215.6, losing four *Tigers*. On the seventeenth during a local counterattack, another *Tiger* was hit by antitank gunfire and sustained damage near Michailowka. On the eighteenth, the attack that was conducted on the sixteenth was repeated, but the results were the same. The attack started out from Petrowka but came under heavy antitank gunfire west of Alexandrowka. On the nineteenth, the *gepanzerte Gruppe* redeployed into the area of Nowo Ukrainka. The following day, uniform inspection and weapon cleaning were carried out.

Eric Lehmkuhl recorded in his diary:

> On 16 January 1944, we attack with 6 Tigers in the direction of Petrowka (Petrovka). The attack breaks down under heavy Russian defensive antitank gun fire. The *Tiger* of *SS-Unterscharführer* Pavlu is knocked out. Radio operator Franz Nawatril is seriously wounded. On the eighteenth, we repeat the same attack but with some slight changes over the same ground, but again we have the same results—nearly all the *Tigers* come to grief. In February, the divisional command post is located in Bolschaja Wyska. Along our front, all is quiet; nothing remarkable happened. To our north, the *5. SS-Panzer-Division Wiking* is encircled in the Korsun-Cherkassy pocket.
>
> On 28 February, the divisional command post is in Alexejewka. Early morning, the Russians open up with a massive artillery barrage; this announces the beginning of a new Russian offensive. On 3 March, the Russian offensive is in full swing; we receive orders to move out toward Iwanowka, form a *Kampfgruppe*, and reinforce the units of the *Großdeutschland*. A signal comes from Nowo Ukrainka: *SS-Obersturmbannführer* Baedke will lead with four *Tigers*. We start out for Iwanowka via Nowo Alexandrowka in the direction of Bolschaja Wyska. Our *Tiger* takes a hit in the main gun from a shell. We try firing a test round, but the main gun is no longer of use. We remain at the command post in Nowo Ukrainka and recalibrate the main gun.
>
> Baedke receives a signal from the tank regiment ordering him to return to Nowo Ukrainka since the Russians there have broken through. *SS-Obersturmbannführer* Baedke turns around and leads a relief assault on Nowo Ukrainka, during which he his killed after a shell hits the commander's cupola. *SS-Sturmann* Mucke is killed by an artillery shell.

Between 20 and 24 January, the days are spent quietly in a village; the crews caught up with personal hygiene, washing uniforms, and cleaning weapons. On the twenty-fifth, the Russians shelled the German front lines with artillery and mortar fire, following up with infantry attacks which were beaten back with heavy defensive fire. On the same day, the *Instand Staffel* repaired several *Tigers* which were test-driven before being returned to the company. On the twenty-sixth, the company had a roll call and a winter uniform inspection. Baedke had much to complain about. On the twenty-seventh, it was announced that the town of Krakow had become the company sponsor. On the twenty-ninth, the company engaged Russian troops south of Petrowka and southeast of Wesslowka, where a Russian antitank front was destroyed. On the thirtieth, the *Tigers* needed ammunition and required urgent repairs because of the recent support provided to the grenadiers along the front line. On the thirty-first, one *Tiger* was damaged after being struck by Russian artillery fire. The radio operator, Nawratil, was wounded. Another *Tiger* had to be towed after breaking down, but the *Tigers* of *9. Kompanie* did manage to knock out nine Russian tanks.

On 1 February, in the early morning, the *Tigers* were in the assembly area of *II/SS-Panzer-Regiment 3*. One *Tiger* had to tow a self-propelled gun; both vehicles came under Russian artillery fire near Petrowka. Over the next couple of days, the crews conducted signal, technical, and firearms training. On the sixth, the alarm was given in readiness for departure movement. The Russians occasionally shelled the company area, but this ceased in the afternoon; the crews removed the winter camouflage from the *Tiger* tanks. On the seventh, *SS-Panzer-Regiment 3* reported that it had forty tank crews without tanks; this was reported to *A.O.K. 8* as well. On the ninth, the company commander conducted a test on all the communication equipment. On the tenth, the crews carried out technical service on the *Tigers*. Some thirty men went on home leave the following day. On the twelfth, the company rations were running low, and the use of iron rations was being considered, but on the thirteenth, the situation was alleviated with a new allocation of rations. The crews made potato pancakes. On the fifteenth, post arrived from the home front; in some of the packages schnapps and beer were found. The sixteenth was very cold, and a heavy snow storm closed in, making matters worse. On the eighteenth, a *Tiger* had to recover a stuck *Panzer IV* in severe conditions. The snow storm had abated, but it was still very cold. On the twenty-first, three *Tigers* broke down and had to be towed to the regimental *WerkStatt* company for repairs. On the twenty-second, the front line was quiet. The crews started the engines on the *Tigers* and kept them running. Radio and frequency checks were conducted as well. The company support units were inspected by Baedke on the twenty-third.

On the twenty-fifth, the *Tigers* were deployed to observe Russian movement after an alarm was raised, but nothing was noted after the stand-down order was given and the *Tigers* pulled back to Bolschnaja Wyska. During the march back, a *Tiger* broke down and had to be towed. Both *Tigers* returned to the company later in the day. On the twenty-sixth, the company conducted technical maintenance, and on the twenty-seventh, *SS-Sturmbannführer* Laackmann assumed command of *SS-Panzer-Regiment 3* after being appointed on the tenth. The twenty-eighth was a very quiet day. The crews managed to bathe and carry out personal administration.

On 3 March, four *Tigers* from the company were involved in a counterattack in the area of Nowo Alexandrowka after being sent to Iwanowka. The barrel of *SS-Obersturmbannführer* Baedke's *Tiger* was hit. A test round was fired, but the test failed; the barrel was a total write-off. Baedke changed *Tigers* and continued the attack, during which the commander's cupola was struck, killing Baedke. (Another report stated he was killed on the eleventh.) On the fifth, the combat-ready tanks from *SS-Panzer-Regiment 3* were split and spread along the *Totenkopf's* front line to provide support. On the eighth, one of these small groups was sent to assist *320. Infanterie-Division*. The same day, *A.O.K. 8* ordered the *Totenkopf* to ready to relocate to the area of Balta. On the ninth, *9. Kompanie* was used to secure the eastern exit of Bolschnaja Wyska. Another mixed *Kampfgruppe* was sent to Iwanowka along with *I/SS-Panzer-Grenadier-Regiment 5 (gep) Totenkopf*, under the command of Laackmann, to assist *Großdeutschland* after a Russian breakthrough in the sector of the division south of Nikolajewka.

On the tenth, elements of *SS-Panzer-Grenadier-Regiment 6 Eicke*, along with a handful of *StuG's*, were attached to *Großdeutschland* while *9. Kompanie* was used in defensive actions around Alexejewka and Kolhoz Gurjewka. On the following day, the *Totenkopf* began loading onto rail transports, but the *Tigers* and available *Panzer III's* and *IV's* were still south of Raskopana, engaging Russian tanks that had forced a breakthrough of the German lines. The same process was repeated in the afternoon, but the Russian attack was beaten back. The *A.O.K. 8* leadership requested that the *Totenkopf* relocate to the area of Kriwoj Osero as quickly as possible.

Walter Nahm, who served in the *Panzer* regimental *Aufklärungs Zug* (armored reconnaissance platoon). He was later transferred to the *Tiger Kompanie*.

On maneuvers in Fallingbostal, January 1943.

The same *Panzer III*, but from the front.

Group photograph taken in Fallingbostal on 2 January 1943. The *Kompanie's* ten new *Panzer III 5cm lang* (long—5 cm L/60) *Ausf. L* were delivered on 1 January 1943. WERDEHAUSEN

Panzer III Ausf. L of the *Stabs.Kp., Aufklärungs Zug*, late 1942. Wolfgang Barth served as a gunner during this period and is seen here sitting with the gunner's double hatch open.

Portrait of Barth taken on 4 July 1943. At this time he served in the *Aufklärungs Zug, Stabs.Kp., SS-Panzer-Regiment 3.* The *Panzerkampfabzeichen* (Tank Battle Badge) in Silver is evident, awarded for participation in three separate armored assaults.

Barth and three other comrades pose for the camera, April 1943.

Rail transports being loaded in France before the departure for Russia. SCHILLING

The crews from the *Aufklärungs Zug, Stabs.Kp., SS-Panzer-Regiment 3*, do not, it seems, get to travel first class.

4(s) Pz.Kp. in the Krassnogrod area, February 1943. The spaced armor of the *Ausf. L* variant is evident. WERDEHAUSEN

Panzer III Ausf. J's on the move. The high-velocity main gun was only effective against the Soviet T-34 frontally at close range, if at all. As for the heavy KV-1, even its side armor could only be penetrated at close range. WERDEHAUSEN

SS-Oberscharführer Rathsack throwing a snowball at Alfred Hargesheimer during the early part of 1942. Rathsack at this time was a *Zug Führer* in *3. Kompanie, SS-Panzer-Abteilung 2*, before being transferred to *SS-Panzer-Regiment 3* later in the year. RÜDIGER WARNICK

An overturned truck that had fallen through a bridge in Walki, February 1943.

Panzer III Ausf. L's and *Panzer. VI Ausf. E* (*Tiger*) assembled after unloading in Poltawa, February 1943. The *Tigers* are the early-production variant.

An overturned *Panzer III* from *4(s) Pz.Kp.* during the late winter of 1943.

A *Panzer III Ausf. L* from *4. Kompanie* moves across the open Russian countryside. WERDEHAUSEN

Tiger 411 had broken through the ice near Pereschtschepino, while another source says this happened near Walki in March 1943.

Tigers and *Panzer III's* on the move in the area of Poltawa, February 1943.

The crew of 412, a *Panzer III*, being utilized as a towing vehicle helping to recover a bogged-down truck, March 1943.

A Russian village looking desolate after the fighting in March 1943.

The crew of 412 getting dinner ready.

SS-Unterscharführer Lahm sits on top of a T-34/76, which is reportedly the *Tiger Kompanie's* first tank knocked out near Kirowograd. Note the mix of steel and rubber-tired roadwheels—this was not due to a shortage of rubber in the Soviet Union as has often been claimed. The photograph was taken in March 1943. *4(s) Kompanie's* first actions were recorded on 3 March 1943. WERDEHAUSEN

On the move to the loading ramp in Fallingbostal, February 1943. WERDEHAUSEN

Stuck in the mud near Walki. Note the divisional "Death's Head" emblem on the fender of the light personnel car.

In the woods near Budy, May 1943.

Entry into Charkow, 15 March 1943. A mixture of armored half-tracks, assault guns, and tank destroyers. The third of the four battles for Charkow (Kharkov) was a marked success for *General* von Manstein and the SS divisions involved.

Fritz Hitz, Fritz Lau, and Jupp Franz, May 1943.

Fritz Hitz stands next to an eighteen-ton *"Famo" Sd.Kfz. 9* heavy prime mover from the maintenance section on the Mius Front, August 1943. The tactical symbol on the fender indicates a heavy tank company.

The *Kompanie* female volunteer, Magda. Charkow, May 1943.

The latest *Opel Blitz Tiger* under wraps, May 1943. The *Opel Blitz* was the standard German medium truck.

In April 1943, *SS-Sturmbannführer* Kunstmann took command of *SS-Panzer-Regiment 3* after *SS-Sturmbannführer* Leiner was relieved of command. Standing in this group are *SS-Sturmbannführer* Kunstmann, *II/SS-Panzer-Regiment 3* commander; *SS-Hauptsturmführer* Beiermeier, *4(s) Kompanie* commander; *SS-Obersturmführer* Schroder, platoon commander in the *Tiger Kompanie*; and Karl Frank, engineer from Maybach. Standing off to the side is *SS-Oberscharführer* Baumann.

Artur Privatzki standing in front of *Tiger 933*, June 1943. Privatzki is wearing the camouflaged tanker uniform particular to the *Waffen-SS*.

SS-Untersturmführer Quade shows where a shot from a Russian antitank rifle bounced off the *Tiger's* cupola, July 1943. The Soviets used antitank rifles extensively, and they could be effective even against heavy armor if fired against visors, as in this case.

Maintenance being conducted in Makiewka, August 1943. Standing in front of the *Tiger* are *SS-Untersturmführer* Hadera and *SS-Oberscharführer* Biermann.

Group photograph of the supply section in the area of Bjelgorod, July 1943.

Tiger 911 on the Mius Front, with Schulze-Berg and the driver, Hoffmann. The *Tiger* was commanded by *SS-Untersturmführer* Kohler. The photograph was taken at the end of July 1943.

The *Tiger* of *SS-Unterscharführer* Gockl, July 1943.

SS-Untersturmführer Quade in Walki, August 1943.

Brand-new *Tigers* drive to the assembly area of Budy after being unloaded, May 1943.

A *Tiger* crosses a shallow stream in the area of Charkow, August 1943.

Tiger 924 under cover in the woods around Bjelgorod, June 1943.

Tiger 911 under the command of *SS-Untersturmführer* Kohler, May 1943.

The *Tiger* of *SS-Oberscharführer* Tassler in the area of Bjelgorod, June 1943.

On 3 October 1943, *9. Kompanie/SS-Panzer-Regiment 3* took delivery of five new *Tigers* in Protopopowka. From the left: *SS-Mann* Fritz Winter, *SS-Oberscharführer* Peters, and *SS-Sturmmann* Heinz Krummel. This mid-production *Tiger* is covered in *Zimmerit*, an antimagnetic paste applied to counter magnetic and "sticky" antitank mines.

In May 1943, the *Kompanie* received nine new *Tigers*. The collection party had left on 26 March 1943. Note the narrow transport tracks, fitted when the *Tigers* were transported by rail.

Standing on the air intake attached to the winch of the portal crane is Josef Hodapp from the maintenance section, summer 1943.

A *Tiger* undergoes repairs under the supervision of the *WerkStatt.Kp.* from *SS-Panzer-Regiment 3*. The massive crane could lift up to sixteen tons and was necessary for maintenance work on the heavy *Tiger*. WERDEHAUSEN

The *WerkStatt Zug* (workshop platoon) bus in the area of Budy, May 1943.

In May 1943 near Charkow, the *Kompanie* personnel make time for some water sports.

One of the five new *Tigers* delivered on 3 October 1943. This is a mid-production version, as evidenced by the smaller cast commander's cupola. WERDEHAUSEN

For any soldier in the field, personal hygiene is a must. This crewman is hand-washing his uniform, May 1943.

SS-Mann Rex stands in front of *Tiger 911*, June 1943.

The grave of *SS-Untersturmführer* Quade, killed on 30 August 1943 and buried in the German Military Cemetery in Charkow.

Crew of *Tiger 924*, area of Bjelgorod, May 1943.

9. Kompanie personnel inspect the remains of a *Tiger* knocked out on 22 August 1943 near Stepanowka. The *Tiger* has shed the righthand track and received a hit on the barrel.

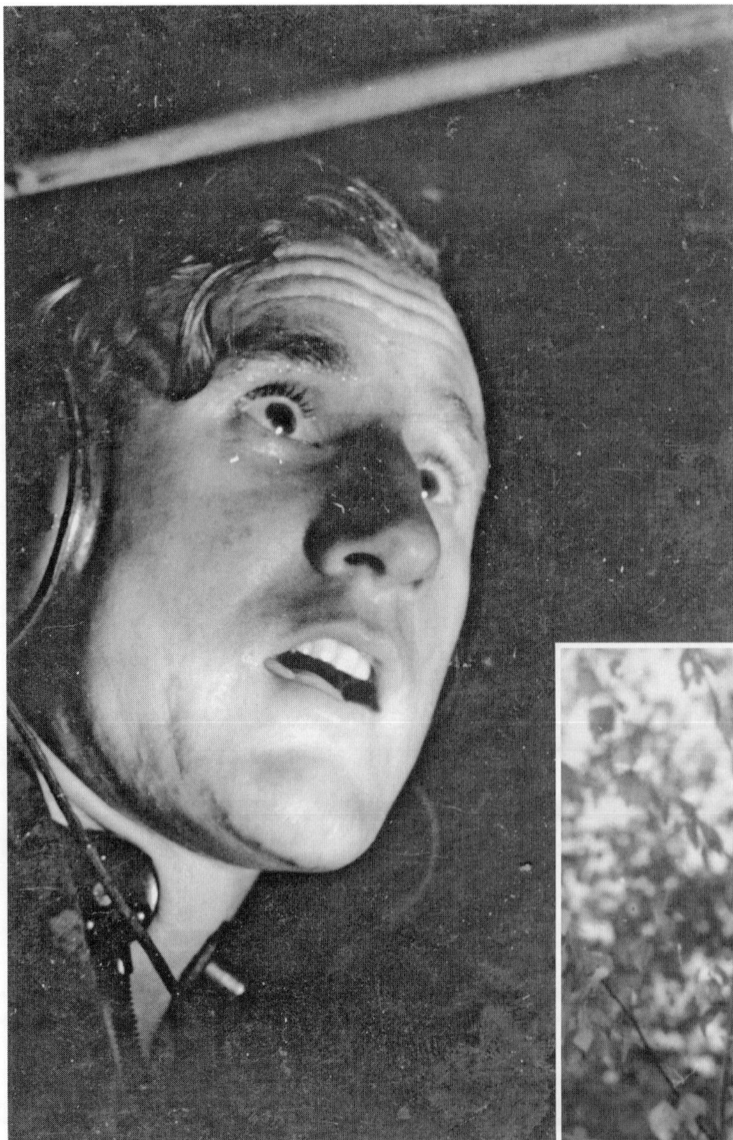

SS-Unterscharführer Emil Weitner.

SS-Unterscharführer Weitner receives the Iron Cross, Second Class. FR WEITNER

Tiger 932 under camouflage netting, May 1943. BENEKE

On 29 July 1943, *9. Kompanie* took over eight *Tigers* from *SS-Panzer-Regiment 1*. Here one of those *Tigers* has been renumbered 933.

Tiger 923 and crew during a pause in the fighting, summer 1943.

Another photograph of *Tiger 924* in the woods near Bjelgorod, June 1943. Standing in front of the tank are Hoffmann and Rex.

Tiger 924, Bjelgorod, June 1943.

Repairs being conducted to the running gear by the *WerkStatt Zug*, September 1943.

Due to the weight of the *Tiger*, the workshop companies were supplied with specialized maintenance equipment, including heavy cranes.

After repairs are completed, it's time for a test drive. Despite its size, the *Tiger* was very well designed mechanically and relatively easy to work on.

In the *Kübelwagen* is the *Kompanie Spieß, SS-Oberscharführer* Berger. June 1943.

A *Panzer III Ausf. L* and crew from the *Panzer-Aufklärungs-Zug/Stabs.Kp./SS-Panzer-Regiment 3*, September 1943.

A crew of a *Panzer III Ausf. L* from the *Stabs.Kp.* of *I/SS-Panzer-Regiment 3*, September 1943. Wolfgang Barth is standing in the middle. The company still had a full complement of eight *Panzer III's* during September 1943 but later lost seven during a single action. Because of this, the *Panzer-Aufklärungs-Zug* was disbanded on 1 October 1943 and the crews dispersed to other units within the *Panzer* regiment. The crew of *SS-Unterscharführer* Nutzenberger was sent to *9. Kompanie*. BARTH

403, a *Panzer III*, in some slight trouble, February 1943.

Wolfgang Barth poses in front of a *Panzer III Ausf. L*, April 1943.

Orders group conducted by *Panzer* commanders from the *Panzer-Aufklärungs-Zug, Stabs.Kp., SS-Panzer-Regiment 3*, September 1943. The *Panzer-Aufklärungs-Zug* had been commanded by *SS-Untersturmführer* Lummitsch before he was transferred to *I/SS-Panzer-Regiment 3. SS-Untersturmführer* Palm assumed commanded thereafter.

Crew of a *Panzer III*, possibly an *Ausf. N* with the 7.5cm L/24 main gun, pose for the camera, September 1943. Barth is sitting on the armored side skirt (*Schürzen*), while sitting directly behind him is *SS-Unterscharführer* Achim Nutzenberger, who served as a *Tiger* commander in *9. Kompanie* for a short period before being posted to *7. Kompanie* of *II/SS-Panzer-Regiment 3* as a *Zug Führer*.

A *Panzer IV Ausf. G* from *I/SS-Panzer-Regiment 3* knocked out, August 1943.

Another *Panzer IV Ausf. G* knocked out on 10 August 1943. This *Panzer IV* belonged to the *Panzer-Aufklärungs-Zug* of *I/SS-Panzer-Regiment 3.* BARTH

Examining a captured Russian T-70, February 1943. Even this late in the war, the Soviets still fielded large numbers of light tanks despite their being easy prey for *Panzer III's.* WERDEHAUSEN

4(s) Pz.Kp. crewmen examine a knocked-out T-34/76, March 1943. The T-34 with the 7.62cm main gun was no match for the *Tiger* in frontal engagements, and the *Tiger's* side armor could be penetrated only at very close range.

Before the introduction of *Berge-Panthers* (a recovery vehicle based on the chassis of the *Panzer V Panther*) in large numbers during 1944, eighteen-ton prime movers were the work horse of the recovery platoons for the *Tiger* units. Here two such vehicles are being used to tow a *Tiger* back to the *WerkStatt* for repairs.

Tiger 923, summer 1943. The three vertical bars on the left hull front are a temporary unit marking designed to deceive Soviet intelligence prior to the Battle of Kursk in July 1943. BENEKE

Tiger 911, end of May 1943. Note the six "kill rings" on the barrel.

From the left: Lachner, van Kerkhom, and Godecke, autumn 1943. It seems that van Kerkhom has just been awarded the Iron Cross, Second Class.

Tiger 912. From the left: Kuster, Rex, unknown, and Hoffmann.

Tiger 914, commanded by *SS-Unterscharführer* Muller, who was killed along with loader Zimmermann after being hit by a Russian artillery round on 7 July 1943. This photograph was taken on 5 July 1943. JOHN KOSER / NARA

SS-Oberscharführer Baumann, who served in *9. Kompanie / SS-Panzer-Regiment 3* during 1943 as a *Tiger* commander. On 3 October 1943, he was serving in *8. schwere Panzer-Kompanie / SS-Panzer-Regiment 2.* He eventually ended up commanding a *Tiger I* and a *Tiger II* in *schwere SS-Panzer-Abteilung 102/502, 1. Kompanie.* RUEDIGER WARNICK / STEPHAN CAZENAVE

SS-Untersturmführer Ebeling was posted to *9. Kompanie* during September 1943 and served as a platoon leader. On 31 December 1943, he was wounded. In June 1944, he was still recovering with the *SS-Panzer-Ausbildungs-und-Ersatz-Regiment* (a replacement unit) in Fallingbostal. Ebeling's treatment continued right up to the war's end. He tried to volunteer for a suicide mission but was rejected for service. He spent the early part of 1945 in the Prague Military Hospital, where he met his future wife. RUEDIGER WARNICK / STEPHAN CAZENAVE

SS-Untersturmführer Friedl Schinhofen served with *9. Kompanie* from early November 1943 to March 1944. He was transferred to *schwere SS-Panzer-Abteilung 102/502*. During the Normandy battles, he was the battalion adjutant until he took command of *3. Kompanie* on 8 August 1944. He remained *3. Kompanie* commander until March 1945, when he again assumed the post of adjutant in the *Stabs.Kp.* until the war's end. RUEDIGER WARNICK

Tiger 933 pauses for a halt in Dolinskayia. The turret number has been painted on a board and hung on the turret as the original number is now covered in whitewash. LACHNER

Soldiers from the *Kompanie* support units marching out for a field training exercise near Merefa, Charkow, April 1943.

SS-Unterscharführer Alois Tassler, 1943.

SS-Sturmmann Frank Sklenzky in Angouleme early 1943. Sklenzky served as a gunner in *9. Kompanie*. Note the distinctive *Totenkopf* armband.

Two *18t Zgkw* towing a broken-down *Tiger*, early August 1943. The *Untersturmführer* with his head turned away from the camera is Rathsack, who was wounded that month.

After the Charkow (Kharkov) campaign, *4(s) Kompanie* personnel managed to get some much-needed rest. During rest periods soldiers catch up with their personal tasks, but here it seems that a soldier is about to get a bucket of cold water thrown over him.

On the left is Munch, and at the end is Adamiak, in front of *Tiger 922* during late 1943.

Graves of three fallen comrades. In the middle is the grave of *SS-Sturmmann* Walter Weber.

Karl Blattmann during the winter of 1942–43. Blattmann was later wounded during the fighting for Vienna on 10 April 1945, was evacuated to an SS hospital in Prague, and was taken prisoner by the Russians.

Lachner (second from left) and Privatski standing next to the graves of fallen comrades, late summer 1943.

Four crew members of *Tiger 933* pose for the camera while carrying out track repairs, December 1943.

Tiger 933 having extensive repairs carried out on its running gear by the *WerkStatt.Kp. / SS-Panzer-Regiment 3* during December 1943. The interleaved and overlapping roadwheels gave the *Tiger* great mobility and a stable ride over soft ground as the ground pressure was low for a tank of its weight. However, this complex arrangement was difficult to work on, particularly if an inner roadwheel or a suspension component was involved.

The driver of *Tiger 933*, Hans-Ludwig Bachmann, takes time out for some light refreshment. Bachmann was killed in action on 30 August 1943.

Tiger 913 commanded by *SS-Unterscharführer* Fein, July 1943. The right track of the *Tiger*, it seems, was being repaired when the photograph was taken. The number of kills on the barrel of the 88 is impressive.

Senior NCO's sit on the *Kompanie* commander's *Tiger* with its newly applied turret number 901, May 1943.

Lachner standing on the left in front of *Tiger 933*, August 1943.

SS-Sturmmann Herman Mocnik standing in front of *Tiger 911*. Mocnik was killed during the fighting for Balta in late March 1944.

Panzer III's (one *Ausf. J* and one *Ausf. L*) of the new *4(s) Kompanie* at Fallingbostal, January 1943.

SS-Sturmmann Werner Hoberg, who was killed in action on 30 August 43 near Kalontajew.

Crew with their brand-new *Panzer III Ausf. L*, Fallingbostal, 1 January 1943.

Photograph taken by Lachner on 29 October 1943 at the Alexandria Air Field showing *Ju 87 Stukas* under going repairs. *9. Kompanie* arrived at the air field in order to meet up with *4. Kompanie (Panther) / SS-Panzer-Regiment 2. 4. Kompanie* was attached to *SS-Panzer-Regiment 3* for about two weeks.

Panzer III and two crew members, Fallingbostal, 1 January 1943

CHAPTER 4

The Long Retreat

Balta, March 1944

On the thirteenth, the company was loaded after the burial of Baedke. Neff took command of the company, which was loaded in Nowo Ukrainka. The transport left at 2000 hours and traveled in the direction of Kriwoje Osero (Kryve Ozero). As the units of *Totenkopf* approached the area of Balta, the unloading area was Sawronka. On the fourteenth, the transport carrying the *Tiger* company arrived in Pomoschnaja (Pomichna). The transport came under a Russian airstrike that wounded several soldiers. In Nowo Ukrainka, twelve trucks from the company began a road march. After some forty kilometers, some of the trucks got stuck. An *18t Zgkw* driven by *SS-Rottenführer* Kurt Heller provided assistance by towing the trucks out of the mud. Later, Heller was rewarded for his efforts. The vehicle column was assembled in Perwomaisk (Pervomais'k). On the fifteenth, the company was diverted to Balta and was unloaded on the sixteenth.

On 18 March, the tank regiment assembled to the west of Balta. Some of the wheeled elements of *Totenkopf* had still not reached the area of Balta. On the nineteenth, *SS-Panzer-Regiment 3* moved into the area of Pereima and was involved in a counterattack with *SS-Panzer-Grenadier-Regiment 6 Eicke* near Ljubomirka (Lyubomyrka). On the twenty-second, Russian troops attacked out of the area of Perwomaisk (Pervomais'k), forcing German forces to withdraw after crossing the Bug River. On the twenty-fourth, Russian forces attacked Lesnitschewka (Lesnychivka) and forced elements

of *Totenkopf* back to the northern edge of Balta. *Kampfgruppe Pitschellis*, with two *Tigers*, provided cover for the withdrawal. The 26th Guards Rifle Corps claimed two *SPW's* (armored half-tracks) and one self-propelled gun during the day's fighting against *Totenkopf*. On the twenty-fifth, *Kampfgruppe Pitschellis* was covering the eastern edge of Balta and forced Russian troops to pull back to Bendsari (Bendzary) after launching a counterattack.

Also on the twenty-fifth, *SS-Untersturmführer* Neff ordered all non-essential company soldiers, *Berge-Zug*, the *Instand-Staffel*, and seven *Tigers* requiring maintenance to be transported by rail from Balta and sent to Romania. The transport moved south via Kotowsk and then passed through Wessely Kut (Novoborysivka) before coming to a halt in Rozdil'na. One other transport made it to Romania after leaving Wessely Kut at 1435 hours in the afternoon on 2 April. This transport had one *Tiger*, one *Befehlspanzer III*, and a *Panzerbeobachterswagen III*. Neff commanded the group of the remaining three *Tigers*; this unit was designated *Panzergruppe Neff*. The three *Tigers* were commanded by Neff, *SS-Oberscharführer* Weitner, and *SS-Oberscharführer* Tonges. The remaining twenty men later fought on as infantry along with units from the *Wehrmacht*. During the retreat from Balta, the company's soldiers and other *Totenkopf* units had to withdraw via Kotowsk on the thirtieth.

On the twenty-sixth, the Russians attacked Balta on the southern edge of the town. This attack was beaten back. Another Russian attack was forced to pull back on the northwestern edge of Balta after a *Kampfgruppe* launched a counterattack from the northern edge of the town with 200 men and three *Tigers* at 1800 hours. This attack was repulsed by the 81st Guards Rifle Regiment/25th Guards Rifle Division, resulting in one *Tiger* being captured intact. Long columns of German vehicles were trying to leave Balta. The rail line leading to Kotowsk (Kotovs'k) had to be recaptured to allow rail transport to move after the Russians temporarily closed the rail corridor. The Russian 26th Guards Rifle Corps claimed one rail transport captured with three tanks on board and one *SPW* knocked out, while the 25th Guards Rifle Division claimed two tanks and two *SPW's* knocked out.

On the twenty-seventh, the Russians managed to capture the main rail station in Balta town center and also captured a rail transport with five tanks and two *Hummel* self-propelled artillery guns from *I/SS-Panzer-Artillerie-Regiment 3*. In the northern suburbs of Balta, the Russians found four tanks and eight trucks abandoned because of lack of fuel. One *Tiger* was lost during the day due to Russian antitank gunfire. The two remaining *Tigers*, under the command of Neff and Weitner, pulled back to the southern area of Balta. On the twenty-eighth, more counterattacks were launched from Balta's second rail station in the direction of Perelty (Perel'oty) and Possizely (Pasytely). No *Tigers* were involved. On the twenty-ninth, a counterattack was launched to the south of Balta. During the day the Russians took in a massive haul of German equipment, finding in and around Balta (and to the south of the town as well) twenty-one self-propelled guns (various types) and thirty tanks (none operational). This was reported by the 94th Guards Rifle Division and the 26th Guards Rifle Corps.

On the thirtieth, while the Red Army began clearing the southern suburbs of Balta, they found one *Tiger* tank abandoned due to lack of fuel. One kilometer south of Balta rail station, the Russians also found a rail transport (reported by the 94th Guards Rifle Division) with twenty-two tanks on board from *II/SS-Panzer-Regiment 3*. The tank group from *SS-Panzer-Regiment 3* reached Kotowsk on the thirtieth and loaded onto rail transports. The direction of travel was Wessley Kut (Novoborysivka) and Rasdelnaja (Rozdil'na). Those crews without tanks followed the bulk of the division toward Dubossary (Dubasari). On the thirty-first, the Russians captured Kotowsk and found one rail transport loaded with three tanks and four assault guns at 0700 hours. *Totenkopf*, withdrawing to the

southeast, formed a blocking position on both sides of the road near Jelissawetowka (Bochmanivka). The bulk of *Totenkopf* withdrew to Dubossary (Dubasari) and then reassembled in Kishinev (Chisinau).

Between the thirtieth and thirty-first, the last three operational *Panzer IV's* from *II/SS-Panzer-Regiment 3* were lost. In Balta, *3. SS-Panzer-Division Totenkopf* was forced to abandon around 1,000 wheeled vehicles. *9. Kompanie* personnel without tanks arrived in Dubossary (Dubasari) on 2 April and reached Kishinev (Chisinau) the next day. The company personnel spent five to six days in the town before moving on to Lapusna on the tenth. On the eleventh, they assembled in the area of Negresti. On the twelfth, *Totenkopf* assembled in the area of Husi-Vaslui-Krassna (Crasna) for rail transport to Bacau and Roman. The Romanian rail authorities were informed that transport was urgently required, but it was reported that they seemed slow in helping with German requests. Personnel from *SS-Panzer-Regiment 3* assembled in Krassna (Crasna) on the twelfth for rail transportation. The first transport left on the thirteenth.

Bacau, April–June 1944

On 2 April 1944, the transport carrying seven *Tigers* from *9. Kompanie* was brought to a halt in the town of Rozdil'na along with thirty other rail transports. The rail line leading to Tiraspol from Rozdil'na was a single line. A German Army officer of the General Staff walked from the Rozdil'na rail station and approached Neff and ordered him to blow up his remaining *Tigers* as the Russians were not far away. Eric Lehmkuhl remembers this event:

> The remnants of the tank regiment were loaded on rail transports heading in the direction of Tiraspol when we came to a standstill along with thirty other rail transports. Because of the Russian rapid advance, we are ordered to blow up our remaining *Tigers*. We had hoped that our transport carrying the *Tigers* would have been given priority and forwarded onto Tiraspol. The crews had to provide themselves with supplies which were gathered from other transports.
>
> We have to make our way westward on foot, but to add insult to injury, we are hit by a snow storm, so we have to sit down with packs, ammunition, and weapons. Slowly, the storm rolls westward. As we move along, we notice many vehicles stuck in the mud. Some of these have to blown up with hand grenades so the Russians cannot use them, but unfortunately, the crews have to get rid of certain items and carry the barest minimum. The crews always try to hitch a ride, but this rarely happens as operational vehicles are scarce.
>
> At night we sleep in barns or haystacks, but we are always in fear of the advancing Russians. The next day, the column is scattered by a small group of Russian tanks. We reply with machine-gun fire. We manage to reach Tiraspol, where large groups of soldiers are gathered by the military police. These soldiers are formed into alarm groups for use in infantry *Kampfgruppen*. We are lucky—the field police let us by and pass through, and we find that *9. Kompanie* had set up a reporting center for the company's soldiers. The soldiers are assembled and transported by rail from Tiraspol to Kishinev (Chisinau), and from there we are transported to Bacau. I later found out that *SS-Mann* Werner from the *Instand-Staffel* was given fourteen days of hard labor for trying to sell his pistol for some rations.

II/SS-Panzer-Regiment 3 and the regimental headquarters company arrived in Krassna (Crasna) on the twelfth and had to wait until the thirteenth for loading. They arrived in Bacau on the fourteenth. On the seventeenth, the army vehicle officer for Kishinev (Chisinau) informed *Totenkopf* that a new allocation of specialist tools for repairing *Tigers* had arrived by air and

could be collected from the maintenance stores in Kishinev. The regiment had no tanks at all. During April 1944, it was planned that *9. Kompanie* should form the new *3. Kompanie/schwere SS-Panzer-Abteilung 102*, but Hitler rescinded this order and instructed that the company remain with *SS-Panzer-Regiment 3* (*schwere SS-Panzer-Abteilung 102* was reinforced by personnel from *schwere SS-Panzer-Abteilung 103* during May 1944).

On 14 April, *9. Kompanie* personnel arrived in Bacau by rail from Krassna (Crasna) and were quartered at a hotel in the center of the town. On the thirtieth, a tank collection team of fifty men was organized under the command of *SS-Untersturmführer* Neff, and on 1 May, they were flown to Belgrade for rail transport to *HZA Magdeburg* by *Ju-90*. On the second, two transports were loaded with eight *Tiger I's*. The first transport arrived with four *Tigers* on 6 May in Bacau but was ordered to be forwarded onto Roman. After unloading in Roman, this took two hours to complete. The four *Tigers* were deployed near Targu-Frumos until the tenth. Between the eighth and tenth, the *Tigers* would come under repeated air strikes from Russian ground-attack aircraft but suffered no losses or casualties. On the eleventh, the *Tigers* withdrew to a village for maintenance. On the twelfth, the *Tigers* moved into position along the Balatati-Jassy (Iasi) road. During the night of the thirteenth–fourteenth, the company claimed one Russian night-bomber shot down. The second transport was delayed because of severe bomb damage to the rail network in the region of Siebenburgen (Transylvania) and stayed in the village of Gross Schogen (Nagysajo). After successive RAF bombing raids on the nineteenth, the second transport arrived in Bacau, but was ordered to be moved onto Roman, where it unloaded on the twentieth.

Eric Lehmkuhl reports:

> The transport took fourteen days; the Pentecostal festival was spent in a *Volksdeutsche* village of Gross Schogen (Nagysajo, about 250 kilometers west of Roman) because the railway had been bombed by the British. The rail line had to relayed. Upon arrival, the new *Tigers* were used around Iasi and Targol Frumos. Another collection commando takes fourteen days and returns with six new *Tigers* from Germany.
>
> Until the end of June, the company command post is in Bacau. Because of the catastrophic situation, we are loaded onto rail transports in Roman on 7 July and head toward southern Poland, Radom, and Warsaw through the area of Brest and unload in Osowice and deploy for operations in the direction of Grodno.

On 31 May, *SS-Panzer-Regiment 3* organized a quick-reaction force near Targu-Frumos, with twenty-four *Panzer IV's* and two *Tigers*. On 7 June, the *LVII. Panzer-Korps* ordered the division to make ready a *Panzergruppe* for deployment along the road to Iasi. The group was commanded by *SS-Sturmbannführer* Laackmann and consisted of twelve *Panzer IV's* and eight *Tigers*, with additional support from *III/SS-Panzer-Grenadier-Regiment 5 Totenkopf*. At 0200 hours, the *Panzergruppe* moved into the area near Podul-Iloaei and came under the command of *24. Panzer-Division* on the eighth. The remaining tanks from *SS-Panzer-Regiment 3*, with thirteen tanks, were placed under the command of *SS-Sturmbannführer* Beiermeier and held in reserve.

On 8 June 1944, the *Panzergruppe*—with twenty tanks (twelve *Panzer IV's* and eight *Tigers*)—and *III/SS-Panzer-Grenadier-Regiment 5 Totenkopf* saw action in the area of Hill 177.0 and along the heights northwest of Damian. This was repeated the next day. The *Panzergruppe* helped secure Hill 176.0 on the tenth and remained there until the eleventh. The *Tigers* were recalled on 13 June. The *Panzer IV's* eventually returned to divisional control on the fifteenth. During the fighting, the *WerkStatt* company for *SS-Panzer-Regiment 3* was located in a wood five kilometers east of Roman.

On 15 May 1944, another tank collection team was organized with a strength of thirty men and departed for *HZA* Magdeburg and left Germany on 17 May with six *Tigers* (which ahd belonged to *schwere SS-Panzer-Abteilung 103*) and arrived in Bacau on the thirty-first. On 7 June, six *Tigers* arrived in Bacau. Two of the *Tigers* were taken over by *9. Kompanie*, but on the eleventh, Army Group South ordered *Totenkopf* to hand over the two *Tigers* to *Panzer-Regiment Großdeutschland. Totenkopf* reported to Army Group South that the two *Tigers* in question had been handed over to a collection team from *Panzer-Regiment Großdeutschland* and loaded onto a rail transport on the same day. On the twenty-first, *SS-Sturmmann* Wolfgang Barth, Gunther Grimm, and Friedrich Schiechel attended the fourth *SS-Panzer-Sonder-Lehrgang* in Königsbruck bei Wien from 4 July to 11 November.

On 7 July, just as *Totenkopf* was being loaded for a major redeployment to Army Group Center, the last tank collection commando of twenty-five men under the command of *SS-Hauptscharführer* Berger drove from Romania to Germany to collect five *Tigers*. These five *Tigers* departed *HZA Magdeburg* on 26 July and arrived in Warsaw on the thirty-first, one day before the Polish Home Army uprising in the city. Originally, this transport should have unloaded in Lochow.

On 5 May 1944, *SS-Untersturmführer* Wenzal joined the company after being transferred from *SS-Panzer-Ausbildungs-und-Ersatz-Regiment* in Sennelager and took command of the 2nd Platoon. Wenzal had been promoted to *Untersturmführer* on 1 March while serving as an instructor at the *Panzer-Truppen-Schule Putlos*. The 1st Platoon was under the command of *SS-Untersturmführer* Hans Kriescher, who joined *9. Kompanie* on 10 November 1943 after completing the first *SS-Panzer-Junker-Sonder-Lehrgang* from 16 August to 6 November 1943; he was promoted to *Untersturmführer* on 1 March 1944. The 3rd Platoon was commanded by *SS-Untersturmführer* Helmut Neff, who was also acting company commander at the time. He had originally enlisted in the *Luftwaffe* in 1937, and before he was transferred to the *Waffen-SS*, he had reached the rank of *Feldwebel*. Neff was transferred to the *Waffen-SS* on 11 February 1943 and given the rank of *Oberscharführer*. Neff undertook a series of officer-cadet courses. He was promoted to *Untersturmführer* on 1 October and joined *9. Kompanie* on 1 November.

SS-Hauptsturmführer Hans Fischer was nominated as the company commander on 20 March 1944 but wasn't officially confirmed until the thirty-first. He eventually joined the company on 18 July. During March 1944, Fischer was acting commander of *schwere SS-Panzer-Abteilung 102*. In May 1944, he was in Vienna with his wife as they were expecting the birth of their first child; he was still in Vienna on 5 July.

Organization

During May 1944, the company support units remained in Bacau. The only major change to the organizational structure was the integration of the *WerkStatt* platoon from the company into the regiment's *WerkStatt* company. The company's support units still on strength were the *Instand-Staffel* (maintenance section), which was led by *SS-Oberscharführer* Henker; the *Berge-Zug* (recovery section) under *SS-Oberscharführer* Bauer; and the *Nachschub Zug* (supply platoon). *SS-Untersturmführer* Greisinger was posted to the regiment as the new *TFK*. On 10 May, *Der Generalinspekteur der Panzertruppen 013/44 g.Kdos* requested during a *Führer Vortrag* (leader conference) that *9. Kompanie* have a strength of 125 men and, in another *Führer Vortrag* dated 11 May 1944 (*019/44 g.Kdos*) that *9. Kompanie* was to be allocated ten new *Tigers*.

SS-Panzer-Regiment 3, April–July 1944

When *II/SS-Panzer-Regiment 3* unloaded on 14 April in Bacau, the battalion had no tanks at all. On the fifteenth, the *LVIII. Panzer-Korps* ordered *Totenkopf* to provide fifteen tank crews to help train the Romanian tank crews on the

Panzer IV belonging to the 1st Romanian Armored Division *Romania Mare*. These crews returned to *SS-Panzer-Regiment 3* on the twenty-seventh. On the twentieth, the battalion commander, *SS-Hauptsturmführer* Beiermeier was promoted to *Sturmbannführer*. The first two *Panzer IV's* were handed over by *Panzer-Regiment Großdeutschland* on the twenty-eighth and issued to *5. Kompanie* as training tanks. On 2 May, rail transports carrying thirty-four new *Panzer IV's* for *24. Panzer-Division* and *Panzer-grenadier-Division Großdeutschland* unloaded in Roman. A collection team (*6.* and *7. Kompanien*) from *II/SS-Panzer-Regiment 3* collected twenty-two *Panzer IV's* from this delivery as an emergency issue. On 19 May, a new delivery of four *Panzer IV's* arrived in Bacau. These tanks were meant for *Panzer-Regiment Großdeutschland* but were handed over to *SS-Panzer-Regiment 3* on the twentieth.

On the second, the *Panzer IV's*, after being collected, were deployed under the leadership of *SS-Sturmbannführer* Beiermeier near Helestieni in support of *II/SS-Panzer-Grenadier-Regiment 6 Eicke*. Also attached was a single battery from *StuG Brigade 325*. On the third, the *Panzer IV* group engaged a Russian tank force two kilometers south of Ruginoasa, knocking out four Russian tanks. On the fourth, the group was still supporting *II/SS-Panzer-Grenadier-Regiment 6 Eicke* near Ruginoasa.

SS-Sturmgeschütze-Abteilung 3

SS-Sturmgeschütze-Abteilung 3 was quartered in the village of Parincea on 15 April for refitting under the command of *SS-Sturmbannführer* Pitschellis. The battalion still possessed two *StuG's* and two *PaK (Sfl)* on strength, but on the twenty-eighth, it received eight *StuG's* from *Sturmgeschütze-Brigade 228* of the German Army. A further seventeen *StuG's* were handed over to *SS-Sturmgeschütze-Abteilung 3* on the fifth. It received nine *StuG's* plus another eight on the sixth from *Sturmgeschutze-Brigade 228*. A new delivery of sixth *StuG's* was unloaded on the eighth in Roman, and three were taken over from *46. Infanterie-Division* on 10 June. On the eighteenth, one more *StuG* was delivered to the battalion. On the fourteenth, the battalion rejoined the front line. On 1 July, the battalion was ordered to hand over seventeen *StuG's* to *II/SS-Panzer-Regiment 3*, which formed the basis of the new *8. Kompanie*. *SS-Sturmgeschütze-Abteilung 3* was redesignated *SS-Panzerjäger-Abteilung 3*, with thirty *StuG III's* (two in the headquarters company, fourteen each in *2.* and *3. Kompanien*), two *schwere PaK Sfl*, and four heavy antitank guns in the *1. Kompanie*.

On 12 May, *SS-Sturmgeschütze-Abteilung 3* deployed a single company under *SS-Obersturmbannführer* Muller toward Oboroceni. On the twenty-sixth, it relieved elements of *Sturmgeschütze-Brigade 228* assigned to the Romanian Brigade *Opris*. Another *StuG* company with eight *StuG's* was deployed on 23 June and attached to the Romanian Guards Brigade and returned to divisional control on 1 July.

Overview

On 1 July, *SS-Panzer-Regiment 3* could field twenty-eight *Panzer IV's*, seventeen *StuG III's*, and fifteen *Tigers*. A further seventeen *Panzer IV's* and two *Panzerbeobachterswagen IV's*, five *Tigers*, and four *StuG's* had been allocated as a new issue. During July 1944, *I/SS-Panzer-Regiment 3* was completing its refurbishment and issued with seventy-eight *Panther* tanks, along with four replacement *Panthers*, which arrived on the thirty-first. The *Panzerjager-Abteilung's 1. Kompanie* was transported from Poland on 6 August for conversion to the *Panzerjäger IV*. On 5 September, *1. Kompanie/SS-Panzerjäger-Abteilung 3* was issued twenty-one *Jagdpanzer IV's* at Troop Training Grounds Mielau and rejoined the division on the fifteenth.

Poland 1944

On 6 July, *3. SS-Panzer-Division Totenkopf* received orders for reallocation from Romania to Poland. Army Group Center had been the subject of a huge Russian offensive launched on 22

June—Operation Bagration involving the 1st Baltic, 1st Byelorussian, 2nd Byelorussian, and 3rd Byelorussian Fronts. *9. Kompanie* loaded in Roman on the seventh on two transports and traveled through Warsaw and unloaded in Osowice on the sixteenth. *Totenkopf* came under the command of *A.O.K. 4. 9. Kompanie*, after unloading, assembled in Mieleskowcze, southwest of Kuznica.

On 17 July, *9. Kompanie* was assigned to *Kampfgruppe Kuhn*, which, with another *Kampfgruppe*, was to stop a Russian advance. *III/SS-Panzer-Grenadier-Regiment 6 Eicke* advanced toward Adamowicze, supported by *9. Kompanie*. Two kilometers north, near the village of Mickiewicz, *I/SS-Polizei-Regiment 34* was deployed. Both units were to try to eliminate the Russian bridgehead near Zarzyczach. Throughout the day, both *Kampfgruppen* were making gains. *III/SS-Panzer-Grenadier-Regiment 6 Eicke*, with the *Tigers* from *9. Kompanie*, was involved in fighting for Adamowicze. The *Tiger* of *SS-Untersturmführer* Wenzel was hit and immobilized. Russian troops dragged the crew out and executed them, sparing the radio operator, *SS-Rottenführer* Heinz Rudolf, who was taken as a prisoner of war. But Wenzel, *SS-Unterscharführer* Siebenaler (driver), *SS-Sturmann* Lau (gunner), and *SS-Sturmmann* Metzger (loader) were all executed. During the evening, *I/SS-Polizei-Regiment 34* entered Mickiewicz.

On 18 July, Russian forces were trying to assault Hill 67 near Adamowicze. Due to the situation, *III/SS-Panzer-Grenadier-Regiment 6 Eicke* had to withdraw in coordination with *Korps von Gottberg*. *Kampfgruppe Kuhn* sent elements to support *I/SS-Polizei-Regiment 34* in order to try to retake Adamowicze. The *Tigers* provided covering fire near Kilbaski, while *I/SS-Polizei-Regiment 34* (supported by fifteen *StuG's*) and *Kampfgruppe Kuhn* attacked Adamowicze. It was during this operation that the company commander, *SS-Hauptsturmführer* Fischer was fatally wounded. A *Tiger* commanded by *SS-Unterscharführer* Schulz requested assistance because of technical damage. Fischer arrived and hooked up Schulz's *Tiger* and towed it back to German lines. As they moved along the road, an antitank gun from *SS-Polizei-Regiment 34* fired at Fischer's *Tiger* and wounded Fischer (fatally) and the driver, *SS-Unterscharführer* Aage Skjodt. When the gun commander found out, he was shocked. Fischer died on the twentieth in Lojki. *SS-Hauptsturmführer* Neidhardt took over the company; he was transferred from *7. Kompanie*.

On 19 July 1944, *9. Kompanie*, along with *3. Kompanie/SS-Panzer-Aufklarungs-Abteilung 3*, advanced on Sopockinie. This was met with strong Russian defensive fire, and the attack was made in conjunction with *SS-Kampfgruppe Pitschellis* (Pitschellis was commander of *SS-Panzerjager-Abteilung 3*). During the day, *SS-Sturmann* Heinz Bartl (vehicle diver) was killed and Josef Hodap from the maintenance section was wounded during a Russian air strike; *SS-Untersturmführer* Kriescher was lightly wounded. On the twentieth, *9. Kompanie* was still attached to *III/SS-Panzer-Grenadier-Regiment 6 Eicke* and fighting near Kilbaski. During the day, the *Tiger* of *SS-Untersturmführer* Wenzel was destroyed in Adamowicze after German forces launched a limited counterattack and seized temporary control of the *Tiger*; petrol was poured inside and outside the *Tiger*, which was then set on fire.

On 21 July 1944, *9. Kompanie* fought off a Russian armored attack using SU-85 self-propelled guns. The company knocked out several of these guns in the course of a Russian attack on Mankowiec. Next, the *Tigers* had to support *II/SS-Panzer-Grenadier-Regiment 6 Eicke* in defending against a Russian attack near Sylwanowicz, but the Russians were putting pressure along *SS-Panzer-Grenadier-Regiment 6 Eicke's* front line from Wasilewicz-Nowosady with three strong attacks. The grenadiers were supported by *9. Kompanie*. In the evening and the early hours of the twenty-second, *9. Kompanie*, in support of *I* and *II/SS-Panzer-Grenadier-Regiment 6 Eicke*, launched a counterattack trying to restore the regimental

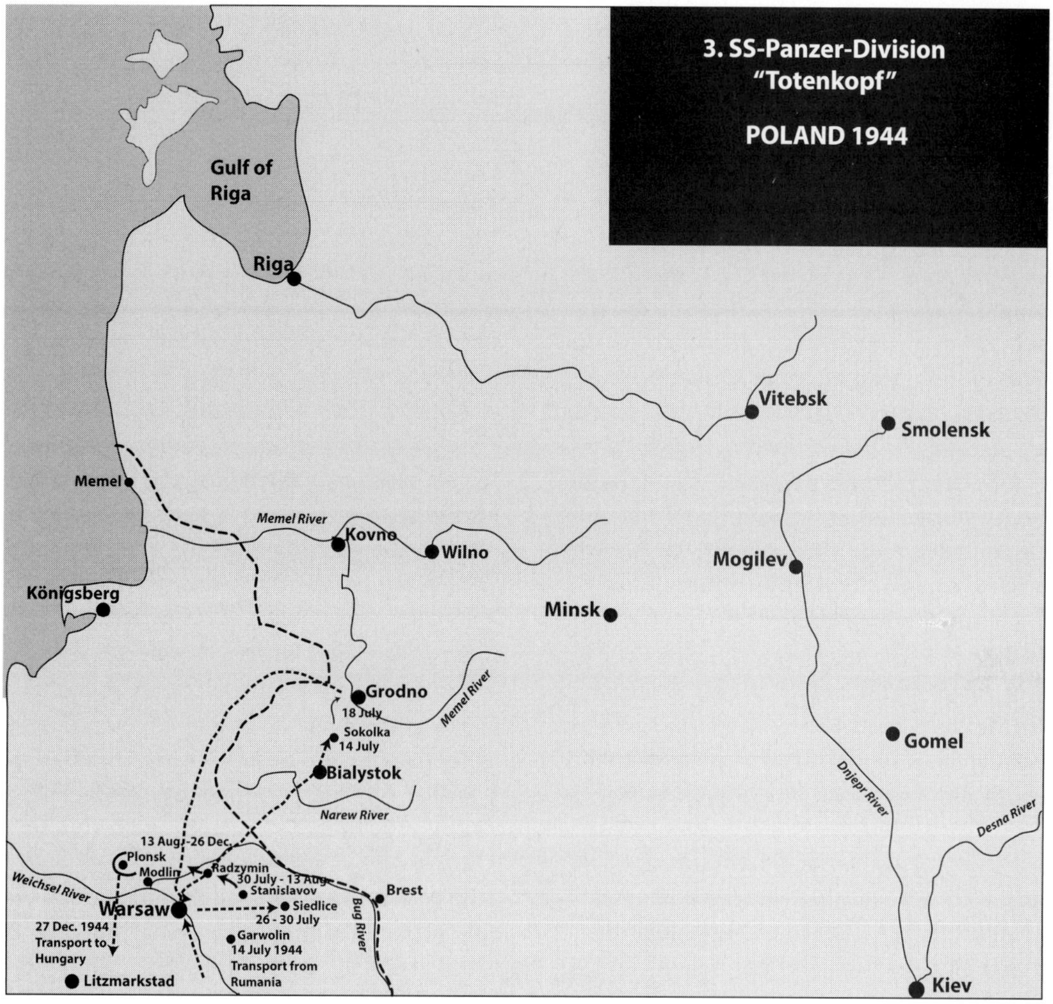

front line. Despite some limited success, *Totenkopf* had to withdraw.

On 23 July, Neff had to report to divisional headquarters and receive movement orders for rail transfer from *A.O.K. 4* to *A.O.K. 2* for redeployment in the Siedlce area. Despite these orders, *9. Kompanie* was still committed. Four *Tigers* were sent to Osowiec on the twenty-fifth for loading, but only three rail flat cars were available to carry the *Tigers*. The remaining *Tiger* had to wait until 3 August before it could be transported. The *Tiger* was unloaded in Warsaw-Praga on the fifth. The three *Tigers* loaded in Osowiec and arrived in Sokolow in the evening. One *Tiger* entered Siedlce at 1950 hours; the other two left Sokolow at 2205. On the twenty-sixth, five *Tigers* were still in action five kilometers east of Dabrowa, attached to *III/SS-Panzer-Grenadier-Regiment 6 Eicke* at 2000 hours. These were eventually released for transport on the twenty-seventh, being ordered to move from Dabrowa to Zamborow. The transfer to Siedlce began on the twenty-eighth with one transport carrying the *WerkStatt* company, loading two damaged *Tigers*. *SS-Panzer-Regiment 3* required fifteen flat cars to take all of its damaged tanks and *StuG's*. This transport left Osowiec at 1515 hours.

One transport was loaded on the twenty-ninth at 0530 with five *Tigers* in Osowiec and arrived in Sokolow at 1725 hours on the thirtieth. Another three *Tigers* were loaded and left Osowiec at 2230 hours, but due to the combat situation, the transport was diverted from Sokolow to Warsaw and arrived at 2315 hours on the thirty-first. The transport with five new *Tigers* from *HZA Magdeburg* arrived in Warsaw-Praga on the thirty-first. The new *Tigers*, under the command of *SS-Hauptscharführer* Berger, were directed by *SS-Obersturmbannführer* Wolf to proceed to the Stauffer *Kasserne*. On the twenty-fourth, *I/SS-Panzer-Regiment 3* returned with seventy-eight *Panthers*; five of these were command versions commanded by Knight's Cross and Oak Leaves winner *SS-Sturmbannführer* Meierdress.

Eric Lehmkuhl reported:

> On 18 July 1944, we receive the order from the new company commander, *SS-Hauptsturmführer* Fischer, to move toward the Niemen bridgehead. The village of Kilbaski is being attacked on three sides by the Russians, and so we have to secure the village. To the north, the *Tiger* of *SS-Unterscharführer* Schulz has engine trouble, and Schulz is requesting help—he is stuck in the middle of the village surrounded by burning thatched houses. We go directly to his aid, attach tow cables, and head west. Suddenly, we are hit from the front by antitank fire. The first shot hits the main gun of Schulz's *Tiger*, and we immediately close the hatches, but *SS-Hauptsturmführer* Fischer is not so lucky—he is killed while trying to close the commander's hatch as another round hits our *Tiger*. Our driver, Sepp, fires a flare signal; the antitank gun quickly recognizes us and stops firing. The antitank gun belongs to an *SS-Polizei-Regiment*. We drive along the road toward a road block; the antitank crew is naturally horrified by their mistake. However, a properly trained gun commander would never have made this mistake.

A *Tiger* commander recorded the following about Siedlce on 31 July 1944: "Our *Tiger* turns on the spot and fires toward the end of the street. On our right is a rail embankment and behind that is the road leading to Chodow. The cannon fires an 88cm shell from the barrel. The turret is full of smoke, so we leave the hatches open to allow the fumes to ventilate. Behind me is *SS-Unterscharführer* Holtorf, who hits a third Russian tank with a single shot. It catches fire. The crew bail out."

During the withdrawal from Siedlce, the *Panther* battalion and *9. Kompanie* pulled back to the west and then headed north to Chodow along the road to Kopcie and eventually assembled in the area of Suchdol. On 3 August, two *Tigers* supported *I/SS-Panzer-Regiment 3* near Banachowizna, just east of Nadbiel, defending against the Russian III Tank Corps. The *Panther* battalion launched a counterattack along the Kolno-Zambraniec road. Two *Tigers* were involved in a counterattack on Stawiska. On the fourth, three *Tigers* were supporting *I/SS-Panzer-Regiment 3* during the fighting near Okuniew. A single *Panther* company from *I/SS-Panzer-Regiment 3* supported *SS-Panzer-Grenadier-Regiment Germania* from *5. SS-Panzer-Division Wiking* during the fighting in the area of Chobota and Mrowiaska.

On the fifth, *9. Kompanie* saw defensive actions near Lesnogora, about twenty-five kilomters east of Stanislawow, supporting *II* and *III/SS-Panzer-Grenadier-Regiment 6 Eicke*. Three Russian T-34 tanks were knocked out, and one *Tiger* sustained battle damage which required maintenance. Between the sixth and seventh, the company was able to enjoy a quiet period before being recommitted on the eighth to the west of Gozdiowka.

On the nineteenth, *9. Kompanie* and elements of *I/SS-Panzer-Regiment 3* were involved in a series of counterattacks near Krusze during the day. At the start in the morning, the task was to clear a Russian antitank gun front in the area of east of Wola-Roszczep. *9. Kompanie* had the support of *1. Kompanie*. The antitank gun front was breached, but one *Panther* required repairs to the main gun after it was hit by Russian anti-tank gunfire. Later, Russian tanks were reported in the woods 1.5 kilometers southeast of Krusze. *1. Kompanie* and *9. Kompanie* were tasked again with clearing the area. *1. Kompanie*, with seven operational *Panthers*, and *9. Kompanie*, with four *Tigers*, advanced across the open terrain. At a range of 1,000 meters, JS-2 tanks (based on the KV chassis and mounting a massive 12.2cm main gun) from the 62nd Heavy Guards Tank Regiment opened fire. One *Panther* from *1. Kompanie* was immediately knocked out. A second *Panther* (*SS-Obersturmbannführer* Schramm's) took hits to the track, wheels, and hull and needed to be recovered and towed away. Two *Tigers* were also knocked out (trophy numbers 123 and 124), and a third *Tiger* was so badly damaged that the crew bailed out and abandoned the *Tiger*. The Tigers were commanded by *SS-Untersturmführer* Neff, *SS-Unterscharführer* Sandler, and *SS-Oberscharführer* Weitner. Weitner was killed along with *SS-Sturmmann* Schmidt (radio operator) and *SS-Sturmmann* Meier (driver).

In the afternoon, another counterattack was ordered, with better results. The *Tigers* knocked out one JS-2 tank and immobilized two other JS-2's. The tanks of *SS-Panzer-Regiment 5* launched an attack on Kozly which brought some relief to *SS-Panzer-Regiment 3* near Krusze. At the end of the day, the *IV. SS-Panzer-Korps* claimed twenty-one Russian tanks and self-propelled guns as destroyed, while the Russian claimed two *Tigers* and eighteen *Panthers* as destroyed. The Russian 8th Guards Tank Corps on the nineteenth lost two M4 Sherman tanks and a single SU-76 SPG; another nine Shermans and two SU-76 SPG's required repairs due to battle damage during the fighting for Krusze. On the twentieth, the 62nd Heavy Guards Tank Regiment managed to gain control of the left side of Krusze, but on the twenty-second, the *Tigers* from *9. Kompanie* knocked out four Sherman tanks.

Eric Lehmkuhl recalled:

The *Tiger* of *SS-Oberscharführer* Weitner is knocked out. All his crew are killed. The *Tiger* of *SS-Untersturmführer* Neff is hit, sustains severe damage, and the crew bail out. The company carries out several counterattacks in the area of Radzymin and Pustelnik; we suffer some *Tiger* losses. Loader Boxleitner is killed by friendly fire. The Russians constantly attack us with artillery fire. Sleep is hard to come by, and life is to a degree unbearable. Currently, our armor is located in the area of Radzymin. *SS-Obersturmbannführer* Neidhardt is surveying the terrain with binoculars when a grenade explodes nearby, wounding him and killing his dog. The company is taken over by Neff. *SS-Untersturmführer* Kriescher is slightly wounded, and *SS-Sturmmann* Berg is wounded.

The front line has to be pulled back to the area of Jozefow. There are some dominant heights in the area. In the late afternoon, we receive orders to support the *StuG* battalion and take Hill 104 near Rembelszczyzna. The Russians have occupied the hill; we quickly advance up it and knock out a T-34 that is blocking our way at a range of fifty meters. In the morning the Russians open fire on us with artillery from the direction of Solchew. I've never seen anything like this. Thank God for a small ravine in which we take cover. Fountains of earth and trees are thrown through the air. To our front there is a loud bang, and we see a *StuG* get thrown into the air.

The *Tiger* is shaken for about thirty minutes. The Russians laid artillery fire that fell behind us before masses of Russian infantry came toward us. Our own infantry are happy as we open fire with our 8.8cm and MG. This brings the Russians to a standstill. There is hardly any cover for them, but the pressure is so intense from the Russians that we have to fall back from the hill. Soon our own artillery and *Nebelwerfer* units shell the Russians, and then we roll forward back up the hill and try to reach a ravine which leads into a wood. The wood is just a sea of tree stumps and rubble, shot-up guns, and destroyed vehicles—amongst all this carnage are dead bodies from both sides.

The hill is once again back in our hands. On the left is another *Tiger*, and on our right are two *StuG's*. There is a silence, and then we begin to hear the moaning of the wounded. There is a frenzied banging on my hatch. *SS-Untersturmführer* Neff and his gunner had bailed out after his *Tiger* was hit. Loader Mauser, driver Lucht, and radio operator Laux have all been killed. Eventually, things begin to settle down. The Russians don't press us, but on another morning, the third battle begins. There is no cover, no trees—we have to move back with the turret at the six-o'clock position. We have a probation infantry battalion (a penal unit) assigned to us. We are ordered to attack back up the hill under the heaviest fire; in fact, the Russians are so demoralized that they don't even return fire, so we are back on top of the hill. The probation infantry battalion did nothing of note and hid from the Russians. Suddenly, it's midnight.

Then came a radio signal to pull back, so we move to the foot of the hill where there is a wood. Here we find time to catch up on some needed sleep. We sleep inside the *Tiger*. I awake at about noon due to one of my friends snoring loudly, but standing before us is a group of Russians who are shouting at us and at the same time admiring our *Tiger*. I shout at my fellow comrades to wake up. Very quickly, we fire our MG at them, but we get hit from the right by antitank fire, but nothing happens. We are asking ourselves where the gun is. We fire at the closest proximity with our main gun and drive at full gas down the road and reach our nearest infantry, which is still positioned on Hill 104. This was one of the closest experiences I had during the war.

October comes—we have built bunkers in the area of Jozefow. During an artillery raid, I fall over and break my arm. I'm taken to a field hospital in Modlin. On 9 October, I return to the company to recover. Since the tenth, the Russians had started another offensive with 1,000 guns along a five-kilometer front in our divisional sector. Like an earthquake, the barrage reaches Jozefow, and the Russians break through several sectors of our front line, but later in the day, our former front-line positions are restored. On the twelfth, I returned to the company commander's *Tiger* and the crew of *SS-Untersturmführer* Neff. We see action in the area of Legionowo-Jablonna in the so-called wet triangle near the Vistula River. *SS-Unterscharführer* Probst and *SS-Rottenführer* Hodap are both killed near Jablonna. One of our cooks is killed on a farm near Jablonna by a mortar round.

In November, the division is pulled out of the line and sent to rest. On 24 December, we celebrate in a school house. By 2200 hours, we continue in our quarters. I set up a radio and try to get the nighttime broadcasts. Suddenly, a comrade comes in saying that the division is to load on transports immediately and is being sent to Hungary. That night we packed all our equipment. I pack our radio sets and my personal possessions and store them inside the tank, including ammunition.

On 25 August, *9. Kompanie* was on the defensive near Klembow, then Kraszew and Zawada, three kilometers northeast of Radzymin. On the twenty-sixth, the *Tiger* of *SS-Unterscharführer* Kronmuller was hit by Russian antitank gunfire near Klembow, eight kilometers east of Radzymin. Kronmuller and the radio operator, *SS-Rottenführer* von Berg, were both killed. *9. Kompanie* was taken over by *SS-Untersturmführer*

Neff because *SS-Hauptsturmführer* Neidhardt took command of *5. Kompanie* of *II/SS-Panzer-Regiment 3*. Between the thirtieth and thirty-first, *9. Kompanie* saw defensive actions in the area of Wiktorow and Marianow. During August 1944, Gunther Schulz arrived. *SS-Oberscharführer* Wendt, *SS-Rottenführer* Of, and *SS-Rottenführer* Schulz-Berge all did limited time in the *Bewahrungs Zug* (probationary platoon) for breaches of discipline. On 1 September, *9. Kompanie* pulled back to the area of Hill 104 and the villages of Struga and Nadma. Former company commande Neidhardt was killed while leading *5. Kompanie*.

9. Kompanie's manpower strength on 1 September 1944 was three officers, nineteen NCO's, and sixty-six other ranks, for a total of eighty-eight.

On 2 August, the *Tigers* of *9. Kompanie* were fighting in the woods northwest of Nadma. Some *Tigers* in Warsaw crossed Pontiatowski Bridge after conducting maintenance en route to Struga. On the sixth, the company was involved in security and defensive duties in the area of Wolka-Radzyminska. Between the twelfth and thirteenth, *9. Kompanie* was supporting grenadiers launching attacks around Hill 104. The Russians would later capture the hill, forcing the German front line. On the thirteenth, the *Tiger* of *SS-Unterscharführer* Probst was destroyed by Russian artillery fire on Hill 104, one kilomter west of Slupno. Probst was killed.

Walter Weber of *5. Kompanie* reported:

> Afternoon in Radzymin and our positions on the outskirts of town, there is a 2,000-meter strip ahead of us near a wood where the Russians are deploying tanks. We watch the trees and bushes move. We listen in to the Russian radio traffic—mind you, we don't know what they are saying. In support of us are three *Tigers* from the heavy company.
>
> We pulled back farther inside the town. Alongside use are two *Tigers* that were involved with skirmishes with JS-2 heavy tanks. The two *Tigers* left the town. We wanted to pull back as well, but we received orders by radio to stay put, so we strengthened our positions, and—lo and behold—Russian JS-2 heavy tanks appear.

After losing Hill 104, *9. Kompanie*, along with other *Totenkopf* divisional units, pulled back to a new front line during the night of 14–15 September into the area of Jozefow. On the fifteenth, *9. Kompanie* was attached to *SS-Panzerjäger-Abteilung 3*. On 16 September 1944, *9. Kompanie*, along with grenadiers of *III/SS-Panzer-Grenadier-Regiment 6 Eicke* and *2./SS-Panzerjäger-Abteilung 3*, was sent to the area of Rembelszczyzna and Tomaszow to support Hungarian forces that were coming under increasing Russian pressure. The *Tigers* and *Totenkopf* grenadiers launch a counterattack on Hill 103, two kilometers south of Rembelszczyzna. During this attack, the *Tiger* of *SS-Untersturmführer* Neff is hit by Russian artillery fire, destroying the *Tiger*. Neff managed to bail out, but *SS-Rottenführer* Kowalski (gunner), *SS-Sturmmann* Lucht (driver), and *SS-Sturmmann* Laux (radio operator) were all killed. In a separate engagement, *SS-Sturmmann* Weber was killed by Russian infantry fire. Neff had to hand over command of *9. Kompanie* to *SS-Untersturmführer* Kriescher as he had been lightly wounded. Neff recovered at the divisional hospital. Counterattacks were launched on the seventeenth and eighteenth, but on the eighteenth, the *Tigers* came under heavy Russian artillery fire. On the nineteenth, a partially successful attack on Hill 103 was made, but on the twentieth, the Russians made an all-out effort and took the hill. During the attack, the *Tigers* of *9. Kompanie* found themselves exposed and had to reorient themselves in order to make a successful withdrawal.

9. Kompanie's manpower strength on 20 September was 2 officers, 25 NCO's, and 87 other ranks—a total of 114. On 1 October, it was 2 officers, 25 NCO's, and 90 other ranks—a total of 117 (of this total, 3 NCO's and 8 other ranks were sick or wounded).

At the start of October, the company personnel built bunkers in the area of Legionowo using wood as roof beams. The support units were based in Jablonna, and the combat elements were in the area of Jozefow.

On 10 October, the *Tigers* were involved in heavy fighting for Hill 101, west of Jozefow, along with *II/SS-Panzer-Grenadier-Regiment 6 Eicke*, during the day. *SS-Sturmmann* Kautz (cook), *SS-Rottenführer* Koppen (gunner), and *SS-Oberscharführer* Wendt (tank commander) were killed when their *Tiger* was hit, causing heavy damage, and *SS-Rottenführer* Preisendanz (truck driver) was seriously wounded and died from those wounds on the twenty-fourth. All of this occurred in the area of Jablonna. Wounded during the day as well were Karl Schade (*Kübelwagen* driver), Christian Schuard, and Loidold (company cook).

On the eleventh, former *9. Kompanie* commander, *SS-Sturmbannführer* Biermeier, was seriously wounded while commanding *II/SS-Panzer-Regiment 3*. He was visiting the command post of *2. Kompanie/SS-Panzer-Pionier-Bataillon 3*. On the eleventh, six *Tigers* broke up a Russian attack, which resulted in four *Tigers* being seriously damaged near Michalow-Grabina. On the twelfth, *SS-Untersturmführer* Neff returned to *9. Kompanie* after recovering from his wound and resumed command of the company. *SS-Untersturmführer* Kriescher was transferred to the regiment's headquarters company. *SS-Untersturmführer* Kriescher would later contract pneumonia and had to be hospitalized on 9 December at the SS-Hospital in Modlin. On the twenty-third, he was transferred to the *SS-Panzer-Ausbildungs-und-Ersatz-Regiment* in Sennelager. On 7 February, he was transferred to a specialist in Vienna for further treatment.

Between the twelfth and thirteenth, the front line of *Totenkopf* came under heavy Russian artillery fire, causing the deaths of *SS-Rottenführer* Hodap in Legionowo and *SS-Sturmmann* Priess (both from the maintenance section), near Jablonna during a Russian airstrike. On the fourteenth, the *Tigers* from *9. Kompanie* took part in defensive fighting around Hill 97 and Lapigrosz. On the fifteenth, *SS-Untersturmführer* Neff was promoted to *SS-Obersturmführer*. *Tigers* attached to *I/SS-Panzer-Regiment 3* fought near Jozefow and knocked out six Russian tanks (three claimed by the *Panther* battalion and three by *9. Kompanie*). On the sixteenth, the Russians halted all their attacks trying to break through to the Vistula River. On the nineteenth, another attempt was made but again the attack was beaten back by German defensive fire. On the twenty-second, *SS-Panzer-Regiment 3* reassembled in the area of Jablonna-Legionowo. *9. Kompanie* regrouped as well, with a total strength of thirteen *Tigers* still on hand. Elements attached to *SS-Panzerjäger-Abteilung 3* rejoined the company, and the other elements of the company had been attached to *I/SS-Panzer-Regiment 3* during mid-October 1944.

On the twenty-sixth, five new replacements joined *9. Kompanie*; these men had been transferred from the *Luftwaffe* and reenlisted into the *Waffen-SS*. *Totenkopf* had the following replacements from the *Luftwaffe*: 12 officers, 944 NCO's, and 3,360 other ranks. Of these, 2,086 men had already been assigned to divisional units, 1,277 were still undergoing training behind the front line, and 950 were with *SS-Feld-Ersatz-Bataillon 3*.

On the same day, the Russians began a heavy artillery barrage along the front line of the *Totenkopf*. On the twenty-seventh, *SS-Panzer-Regiment 3* withdrew over the Brodnowski Canal near Lajsk. On the twenty-eighth, the Russians captured Legionowo. On the thirty-first, the Russians tried to capture Nowy Dwor (Bugmunde), but well-hidden German antitank guns and *StuG's* forced the Russians back after heavy fighting near the village of Derlacz. The Russians had to withdraw back to their start positions after a successful counterattack by grenadiers and *StuG's* from *Totenkopf*.

From 5 November, *A.O.K. 9* used *I/SS-Panzer-Regiment 3*, with fourteen *Panthers*, as well as *I (gep)* and *II/SS-Panzer-Grenadier-Regiment 5 Totenkopf*, as a reserve south of

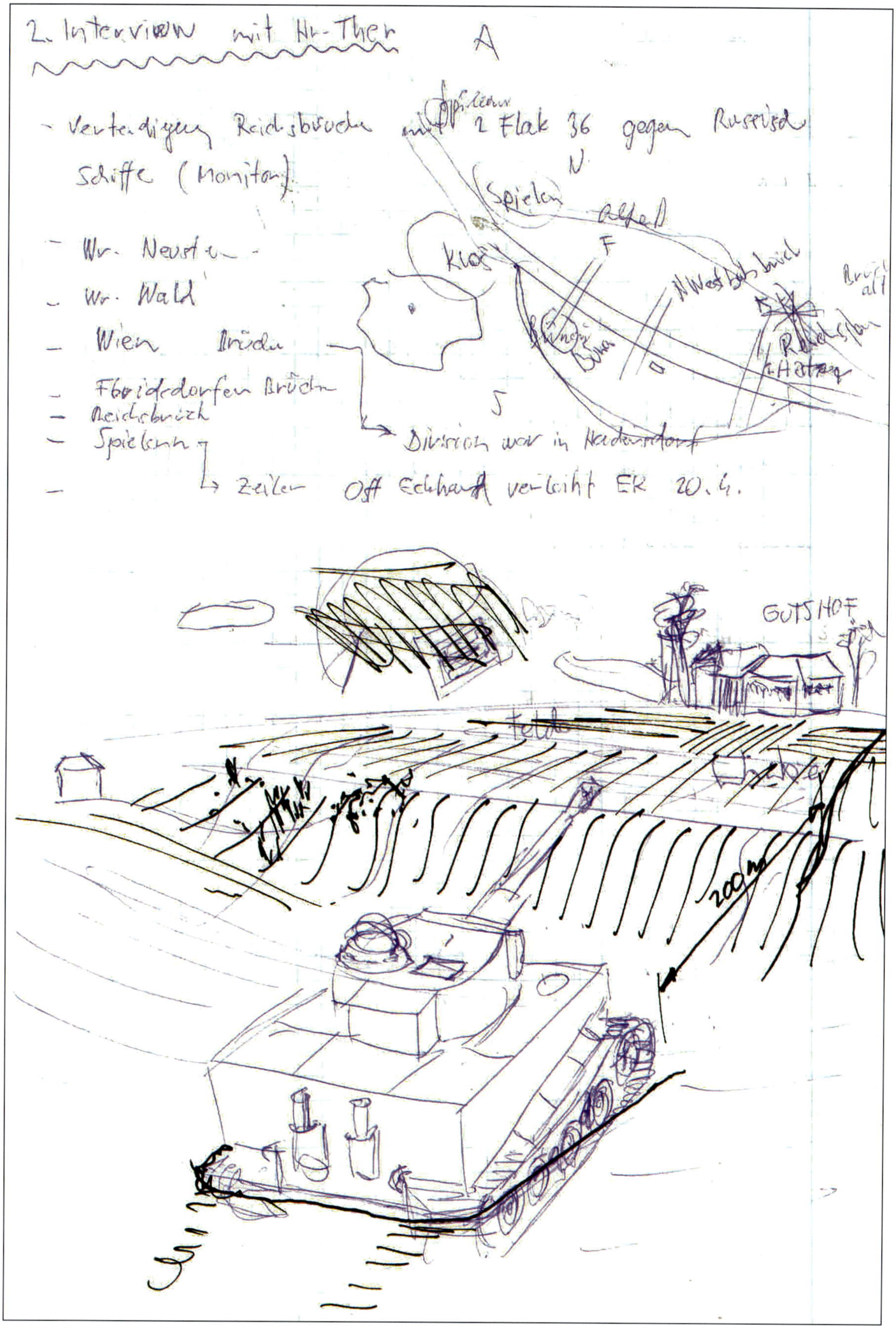

A sketch from memory of the moment when *SS-Hauptsturmführer* Ther had to abandon his *Tiger* on 17 March 45, about 200 meters east of the farmstead Felso Major. KUNO THER / DIETRICH WOLF

Tiger 931, *SS-Untersturmführer* Rathsack, July 1943

Tiger 901, *SS-Hauptsturmführer* Baedke, January 1944

Tiger 913, *SS-Oberscharführer* Wimmer, May 1944

Tiger Cutaway, View 1

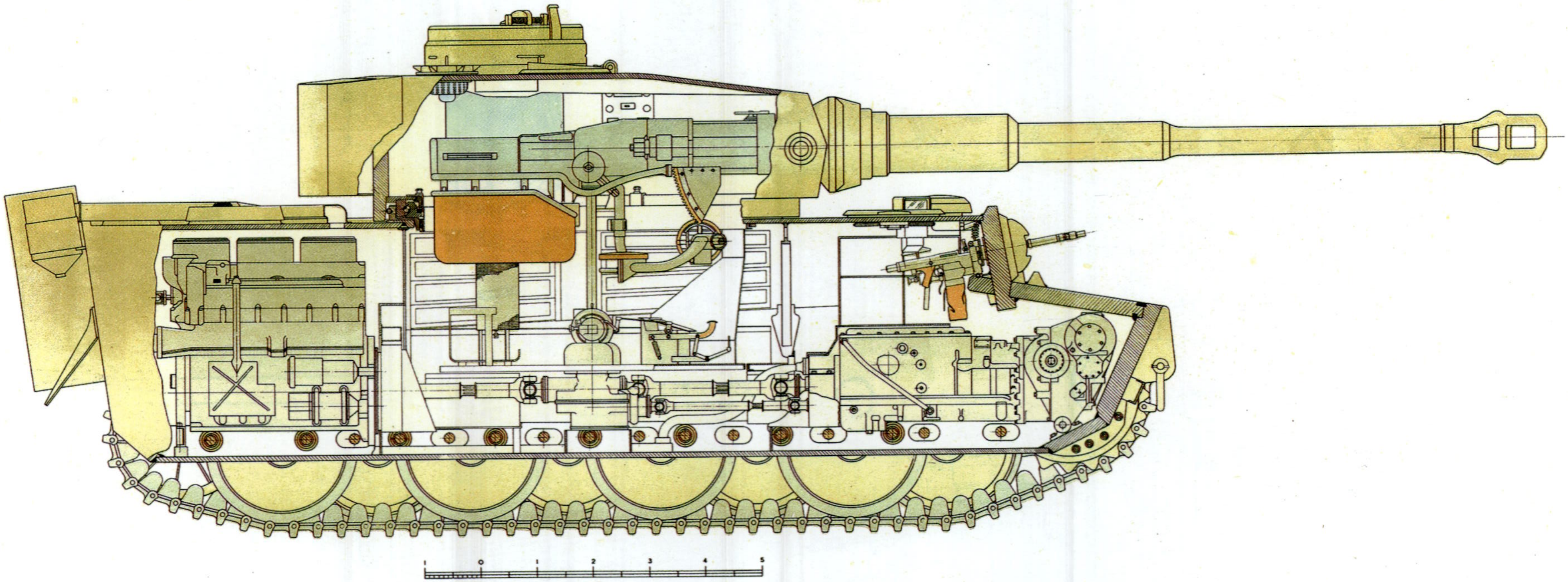

Tiger Cutaway, View 2

Modlin. On the sixth, *SS-Panzer-Regiment 3* assembled in Lomna Niemicki. On the eighth, *SS-Untersturmführer* Heinz Vesterling joined *9. Kompanie* as a platoon leader after completing the third *SS-Panzer-Junker-Sonder-Lehrgang* in Fallingbostal. He had joined the *Waffen-SS* on 15 May 1942, and he was promoted to *SS-Untersturmführer* on 20 October 1944. *I/SS-Panzer Regiment 3* was still south of Modlin on the twelfth, with twelve operational *Panthers* along with *I/SS-Panzer-Grenadier-Regiment 5 Totenkopf (gep)* acting as *A.O.K. 9* reserve.

Before the eighteenth, *II/SS-Panzer-Grenadier-Regiment 5 Totenkopf* was released from *A.O.K. 9* reserve and rejoined its parent division. During mid-November, the rains brought road movement almost to a halt; the use of horse-drawn wagons and sledges was generally the only way to get about. On the seventeenth, *SS-Standartenoberjunker* (*SS-Hauptscharführer* as of 9 November) Rudiger Blau joined *9. Kompanie* after completing the fourth *SS-Panzer-Junker-Sonder-Lehrgang* at Königsbruck bei Wien from 1 July to 9 November 1944. He had joined the *Waffen-SS* on 15 September 1942 after completing his RAD (*Reichsarbeitsdienst*, or Reich Labor Service). He served with the *Tiger* company in *SS-Panzer-Regiment 2* as an *SS-Panzer-Schütze*. He was wounded near Walki on 10 March 1943 and was initially treated by *2. Kompanie/SS-Sanitäts-Abteilung Leibstandarte.*

On the twenty-third, *Totenkopf* had to repel another Russian attack near Jablonna. On the twenty-fourth, the divisional front line came under strong artillery and mortar fire. A local counterattack, with the support of *StuG's*, cleared a bunker system. On the same day, Army Group Center ordered that *Totenkopf* be released from *A.O.K. 9* control and assigned to *A.O.K. 2*. On the twenty-fifth, elements of *Totenkopf* were involved in defensive actions south of Jablonna and Nowe Dwor. On the twenty-sixth, *SS-Panzer-Regiment 3* moved into the area of Nowe Miasto (Neustadt). On the twenty-seventh, *Totenkopf* reported to *A.O.K. 2*. On 2 December, *I/SS-Panzer-Regiment 3* and *I (gep)/SS-Panzer-Grenadier-Regiment 5 Totenkopf* were released from *A.O.K. 9* and rejoined their parent division.

On 2 December, *SS-Obersturmbannführer* Neff went on home leave, and *SS-Obersturmbannführer* Wenke took over *9. Kompanie*. At 2000 hours on the third, *Totenkopf* was assembled in the following areas: Nowe Miasto–Borkowo–Cegelinia–Psucka–Krzycki–Rebkowo–Swiercze and Koty. On the ninth, former *9. Kompanie* officer *SS-Untersturmführer* Hans Kriescher had to be treated in the SS-Hospital in Modlin for pneumonia. On the twenty-third, he was transferred to *SS-Panzer-Ausbildungs-und-Ersatz-Regiment* in Paderborn for further treatment.

During December 1944, *SS-Rottenführer* Ruediger Bernhardt and *SS-Unterscharführer* Dieter Thomas were sent to attend the *SS-Junkerschule* back in Germany.

During the night of 25 December, the *Tigers* of *9. Kompanie* moved to Nasielsk for loading in readiness for departure to Hungary. Loading commenced on the twenty-sixth, and they departed the same day. The route was Bydgoszcz–Poznan–Wroclaw–Wien, and they arrived in Komarom on 30 December 1944. After unloading, the *Tigers* moved through the center of the town and were quartered in an old cavalry barracks. The company still had thirteen *Tigers* on hand, of which eleven were operational, with two *Tigers* in repair. On the thirty-first, the *Tigers* were coated with whitewash for use as winter camouflage. During the afternoon, *SS-Obersturmbannführer* Laackmann issued orders for the up and coming relief operation on Budapest. That evening the company had a New Year's party.

Warsaw

On 31 July, *Tigers* from *9. Kompanie*, after being unloaded, were used to secure the major road heading east in the direction of Milosna Street. The five new *Tigers* under the command of *SS-Hauptscharführer* Berger unloaded in Warsaw Praga on the thrity-first and were directed by *SS-Obersturmbannführer* Wolf, the transport officer, to proceed to the Stauffer *Kaserne* on Rakowiecka Street.

On the morning of 1 August, the *Tigers* underwent technical maintenance and took on a new load of fuel and ammunition. The *Tigers*, along with five *Panzer IV's*, set off and crossed Paniatowska Bridge, which spanned the Vistula River, moving along Pankiewcza Street and then turning onto Marszalkowska Street. Along the way the *Tigers* came under intense fire and bombardment from Molotov cocktails and petrol canisters. The *Tiger* of *SS-Unterscharführer* Sandler was hit by a captured *Panzerfaust* fired from a cellar. The radio operator, *SS-Sturmann* Steinau, was killed. The *Tiger* of *SS-Unterscharführer* Kronmuller was hit, and the driver, *SS-Unterscharführer* Munch, was seriously wounded. Another *Tiger* on the corner of Marszalkowska Street and Koszilkowa Street was set on fire and abandoned by the crew. Another *Tiger* broke down due to technical trouble and had to be recovered.

Another group of *Tigers* provided support to the Narbuta *Kaserne*, which is not far from the Stauffer *Kaserne*, at around 1700 hours. The streets were blocked with steel rails and tram cars. The *Tigers* fired at these street barricades and the surrounding residential buildings, which were occupied by members of the Polish Home Army. The *Tigers* were pelted by homemade bombs.

Most of the *Tigers* unloaded in Warsaw left the city and headed northeast between the first and the eighth. On the same day, *Panzer-Kompanie Totenkopf* was formed under the command of *SS-Obersturmbannführer* Wolf. The company was made up of new replacement tanks. On the second, two *Tigers* were tasked with providing an escort for a convoy of wounded soldiers to Okecie air field.

At the Stauffer *Kaserne*, *9. Kompanie* had four *Tigers* under short-term repair and one *Tiger* in long-term repair. The *Tiger* that was left behind in Osowiec from 24 July was finally unloaded in Warsaw on 7 August (and was still there at the station on the twelfth). On the same day, four *Tigers* were attached to *Kampfgruppe Geibel*. At the Stauffer *Kaserne*, two *Tigers* were still undergoing short-term repair. On the third, *Panzer-Kompanie Totenkopf*, with mounted grenadiers, assisted in a clean-up operation in the southwestern part of the city. They returned to the Stauffer *Kaserne* in the evening.

One of the *Tigers* attached to *Kampfgruppe Geibel* was immobilized by a *Panzerfaust* along Jerozolimskie Street near the main rail station and had to be towed away. On the eighth, *9. Kompanie* had three *Tigers* operational within the areas of Jerozolimiskie and Mokotow. On the tenth, the operational *Tigers* in Warsaw were planned for use in an operation in the Omina area. This task was to be completed on the twelfth. On the same day, *9. Kompanie* had one *Tiger* at the Warsaw Praga rail station and six *Tigers* with *Kampfgruppe Reinfarth*.

On the fourteenth, six *Tigers* from the Stauffer *Kaserne* were attached to *Kampfgruppe Patz*, commanded by *SS-Obersturmbannführer* Patz, which was under the command of *SS-Obergruppenführer* von dem Bach-Zelewski. On the sixteenth, *Panzer-Kompanie Totenkopf*, commanded by *SS-Obersturmbannführer* Wolf, still had two *Tigers* on strength, along with nine *Panzer IV's* and a single *Panther*. Most of the *Tigers* by this date had already returned to the tank regiment. On the seventeenth, *Panzer-Kompanie Totenkopf* was placed under the command of the *Wehrmacht*. On the twenty-second, *Panzer-Kompanie Totenkopf*, along with two *Tigers*, was assigned to *Kampfgruppe Rohr*. *Panzer-Kompanie Totenkopf* conducted maintenance on the twenty-ninth at the Stauffer *Kaserne*; the day itself was relatively quiet. Between the seventeenth and the twenty-fourth, two *Tigers* would remain in Warsaw with *Panzer-Kompanie Totenkopf* before returning to the tank regiment along with the remaining *Panzer IV's*.

SS-Rottenführer Riebow, who served with *SS-Feld-Ersatz-Bataillon 3* in Warsaw, wrote: "At the eastern end of Milosna Street, our *Tigers*

Personnel from *9. Kompanie* loaded onto carriages awaiting departure to Balta, March 1944.

Departure to Balta, 12 March 1944. Contrary to standard practice, the *Tigers* are fitted with their standard tracks, not the narrower transport type.

Standing on the rail flat car from the left: Lachner, Weiler, Gansera, Wendt. Sitting down is *SS-Rottenführer* Adamiak.

Standing in front of the rail flat car, from the left: *SS-Unterscharführer* Hofmann, driver; *SS-Rottenführer* Weiler, unknown. Fourth from left is Blatmann, loader. Standing behind Blatmann is *SS-Unterscharführer* Godecke, driver. Standing next to Blatmann with a pipe in his mouth is Pavlu. Next to Pavlu is *SS-Untersturmführer* Neff. Next to him is Lachner, *Panzer* commander. Standing second from Lachner is Theo Richts. Last is *SS-Rottenführer* Adamiak.

Despite the desperate times, some humor still prevails.

The crew of *Tiger 922* during January 1944. The *Tiger* is an initial-production model from 1942.

The *Kompanie* commander's *Befehls tiger* and crew, 11 January 1944. From the left: *SS-Oberscharführer* Munch, driver; *SS-Sturmmann* Heinz Rudolf, loader; Wolfgang Barth, gunner; *SS-Sturmmann* Lehmkuhl, radio operator; Kuepper.

Crew of *Tiger 901*, this time in February 1944. From the left: Lehmkuhl, Rudolf, Barth, and Kuepper. The youth of the crew is evident. WAGNER

Loipolt and Gunther Schulze with a milking cow, Struga, August 1944. Supplementing rations with produce from local sources was essential. WAGNER

Gocht, Keller, and Schuard photographed in the area of Height 109, August 1944. WAGNER

From the left, Hans Kautz, Gunther Schulze, Schwade, Wagner, Schuard, and female assistants, Struga, August 1944.
WAGNER

The crew of *Tiger 923* cleaning onboard weapons, August 1944: Lachner, Heimbruch, Holzner, Weiler, and Schilling. The *Tiger* had one 7.92mm *MG 34* in the hull front and another coaxial with the main gun. There was also a 9mm *MP 40* machine-pistol for close-in defense and personal weapons such as the *P 08 Luger* and *P 38 Walther*.

Another ration collection from the supply truck, September 1944. WERDEHAUSEN

In the area of Height 104, September 1944. From the left: Volz, Schulze, Heinkel, and Dietz. WAGNER

SS-Sturmmann Schuard in what seems good company, Radzymin, September 1944.

9. Kompanie personnel pose with a Romanian family, June 1944. The Romanians were allied with Germany until 23 August 1944, when they surrendered and changed sides. BENEKE

SS-Rottenführer Georg Preisendanz outside the *Kompanie* command post, October 1944. WAGNER

After collecting their rations, it is time to sit down and eat. September 1944. BENEKE

Tiger 902 towing *Tiger 913* on 11 March 1944. It was strictly prohibited for a *Tiger* to tow another due to the strain on the mechanical components, particularly the engine and transmission. However, in emergency situations, this directive was often ignored.

Tiger and crew in Bolschaja (Bolshaya) Wyska on 5 March 1944.

The barrel of a *Tiger* overlooks a street corner in Balta, 27 March 1944.

Another group photograph taken in May 1944. From the right: Knut, Kronmuller, and *Tiger* commander *SS-Unterscharführer* Blasé.

Rail transport to Balta, March 1944. WENDT

A *Tiger* takes up a defensive position near Balta, March 1944.

Amongst this group standing at the back of a *Tiger* is Krippl (died November 2011), Tassler, Pawlu, and Neff. The *Tiger* was a thirsty tank, and supplementary "Jerry cans" and even large drums of fuel were often carried when the *Tigers* were moving from one location to another. In combat situations, the fuel was, of course, dumped.

A *Tiger* stands in readiness, February 1944. The crewmembers appear to have smeared a coating of mud on the tank as camouflage.
WERDEHAUSEN

Tiger 921 coated in winter camouflage near Balta, March 1944.

Another photograph of *9. Kompanie* moving by rail to Balta.

A *Tiger* in a covering position near Balta, March 1944. The remaining operational *Tigers* in Balta were known as *Panzergruppe Neff.*

Two *StuG III* assault guns from *SS-Sturmgeschütze-Abteilung 3* in Balta, March 1944.

After the fighting in Balta was over, the *Kompanie* personnel ended up in Kishinev/Chisinau during the first few days of April 1944.

Another queue for rations, April 1944.

The maintenance section in Kishinev/Chisinau, April 1944.

Barth after receiving the Iron Cross, Second Class, 20 April 1944.

From the left: Barth, Lehmkuhl, and Schulze in Bacau on 20 April 1944 after being awarded the Iron Cross, Second Class.

Tiger crewmembers show off their new camouflage uniforms, May 1944. From the left: unknown, Schulze, unknown, and Seiler (fourth from the left). Seiler originally came from Austria.

SS-Unterscharführer Berger in April 1944.

Officers and men from *9. Kompanie* gather to celebrate Mother's Day in Bacau on 14 April 1944. The man in the center holding the bouquet of flowers is Beneke, *Kompanie Spieß* (roughly equivalent to master sergeant).

People of Bacau on the move, April 1944.

The Romanian countryside as the train carrying *Totenkopf* personnel approaches Bacau station.

SS-Totenkopf personnel unload from the train in Romania, April 1944.

9. Kompanie personnel assemble outside the rail station in Bacau, April 1944. Standing on the steps in field-grey uniform at the bottom of the steps is the *Kompanie Spieß*, with Beneke next to him. Also in field-grey uniform is the *Werkstatt Zug* leader, Herderer. Sitting along the wall, third from the left, is the *Kompanie* cook, Leutholdt. Sitting behind the officer leaning against the step wall is *SS-Unterscharführer* Hans Holzner, who originally came from Argentina.

The maintenance section poses with its new *Sd.Kfz. 11* prime mover, May 1944.

The *Kompanie* in another group photograph, taken in May 1944. BENEKE

Tiger 913 under the command of *SS-Unterscharführer* Wimmer, May 1944. WERDEHAUSEN

Another *9. Kompanie* group photograph, May 1944. BENEKE

Lining up for rations, Romania, May 1944. BENEKE

Radio operator at his post in a new *Tiger*, May 1944.

The *Kompanie* cook stands in front of his *Gulaschkanone* (field kitchen), Radzymin, August 1944. WAGNER

Mother's Day celebrations, April 1944.

9. Kompanie personnel in Kishinev/Chisinau, April 1944. BENEKE

A *Kompanie* stores issue point, September 1944. BENEKE

On 1 May 1944, *SS-Untersturmführer* Neff and fifty men were flown back to Germany and landed in Ravensburg. These *Tigers* originally belonged to *schwere SS-Panzer-Abteilung 103*, which returned them for re-issue (probably the *Tiger II King Tiger*).

Already set for the return journey from Magdeburg to Poland on 26 July 1944. Standing on the rail flat car next to the *Tiger* is *SS-Unterscharführer* Sandler, *Panzer* commander. Sitting in the front row, third from the left, is *SS-Rottenführer* Weiler. Standing behind the woman's right shoulder is *SS-Hauptscharführer* Berger, commander of the 4th Platoon. The *Tiger* on the flatcar is a late-production model with steel-tired roadwheels.

Another photograph taken in Magdeburg on 26 July 1944.

View of the Polish countryside during the fighting, July 1944. In the background some buildings are on fire.

A Polish village on fire, July 1944.

Barth poses with fellow soldiers and the flight crew of a *Junkers Ju 52* transport aircraft on 1 August 1944. Barth was to begin a four-month officer-cadet course, which saw him promoted to *SS-Untersturmführer der Reserve* on 30 January 1945.

Standing from the left: unknown, Schneider, Pavlu, Barth, and Shieshel, outside Rogan rail station.

Barth, as an officer-cadet, competing in a swimming competition, Königsbrück, 12 August 1944.

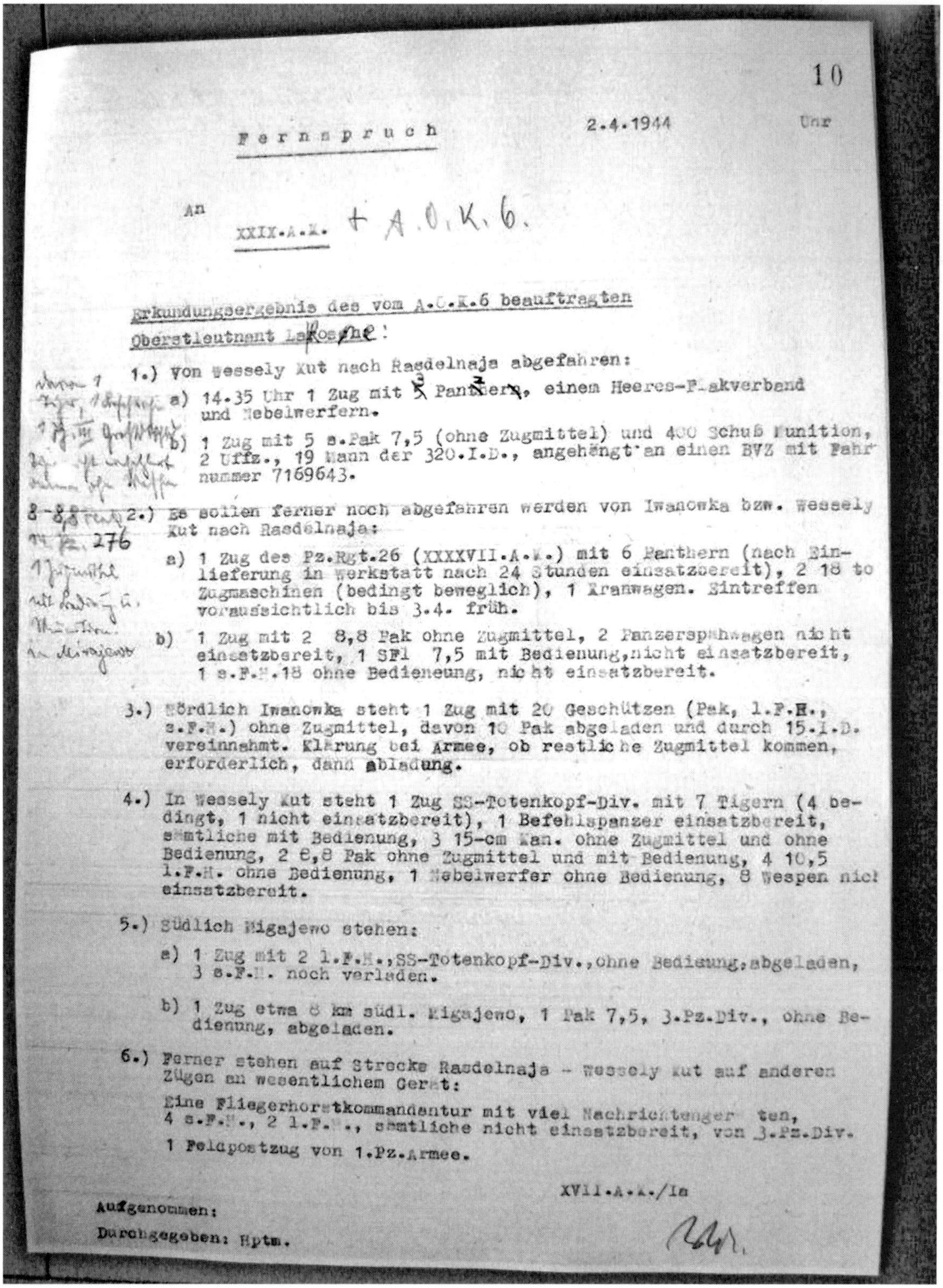

10

F e r n s p r u c h 2.4.1944 Uhr

An

XXIX.A.K. + A.O.K. 6.

Erkundungsergebnis des vom A.O.K.6 beauftragten

Oberstleutnant La Kosche:

1.) Von Wessely Kut nach Rasdelnaja abgefahren:

a) 14.35 Uhr 1 Zug mit 3 Panthern, einem Heeres-Flakverband und Nebelwerfern.

b) 1 Zug mit 5 s.Pak 7,5 (ohne Zugmittel) und 400 Schuß Munition, 2 Uffz., 19 Mann der 320.I.D., angehängt an einen BVZ mit Fahrnummer 7169643.

2.) Es sollen ferner noch abgefahren werden von Iwanowka bzw. Wessely Kut nach Rasdelnaja:

a) 1 Zug des Pz.Rgt.26 (XXXXVII.A.K.) mit 6 Panthern (nach Einlieferung in Werkstatt nach 24 Stunden einsatzbereit), 2 18 to Zugmaschinen (bedingt beweglich), 1 Kranwagen. Eintreffen voraussichtlich bis 3.4. früh.

b) 1 Zug mit 2 8,8 Pak ohne Zugmittel, 2 Panzerspähwagen nicht einsatzbereit, 1 SFl 7,5 mit Bedienung, nicht einsatzbereit, 1 s.F.H.18 ohne Bedieneung, nicht einsatzbereit.

3.) Nördlich Iwanowka steht 1 Zug mit 20 Geschützen (Pak, l.F.H., s.F.H.) ohne Zugmittel, davon 10 Pak abgeladen und durch 15.I.D. vereinnahmt. Klärung bei Armee, ob restliche Zugmittel kommen, erforderlich, dann abladung.

4.) In Wessely Kut steht 1 Zug SS-Totenkopf-Div. mit 7 Tigern (4 bedingt, 1 nicht einsatzbereit), 1 Befehlspanzer einsatzbereit, sämtliche mit Bedienung, 3 15-cm Kan. ohne Zugmittel und ohne Bedienung, 2 8,8 Pak ohne Zugmittel und mit Bedienung, 4 10,5 l.F.H. ohne Bedienung, 1 Nebelwerfer ohne Bedienung, 8 Wespen nicht einsatzbereit.

5.) Südlich Migajewo stehen:

a) 1 Zug mit 2 l.F.H., SS-Totenkopf-Div., ohne Bedienung, abgeladen, 3 s.F.H. noch verladen.

b) 1 Zug etwa 8 km südl. Migajewo, 1 Pak 7,5, 3.Pz.Div., ohne Bedienung, abgeladen.

6.) Ferner stehen auf Strecke Rasdelnaja - Wessely Kut auf anderen Zügen an wesentlichem Gerät:

Eine Fliegerhorstkommandantur mit viel Nachrichtengeräten, 4 s.F.H., 2 l.F.H., sämtliche nicht einsatzbereit, von 3.Pz.Div.

1 Feldpostzug von 1.Pz.Armee.

XVII.A.K./Ia

Aufgenommen:

Durchgegeben: Hptm.

A communications report from *XXIX. Armee Korps* to *A.O.K. 6* dated 2 April 1944.

SS-Junker Barth, 22 December 1944.

SS-Oberscharführer Arthur Privatski in 1944. On his upper left arm, he wears the Demjansk Shield, which was instituted on 25 April 1943 for those soldiers who had fought in the Demjansk Pocket in the winter of 1941–42.

Befehls tiger 901 in full winter camouflage, January 1944. This *Tiger* was delivered in early October 1943 and blown up on 2 April 1944 while still loaded on a rail transport.

9. Kompanie personnel eating rations during September 1944 in Poland. Lachner is sitting on the right, wearing his black *Panzer* uniform. At the back, wearing an M43 field cap, is *SS-Untersturmführer* Neff.

Just visible in the background is a *Tiger* loaded onto a rail transport alongside an armored train, March 1944. Armored trains were used extensively by both the Germans and the Soviets.

9. Kompanie personnel gather outside Bacau rail station just after arriving in the town, 14 April 1944.

Two soldiers from *9. Kompanie* in Bacau, May 1944.

Lachner and another comrade sampling Polish wine during August 1944.

The company cook, *SS-Unterscharführer* Johannes Loidold, during the autumn of 1944 in Poland.

Tiger 911 of 1st Platoon, commanded by *SS-Untersturmführer* Hans Kriescher, August 1944. Kriescher commanded the platoon between May and October 1944.

Tiger 902, commanded by *SS-Oberscharführer* Tonges, undergoes track repairs during late July 1944. This tank is from the final production series (production of the *Tiger I* ceased in August 1944).

Tigers and support vehicles assemble in Nowo Ukrainka (today known as Novo Ukrainka) prior to loading and transport to Balta.

Lachner and a comrade relaxing in Bacau during May 1944.

More *9. Kompanie* personnel arrive in Bacau on 14 April 1944 looking rather dishevelled and tired.

Franz Sklenzky wearing the two-piece camouflage *Panzer* uniform, May 1944.

The *Junkers Ju 90* transport aircraft that took the Neff collection group to Belgrade on 1 May 1944.

CHAPTER 5

The End

Konrad I

SS-Panzer-Regiment 3 started its advance along the Danube shore road at 2300 hours on 1 January 1945 and assembled in Szony. The advance was to begin at 0200 on the second, and the *Tigers* of *9. Kompanie* were posted on point with thc *Panthers* from *I/SS-Panzer-Regiment 3* behind and *II/SS-Panzer-Grenaider-Regiment 6 Eicke* providing support. *SS-Obersturmbannführer* Wenke had to change *Tigers* because of difficulties with the radio equipment in *Tiger 901*.

As the lead *Tiger* approached the western edge of Dunaalmas, a dug-in T-34/85 tank fired one round at the *Tiger*, wounding Eric Lehmkuhl (radio operator). The shell severed his foot just below the ankle. Lehmkuhl was evacuated by motorcycle to the divisional field hospital in Komarom and later in Linz. Also immobilized by Russian defensive fire was the *Tiger* of *SS-Unterscharführer* Lachner, just to the west of Dunaalmas. From behind the damaged lead *Tiger* rolled the *Befehlspanther I01* of *SS-Sturmbannführer* Meierdress, the commander of *I/SS-Panzer-Regiment 3*. His *Panther* now took point in the column. Behind Meierdress's tank was *Panther I02*, commanded by *SS-Obersturmbannführer* Strobl, the *Panther* battalion adjutant. Meierdress ordered a halt. He dismounted and issued new orders. At around 0645, just as he moved out, a dug-in SU-85 self-propelled gun from the 1438th Self-Propelled Artillery Regiment, attached to the 170th Tank Brigade of the 18th Tank Corps, fired a single shot into the rear of the turret, killing Meierdress and the turret crew. Both the driver and radio operator were wounded. The stricken *Panther* rolled off the road in the center of the village and crashed into a nearby house next to the village church. *Panther I03* from the headquarters company detected the SU-85 self-propelled gun and destroyed the vehicle with a single shot. *SS-Obersturmbannführer* Ernst now took command of the *Panther* battalion after leaving *7. Kompanie*.

Later, *Berge-Panther BW 1* was used to recover the stricken *Panther*. During the recovery operation, the Russians tried to hit this *Berge-Panther* four times with antitank gunfire. All four shots missed. Later, the *Berge-Panther* towed the *Panther* to Acs. *Panther I01* was written off as a total loss on 5 February.

After the seizure of Dunaalmas, the tank regiment pushed onto Neszmely and Sutto, then south of the heights of Karva. By midafternoon, the *Panther* battalion shot up a Russian motorized column just outside Nyergesujfalu, which was captured. In Nyergesujfalu the forward elements of *Totenkopf* linked up with *96. Infanterie-Division*, which was attacking from the north. During the approach march along the Danube shore road, the *Tiger* of *SS-Oberscharführer* Tonges was also shot up by Russian antitank gunfire, taking hits to the tracks and running gear. In Nyergesujfalu, the tank regiment regrouped, and *II/SS-Panzer-Regiment 3* now took the lead along with *9. Kompanie*. Seven *Tigers* had fallen out due to battle damage or mechanical failure, including the *Tiger* of *SS-Oberscharführer* Tassler.

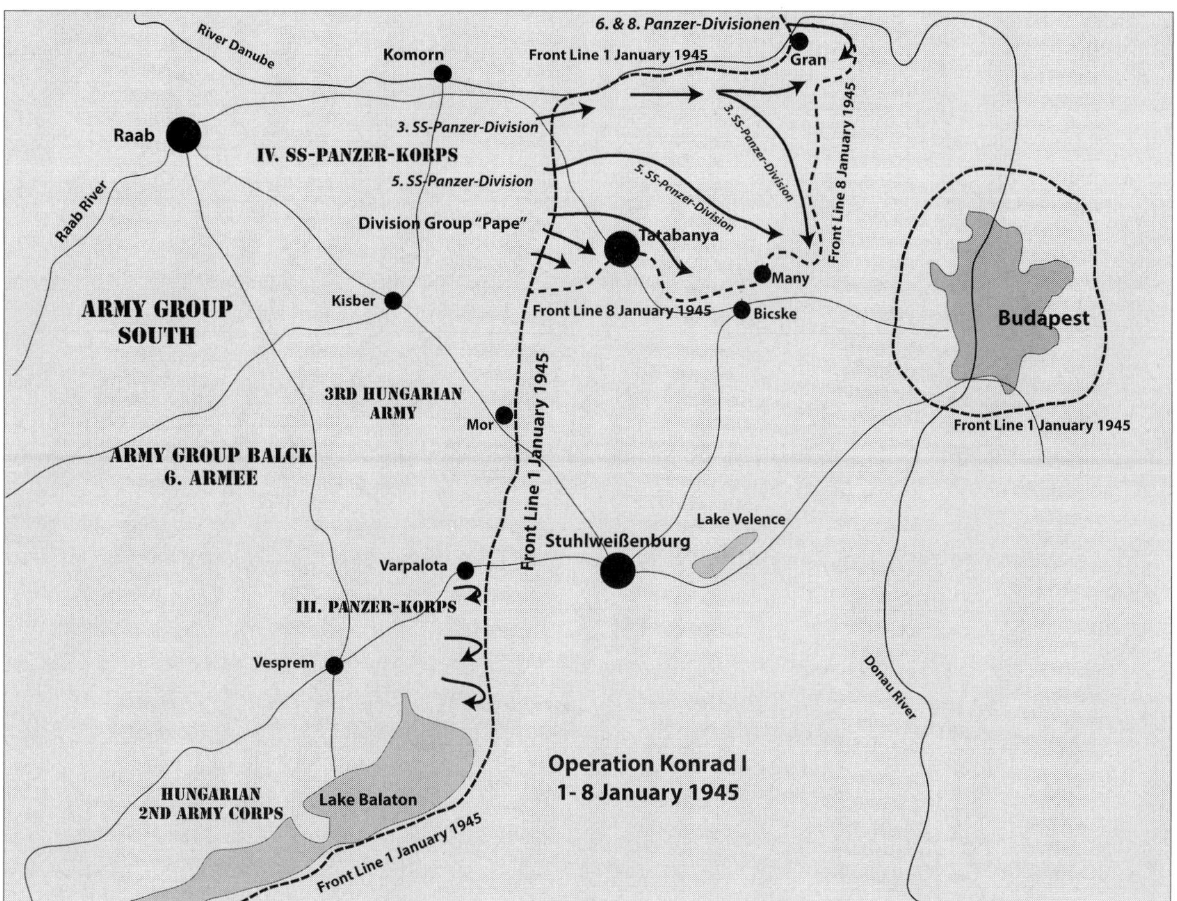

At 0100, the *Tigers* and *Panzer IV's* pushed along the Nyergesujfalu–Bajot road, which led through a wood. Along the road the tank column was strafed by Il-2 Sturmoviks from the 10th Assault Air Corps from the 17th Air Army. One *Panther* was struck by a bomb during the air attack while another was damaged. The grenadiers from *SS-Panzer-Grenadier-Regiment 6 Eicke* attacked to the south of Bajot, overrunning a Russian antitank gun front. The tanks pushed through to Bajot. After Bajot, the tanks took on a new allocation of fuel and ammunition.

In Bajna the *Panzer IV's* of *5. Kompanie* needed the assistance of three *Tigers* from *9. Kompanie*. Two *Panthers* had already turned off the road onto the open terrain in an effort to out flank the village. The lead *Tiger* was commanded by *SS-Standartenoberjunker* Blau, with *SS-Obersturmbannführer* Wenke in the rear. The *Tigers* were required to tackle some T-34/85's that were causing problems for the *Panzer IV's*. Blau drove up to a *Panzer IV* and asked, "Where is the music?" A crewman pointed in the direction of the village church, with a warning to be careful. But as Blau drove past the church, he took multiple hits from Russian tank fire—to the hull, turret, and running gear. The force of the hit to the turret threw Blau out of the turret into the air, killing him. He was promoted to *SS-Untersturmführer* posthumously on 30 January.

The second *Tiger* drove up to the church and was also hit and immobilized. The third *Tiger*, commanded by Wenke, called in air support and proceeded with care to survey the front. Before long Wenke fired and hit a Russian T-34/85. About ten minutes later, two *Ju-88's* flew overhead and attacked the Russian positions. Covering the two stricken *Tigers* was a *Panther*. The two *Panthers* that had moved into the open terrain overcame a Russian antitank gun front.

Blau's *Tiger* had to be towed away and transported to the Vienna Arsenal for factory repairs. On the fourth, the tanks began the advance on Szomor, but 1,500 meters southeast of Bajna, Russian tanks were reported in the woods. As the grenadiers formed up, the tanks started the advance toward Szomor. Throughout the day, the grenadiers and the tanks had to combat Russian tanks and antitank gunfire. There was heavy fighting for Gyarmat Psz and Epol. During the day, five *Panzer IV's* from *7. Kompanie* were knocked out. Two *Tigers* had to provide covering fire to the *Panthers* as they dealt with JS-2 Russian heavy tanks.

On the fifth, the attack on Szomor began from the northwest via Gyermely. The *Panzergruppe* was commanded by *SS-Obersturmbannführer* Laackmann. On the approach from Gyermely to Szomor, two *Panthers* were hit by Russian defensive fire, hitting the tracks, hull, and turret on both *Panthers*. Both quickly caught fire. *III/SS-Panzer-Grenaider-Regiment 6* and *II/SS-Panzer-Grenadier-Regiment 5 Totenkopf* were tasked with attacking on both sides of Szomor to clear Russian antitank gun fronts. The *Tigers* had to repel a Russian counterattack with tanks and infantry from the direction of Somodor Psz, which was turned back. During the day, Laackmann was wounded. The tank regiment was commanded by *SS-Sturmbannführer* Krass, former commander of *I/SS-Panzer-Artillerie-Regiment 3 (sfl)*. By the end of the day, the grenadiers from *SS-Panzer-Grenadier-Regiment 6 Eicke* managed to set up defensive positions between Hill 357 and Hill 289 east of Szomor with the support of the *Panthers*.

On the sixth, the advance on Zsambek began with *III/SS-Panzer-Grenadier-Regiment 6 Eicke* attacking Hill 317, while that regiment's second battalion attacked to the east. The *Tigers* from *9. Kompanie* advanced along the Szomor-Zsambek road, with two *Tigers* moving along in the open terrain just to the right side of the road. The *Tigers* were commanded by *SS-Obersturmbannführer* Wenke and *SS-Untersturmführer* Westerling. The Russians had an antitank gun front positioned near Felsoors Psz. At a range of fifty meters, the Russians opened fire, and both *Tigers* were quickly knocked out. Wenke's *Tiger* was hit in the hull and turret. Inside the turret, the gunner, *SS-Rottenführer* Krippl, was wounded after his left arm was trapped between the deflector shield and the gun breach. Quickly, Wenke dismounted and ran to get medical assistance. He returned with the medical orderly from *II/SS-Panzer-Regiment 3*, who amputated the arm below the shoulder joint without anesthetic; all the while, the Russians were shelling the area with artillery fire. Krippl would later receive treatment in Salzburg. A third *Tiger* quickly moved up to provide covering fire. The *Tiger* of *SS-Unterscharführer* Privatski advanced just to the north of the Many-Zsambek road junction before it was hit by direct fire from 76mm antitank guns. The *Tiger* took hits to the right side of the hull and running gear and the front bow plate. The crew bailed out.

Also wounded during this action were *SS-Untersturmführer* Westerling, who was evacuated on the twenty-third; *SS-Scharführer* Duhmke (radio operator); Gustav Krause (loader); and *SS-Rottenführer* Ludwig Buss (radio operator). Wenke's *Tiger 901* was recovered and transported to the Vienna Arsenal for factory repairs, but Westerling's *Tiger* was left behind in the open terrain halfway between Szomor and Zsambek. This *Tiger* would be later used as a command post by *3. Kavallerie-Brigade* and abandoned on 28 February.

On the seventh, *SS-Obersturmbannführer* Neff returned from home leave and resumed command of *9. Kompanie*. Wenke took command of *5. Kompanie* of *II/SS-Panzer-Regiment 3*. On the same day, another attempt was made to seize Zsambek. At 0700 hours, *SS-Panzer-Artillerie-Regiment 3* laid down an artillery barrage for an hour. This time, ten *Panthers* from *I/SS-Panzer-Regiment 3*, with escorting grenadiers, moved south of Szomor, trying to outflank the Russian positions. The *Panthers* managed to reach the Felsoors Psz–Enes–Many road junction only to come under fire from SU-100 self-propelled guns from the 382nd Guards Self-Propelled Artillery Regiment. This was the first combat commitment of the SU-100. The 382nd had some limited infantry support, which quickly ran away, forcing some of the crews from the SU-100s to dismount and fight as infantry. The 382nd also requested tank support, but the SU-100s managed to knock out one *Panther* and seriously damaged nine more. The 382nd lost eleven SU-100s destroyed or damaged. The tank platoon sent to support the regiment lost some T-34 tanks and one JS-type heavy self-propelled gun. During the action, *SS-Sturmbannführer* Krass in his *Befehlspanther* knocked out two Russian tanks, while *SS-Panzer-Regiment 3* claimed a total of seventeen Russian tanks.

On the eighth, *I/SS-Panzer-Regiment 3*, *5. Kompanie* (*Panzer IV's*) under the command of *SS-Obersturmbannführer* Wenke, and *9. Kompanie* were placed in reserve in Szomor. *5. Kompanie* would later take part in defensive actions repelling Russian attacks to the east of Szomor, while *I* and *III/SS-Panzer-Grenadier-Regiment 6 Eicke*, along with *6.* and *7. Kompanie* attacked Many and Zsambek. *I/SS-Panzer-Grenadier-Regiment 6 Eicke* managed to reach Hill 268 before coming under heavy Russian defensive fire. The *III/SS-Panzer-Grenadier-Regiment 6 Eicke* got into hand-to-hand fighting with Russian infantry near Many. Near Szomor, *Regiment Eicke's* 2nd Battalion had to repel a Russian attack with the support of *Panzer IV's* from *5. Kompanie*.

On the ninth, the Russians tried another attack on Szomor from the direction of Felsoors Psz. It was beaten back; again the *Tigers* provided defensive support to the grenadiers. On the tenth, new replacement personnel arrived for *SS-Panzer-Regiment 3*; they were divided between the *I* and *II* battalions, but there were no new replacements for *9. Kompanie*.

On thirteenth, the first elements of *3. Kavallerie-Brigade* started changing positions with the *Totenkopf*, which was to withdraw and move back to Komarom for redeployment in the area of Berhida for another relief operation on Budapest. The new operation was to relieve Budapest from the south. *SS-Panzer-Regiment 3* and other divisional tracked elements would have to move by road. Some elements were moved by rail, but with only two transports per day, there were insufficient flat cars to carry all the tracked vehicles. The route of approach was by road as follows: Nagyimand, Bana, and Gyorszabadhegy (rail station) via the Bakony Hills, Veszpremvarsany, Bakonyszentkiraly, Magyarszentkiraly, Bakony Oszlop, Cseteny, and Zirc, and then down to the assembly area of Berhida. Those elements transported by rail were unloaded in Veszprem.

SS-Obersturmbannführer Wenke, who served as the company commander from 24 December to 6 January while *SS-Obersturmbannführer* Neff was back in Germany on leave, recorded the following:

> 24 December Company Christmas party. The regimental commander, *SS-Obersturmbannführer* Laackmann, arrives and says a few brief words to the men. During the celebrations, we receive an alarm that we should be ready to move.
>
> 25 December Company moves to the rail station for loading.
>
> 26 December Loading takes place in freezing cold weather. We have eleven *Tigers* operational.
>
> 30 December Transport arrives in the evening and unloaded in Komarom. We drive to a Hungarian barracks and set up quarters. [The old Hungarian Royal Army Cavalry Barracks, where the Hussar regiments had trained. The barracks were housed at Fort Igmand, built between 1871 and 1877. The fort was used as an internment camp for Polish soldiers from 1939 to 1942, after which it was used as a Hungarian labor corps barracks.]
>
> 31 December Battle readiness preparations—we take on fuel and ammunition, the *Tigers* are camouflaged. At midday the regimental commander issues orders. The advance is to begin at 2100 on 1 January; the *Tiger* company will be on point. We are to move along the Danube shore road heading west. The front line is to the west of Dunaalmas; we are to advance toward Nyergesufalu and link up with elements of *96. Infanterie-Division*, where a bridgehead is to be formed.
>
> 1 January The start of the attack is delayed due to operational difficulties. Radio silence is ordered. To hide the sound of our engines, the *Luftwaffe* fly over our location in the direction of Budapest. Around midnight the enemy is reported to be at the western edge of Dunaalmas, where we come under fire. The company commander's *Tiger* comes under fire; the lead *Tiger* of *SS-Oberscharführer* Tassler (Tassler was lightly wounded during this action) is hit with damage to the main gun and tracks. The Russians have laid mines on the road, but we move off to the left and the advance continues without delay.
>
> 2 January During the morning before marching on Neszmely, the fighting in Dunaalmas is still going on. Seven *Tigers* have fallen out due to battle damage or technical failure. We also have some wounded. By the afternoon, we link up with *96. Infanterie-Division* in Nyergesufalu. Shortly the divisional commander appears on the scene, and I give a short report. It's here that I learn that *SS-Sturmbannführer* Meierdress has been killed. Meierdress was a Knight's Cross and Oak Leaves winner. We take on a new allocation of fuel and ammunition, and the company is again placed under the command of *II/SS-Panzer-Regiment 3*. The next objective is Bajot.
>
> 3 January *SS-Oberjunker* Blau is killed while in Bajna. Blau had only recently joined the company. In Bajna there is

heavy fighting around the church. We have to call in air support from the *Luftwaffe*, which blasts a passage for us to continue the advance.

4 January Midmorning, enemy tanks are reported in the woods about 1,500 meters southeast of Bajna. We move out to meet them. The first Russian tank is hit and catches fire. The other Russian tanks quickly turn around and withdraw.

5 January The company is ordered to attack Szomor and protect the flank on the left and repel any enemy attacks. During the advance, we suffer no losses, and later the company assumes security duty at the eastern edge of Szomor. In the evening the enemy attacks with tanks and infantry from the direction of Somodor Psz. One Russian tank is knocked out by a *Tiger* at a range of fifty meters. The remaining Russian force turns around and retreats. Later, the Russians pound our positions with heavy mortar fire.

6 January Three *Tigers* operational. In the afternoon we advance toward Zsambek from Szomor. Moving across open rolling terrain, two *Tigers* are hit by Russian antitank gunfire. The company commander's *Tiger* is hit on the right side of the turret, and the round pierces the turret interior, hitting the main gun mount. The gunner's left arm (Gustav Krippl) is trapped between the deflector shield and the breech. We try to free his arm but with no luck. The *Tiger* is under constant Russian fire and cannot move, but we do have some limited cover due to the wet and misty weather. A medic is brought forward who quickly sizes up the situation and amputates the gunner's arm on the spot. Later, the damaged *Tigers* are recovered.

Eric Lehmkuhl recalled:

By 2300 hours, we finally begin the attack along a road. As we approach a bend in the road, we came under heavy defensive fire. I feel a heavy impact on my left foot. We had been hit by a round that had penetrated the hull. My first thought was that I had lost my right foot. I opened the radio operator's hatch and climbed out and slid down on to the snow. I noticed there were no footprints in the snow, which was not good.

I took cover in a ditch next to the road. I had my leg held against the clear sky, and I saw my foot was gone up to the Achilles heel. I still don't know how everything went, but I was shouting at another tank that went past, but it was knocked out as well. I don't know how long I was lying there, but the next thing I remember was a medic standing over me with a syringe and another man saying he was going to take me away on a motorcycle sidecar combination.

For this, I have to personally thank comrade Herbart Sachs, who rode all the way to come and collect me. I ended up at the divisional field hospital, which was located at the Hungarian Cavalry Barracks in Komarom. I was the first to be operated on. Afterward, I was visited by the company *Spieß*, *Hauptscharführer* Beneke, who awarded me the Iron Cross, First Class, and gave me a small package with some chocolate in it.

Walter Weber of *5. Kompanie* remembered:

At 2000 hours on 1 January, we attacked with the whole regiment. We were all thrilled that we were attacking as a whole unit again. The *Tiger* company leads, with the *Panther* battalion following behind. Later, our battalion takes the lead.

3 January Bajna. Early in the morning, three *Tigers* were required to eliminate

> those annoying Russian tanks. The commander looks down at us from the cupola. He asked where the music was coming from. We pointed toward the church, and the *Tigers* drove off one behind the other. No sooner had the lead *Tiger* edged past the church than it was hit by direct fire. The *Tiger* commander (*SS-Standartenoberjunker* Blau) flies through the air. After this, almost in an instant, the second *Tiger* was hit in the tracks and running gear. It managed to pull back into cover and out of danger. Do not underestimate the T-34/85. Well, the third and last operational *Tiger* tried his luck—carefully, he edged his *Tiger* toward the church. Even before he could fire off a few shots, he was hit by Russian tank fire.
>
> 4 January Then came the pride of the regiment, the *Tiger* company, with two *Tigers*. *SS-Obersturmbannführer* Wenke is behind the lead *Tiger*, and he was wearing a thick fur coat. After a short assessment of the situation, the *Tigers* open fire—lo and behold, there are columns of smoke—three Russian tanks are in flames. Bravo, Wenke. During this period, Wenke led the *Tiger* company.

Endelmann of *5. Kompanie* reported for 5 January: "It is bright. The grenadiers move up and fight the Russian house to house. A *Tiger* tried to break through; it returned later with battle damage. A *Panther* tried the same a little later. *SS-Obersturmbannführer* Wenke came over to us and ask if we get on the radio and request air support."

Wagner recalls Konrad I: "We attack in the direction of Budapest after driving through the night. Three *Tigers* were damaged and fell out. I had to find a map and drive to Esztergom. Neff is on leave and Wenke leads the company. The next day, Blau is killed. Also wounded were Lehmkuhl, August Krippl, and Gustav Krause."

On the fourteenth, the *3. SS-Panzer-Division Totenkopf* had handed over its former sector to *3. Kavallerie-Brigade*. On the seventeenth, elements of *SS-Panzer-Regiment 3* and *SS-Panzerjäger-Abteilung 3* had arrived. The *Tiger* company had not turned up. During the night of 14–15 January, wheeled elements of *Totenkopf* passed through Zirc.

Wagner reported on the early phase of Konrad III:

> The company has one more tank commanded by Tassler. The division returns to Komarom for redeployment via Veszprem for an attack on Szekesfehervar from Falubattyan. Neff returns from home leave. Tonges is slightly wounded after his *Tiger* was hit in the main gun. Dieter Thomas returned after completing an officer-cadet course, and Bernhardt also returned. The company support units move into Agard. We lose one *Tiger*, with Etmayer being killed. Another *Tiger* was lost, with Becker and his crew bailing out; the radio operator was killed.

On the seventeenth, *IV. SS-Panzer-Korps* reported the following units from *3. SS-Panzer-Division Totenkopf* already in the new assembly area:

- *I/SS-Panzer-Artillerie-Regiment 3 (sfl)*
- *II/SS-Panzer-Artillerie-Regiment 3*, with 2 artillery pieces
- *SS-Panzer-Regiment 3*, with 8 *Panzer V's*, 5 *Panzer IV's*, 11 *StuGs*, and to arrive on the eighteenth: 14 *Panzer V's* (2 more in long-term repair), 16 *Panzer IV's*, 11 *Tigers* (2 at the Vienna Arsenal), and 6 *StuGs*
- *SS-Panzerjäger-Abteilung 3*, with 10 *Jagdpanzer IV's*, 4 *StuGs*, and to arrive on the eighteenth: 5 *Jagdpanzer IV's*, 6 *StuG's*

On the eighteenth, *IV. SS-Panzer-Korps* had the following vehicles available for the start of the attack: 42 *Tigers*, 59 *Panzer V's*, 22 *Panzer*

IV's, 58 *StuG's*, 13 *Jagdpanzer IV's*, and 194 *SPW/Panzerspähwagen*.

During September 1944, *schwere Panzer-Abteilung 509* had been transferred from the Eastern Front to Sennelager, where it began conversion training on the *Tiger II*. From 5 December to 1 January, the battalion was equipped with forty-five *Tiger II's*. The *Flak* platoon was formed on 11 October under *Wehrkries IX* and transported to Ohrdorf on the nineteenth for further training. On 12 December, the *Flak* platoon was transported to Sennelager for integration with *schwere Panzer-Abteilung 509* and declared operational on the fifteenth, with eight *Flak Panzer IV's*. The *Berge-Panthers* were issued as follows: the battalion still had one *Berge-Panther* on hand but had two new ones issued on 29 September; another was issued on 2 January. The transports carrying *schwere Panzer-Abteilung 509* to Hungary unloaded in Hajmasker.

On 18 January, *SS-Panzer-Regiment 3* advanced out of the area of Kungos with the attached *schwere Panzer-Abteilung 509* (commanded by *Major* Burmeister) at 0500 hours. On the left in support was *SS-Kampfgruppe Kleffner* (*SS-Panzer-Grenadier-Regiment 6 Eicke*), commanded by *SS-Obersturmbannführer Kleffner*. *SS-Sturmbannführer* Pitschellis led the assault in his *Befehlspanther*. The Russians reported some twenty tanks, including *Tigers*, attacking their forward positions. The first obstacle was a minefield, which had to be cleared by engineers. That took some time. Also encountered were electrically charged cables. *Kampfgruppe Pitschellis* had to turn north and then swung south of Hills 188 and 197 (south of Jeno) and attacked Sandorka, which was captured. The Russians launched a counterattack with tanks from the direction of Fule and were beaten back.

Kampfgruppe Pitschellis turned east and resumed the advance but encountered a strong Russian antitank front to the west of Polgardi. *SS-Panzer-Artillerie-Abteilung 3* had to turn the antitank gun front's flank before the attack could continue in the direction of Falubattyan. *Kampfgruppe Kleffner* advanced south of Felsosomylo and to the north of the Csillagmajorr-Falubattyan road (near Falubattyan, the *Tiger* of *SS-Oberscharführer* Tonges was hit again) with *schwere Panzer-Abteilung 509*. By midday, the *509's Tiger II's* headed northwest of Szabadbattyan and tried to seize the bridge over the Marlom Canal, which was blown up as the *Tigers* got within fifty meters of the bridge. The Russians also used antitank gunfire and air strikes trying to defend the canal. Three *Tiger II's* were immobilized and abandoned by their crews. These *Tigers* were blown up on the twenty-second by a demolition crew from the battalion's *Werkstatt* company.

The tanks from *Kampfgruppe Pitschellis* had entered Szabadbattyan and tried to push onward in the direction of Seregelyes, but as two *Panthers* approached a bridge on the eastern edge of Szabadbattyan which spanned the new Sarviz Canal, the lead *Panther* was knocked out by antitank gunfire after it successfully crossed the bridge. This Panther was knocked out by an antitank gun from the Russian 10th Antitank Artillery Brigade. The second *Panther* started to drive across the bridge, but it collapsed under the weight of the *Panther*. After this, the day's advance had come to a halt, and another crossing over the Sarviz Canal had to be found. The engineers from *SS-Panzer-Pionier-Batallion 3* began repairs on the bridges over the Marlom Canal and the Sarviz Canal and started building a forty-ton bridge as well. *Totenkopf* had lost one *Panzer IV*, two *Panthers*, and one *StuG*. Tonges's *Tiger* took a hit on the main gun, causing a slight wound to Tonges. *Major* Burmeister, commander of *schwere Panzer-Abteilung 509* was wounded, and the *509* was taken over by *Hauptmann* Dr. Konig.

On the nineteenth, the bridge crossing the Sarviz Canal was ready for crossing. It had a forty-four-ton capacity, which allowed the *Panthers*, *Panzer IV's*, and *StuG's* from *SS-Panzer-Regiment 3* to cross, as well as the *Tigers* from *9. Kompanie*. The *Tigers* from *schwere Panzer-Abteilung 509* could not move. *SS-Kampfgruppe*

Pitschellis attacked southeast in the direction of Foveny Puszta. Very quickly, a new crossing area had to be found. After a quick reconnaissance of the area, a shallow part of the Sarviz Canal was found next to the railway bridge near Szabadbattyan. The engineers from *SS-Panzer-Pionier-Batallion 3* began placing wooden railway sleepers into the canal and slowly built up a temporary bridge that allowed the *Tiger II's* of *509* to cross the Sarviz Canal.

After crossing the canal, *SS-Panzer-Regiment 3*, under the command of Pitschellis, advanced on Foveny Puszta, which was taken during midafternoon. Later, a further advance on Seregelyes was halted for the day because of bad weather conditions. On the morning of the twentieth, *Kampfgruppe Pitschellis* advanced on Seregelyes along with *SS-Panzerjäger-Abteilung 3* and became involved in fighting in the northern part of the town, which was also being attacked by the *5. SS-Panzer-Division Wiking*. *SS-Panzerjäger-Abteilung 3*, along with the grenadiers from *I/SS-Panzer-Grenadier-Regiment 5 Totenkopf (gep)*, attacked the southern section of the town. *1. Kompanie* of *SS-Panzerjäger-Abteilung 3* lost two *Jagdpanzer IV's* during the fighting.

By now *Kampfgruppe Pitschellis* had turned northeast and started to advance on Dinnyes, with *schwere Panzer-Abteilung 509* advancing on Borgond airfield, but was struggling with supplies of fuel and ammunition. The tanks from *SS-Panzer-Regiment 3* entered Dinnyes during the afternoon and carried on along the southern embankment road toward Kisvelencze with seven Panzerstanks and 120 supporting grenadiers, but Russian defensive fire damaged two tanks and forced the small *Panzergruppe* to turn back after one Russian antitank gun was knocked out. To the west of Kisvelencze, *Totenkopf* attacked the 63rd Cavalry Division and elements of the 69th Guards Rifle Division near Hill 103 at around 1800 hours. The *Panzergruppe* from *SS-Panzer-Regiment 3* made four attacks against the Russian positions before falling back. That same day, *SS-Sturmbannführer* Anton Berlin assumed command of *I/SS-Panzer-Regiment 3*.

On the twenty-first, the Russians reported that some forty tanks and self-propelled guns were forming up near Gardonny during the early-morning hours, with at least one grenadier battalion in support. *Kampfgruppe Pitschellis* attacked from Dinnyes and headed toward Agard at around 0800 hours. The group captured Agard after breaking through a Russian antitank front. The advance continued across the open terrain south of Gardonny and proceeded to attack Kisvelencze and Kaplosnasnyek from the southeast. The Russians estimated that the group consisted of twenty-five tanks. *SS-Sturmbannführer* Pitschellis was again at point in his *Befehlspanther*. During the attack, *Kampfgruppe Pitschellis* came under murderous Russian antitank gunfire from the southeast. On the western edge of Kaplosnasnyek, the small group of six tanks attacked Kaplosnasnyek from the west, resulting in two *Befehlspanthers* and two *Panthers* of *SS-Panzer-Regiment 3* being knocked out (these wrecks were not recovered until 1950 for scrap by the Hungarian authorities).

The main *Panzergruppe*, with fifteen tanks and mounted grenadiers, tried to break through from the direction of Kisvelencze. This was accomplished at 1700, and the group reached the western edge of Kaplosnasnyek and Hill 120. The Russians decided to move up the 1st Guards Mechanized Brigade to assist in the defense of Kaplosnasnyek; it arrived at about 1600 hours. The Germans noticed the presence of SU-100 self-propelled guns.

Forming up south of Kisvelencze were *I* and *III/SS-Panzer-Grenadier-Regiment 6 Eicke*, supported by *I/Panzer-Regiment 24* (*Panther's*). Their main task was to open up the Vali sector and establish a bridgehead after capturing Kaplosnasnyek. Also in support is *schwere Panzer-Abteilung 509*. *SS-Hauptsturmführer* Leibel, commander of *II/SS-Panzer-Regiment 3*, was ordered by the divisional leadership to take command of the battalion and proceed to the area of Felsobesyno Puszta and then attack

Baracska from the south. This caused a huge protest from the battalion's leadership, especially on such short notice without proper reconnaissance.

During the march, six *Tiger II's* fell out because of mechanical damage, and another two *Tiger II's* collided during the night. During the attack on Kaplosnasnyek by *SS-Panzer-Grenadier-Regiment 6 Eicke*, which lasted over four hours, only a foothold in Kaplosnasnyek was gained before the unit was forced to withdraw. *SS-Panzer-Regiment 3* lost four *Panthers* as total losses and one *Tiger I* damaged by Russian tank fire. *I/Panzer-Regiment 24* lost nine *Panthers*. The Russians lost three T-34's, two self-propelled guns, and twelve antitank guns. The Russians claimed eight tanks and one *SPW* on the twenty-first.

On the twenty-second, the damaged tanks from the previous day were recovered and sent for repairs. The remaining operational tanks were used for an attack on the northern edge of Kaplosnasnyek, which resulted in heavy combat. The attack was conducted in heavy snow drifts and was repelled by heavy Russian defensive fire. All the *Tigers* were hit and had to be recovered and sent for repairs. To the south, *schwere Panzer-Abteilung 509*, along with elements of *SS-Panzer-Artillerie-Abteilung 3*, attacked to the south of Baracska, trying to reach the Vali Canal, but the Russians had built up their defenses in this area and again managed to block any further German advance in this sector. The battalion had managed to reach Kishalom Puszta, but was forced to pull back as shortages of fuel and ammunition increased. During the day, *SS-Panzerjäger-Abteilung 3* lost three *Jagdpanzer IV's*. *SS-Scharführer* Hugo Rise was killed near Agard; he was a truck driver in *9. Kompanie*.

According to Dr. Konig, "During a snow storm, we heard that the *Hauptsturmführer* from the *Waffen-SS* (Leibel) was badly wounded. Of the twenty-six operational *Tiger II's* from the twentieth, I have only twelve available. The other vehicles had fallen out either due to enemy action or technical problems. During the afternoon, we have a convoy of nine vehicles being towed back for repairs just before nightfall."

At around 1100 on the twenty-third, *Totenkopf* made another assault on Kaplosnasnyek, with *III/SS-Panzer-Grenadier-Regiment 6 Eicke* in the lead. The attack was supported by fifteen tanks, but despite heavy fighting, the Russians managed to launch several counterattacks, which were repelled. *I/Panzer-Regiment 24*, with thirty-one operational *Panthers*, saw action in the area between Kaplosnasnyek and Velencze, knocking out four Russian tanks. By the end of the day, Kaplosnasnyek was finally captured by German forces. To the south, *schwere Panzer-Abteilung 509* attempted another advance in the direction of Kishalom, but the battalion spent the day repelling Russian counterattacks before retiring back to Felsobesyno Puszta.

On the twenty-third, the commander of *509* submitted a written complaint about the deployment of the battalion. His main points were late issue of orders; attachment to a tank regiment as opposed to being put under operational control; unsatisfactory engineer support; choice of an incompetent leader; and employment in unsuitable terrain. The complaint was submitted to the General Inspector of *Panzer* Troops, *Generaloberst* Guderian.

On the twenty-fourth, after some reorganization, it was decided to try to clear the Russian troop concentrations to the north of Kaplosnasnyek. Three battle groups from *SS-Panzer-Regiment 3*, *I/Panzer-Regiment 24*, and *schwere Panzer-Abteilung 509* were formed into three *Panzergruppen* of ten to twelve tanks each. The attack was to be in the general direction of Baracska. *509* (nine operational *Tiger II's*) was attached to *Kampfgruppe Eckert* (*SS-Panzer-Grenadier-Regiment 5 Totenkopf*) and was to try again to take Kishalom and Hill 157 and establish a bridgehead over the Vali Canal. The battalion started out in the morning from Felsobesyno and soon got involved in heavy fighting around Hill 157. In a twenty-minute period, the *Tiger*

II's had knocked out fifteen Russian tanks and a huge number of antitank guns.

Kampfgruppe Kleffner (*SS-Panzer-Grenadier-Regiment 6 Eicke*) was to attack from Kaplosnasnyek and take Baracska and establish a bridgehead. Attached to *Kampfgruppe Kleffner* was *I/Panzer-Regiment 24*, whose twenty-two operational *Panthers* would dwindle down to twelve at the start of the attack; by midnight, the number of operational vehicles would be five. Five *Tiger II's* from *509* reported to *SS-Panzer-Grenadier-Regiment 6 Eicke's* command post; by midnight, the number of operational *Tiger II's* was two.

The *Panzergruppe* from *1. Panzer-Division* was to strike north from Kaplosnasnyek. The attack began at 2200. The lead tanks from *SS-Panzer-Regiment 3* came under Russian tank and antitank fire as they advanced along the road to Pettend. About 1.5 kilometers west of Pettend, the *Tiger* of *SS-Unterscharführer* Becker was hit by two 85mm rounds. One round hit the front bow plate near the driver's position; another round hit the right side of the running gear and track. The crew bailed out and managed to escape back to German lines. The Russians examined this *Tiger* on 11 February and assigned it number 60 on their trophy list.

Going into the early hours of the twenty-fifth, *Kampfgruppe Kleffner* was involved in heavy fighting around Pettend. *I/Panzer-Regiment 24* knocked out six Russian tanks. After *Kampfgruppe Kleffner* captured Adam Major, it pushed on to Baracska and, by late morning, had managed to approach the southern section of the village. Two *Panthers* from *I/SS-Panzer-Regiment 3* tried to break through along the Pettend-Baracska road at around 1300. The Russians used air strikes in trying to halt the German attack. The 63rd Guards Cavalry Division was putting up fierce resistance as well.

To the south, *schwere Panzer-Abteilung 509* and *SS-Panzerjäger-Abteilung 3* were fending off strong Russian counterattacks in the area of Nagyhalom. *SS-Panzer-Grenadier-Regiment 6 Eicke* tried to press home the southern foothold it had in Baracska, but the Russians were launching strong counterattacks in the area of Pettend. The *Panthers* from *I/Panzer-Regiment 24* and the tanks from *1. Panzer-Division* knocked out seventeen Russian tanks. By the end of the day, *Kampfgruppe Kleffner* had to transition to defense, but Pettend had been captured by German forces. On the twenty-fourth, *SS-Panzer-Regiment 3* and *SS-Panzerjager-Abteilung* lost the following: three *Panzer IV's*, one *Tiger*, four *StuG's*, and one *Jagdpanzer IV*. *SS-Panzer-Artillerie-Regiment 3* lost one *Hummel*, three *Wespen*, and one *Panzerbeobachterswagen IV*, while *schwere Panzer-Abteilung 509* had a *Tiger II* knocked out one kilomter west of Pettend.

On the twenty-sixth, *Kampfgruppe Pitschellis* launched an attack from the area of Pettend in an effort to reopen the Val sector. Also attached to the *Kampfgruppe* were three *Tiger II's* from *schwere Panzer-Abteilung 509* and five *Panthers* from *I/Panzer-Regiment 24*. The direction of the attack was from Pettend, Baracska, and then Pazmand-Vereb. The attack began with an assault on Baracska, where the *Tiger* of *SS-Hauptscharführer* Berger was knocked out on the main road leading into the village. A 76mm round hit the turret on the left side, which also caused damage to the engine deck. Several other 76mm rounds hit the front bow plate as well, killing the radio operator, *SS-Sturmmann* Etmayer, and the driver, *SS-Sturmmann* Karl Dietz. The turret crew managed to bail out. *SS-Hauptscharführer* Berger was wounded by shrapnel to his back. He was evacuated back to Germany, and on 11 April, he was taken prisoner by British forces after he escaped from the Red Cross hospital at Bad Harzburg.

The *Tiger* was examined by the Russians on 23 February and given trophy number 135. Also knocked out on the northern edge of Baracska were two *Tiger II's* from *schwere Panzer-Abteilung 509* next to the Baracska-Pettend rail line. Here *SS-Panzer-Regiment 3* regrouped. South of Baracska, *Kampfgruppe Eckert* (*SS-Panzer-Grenadier-Regiment 5 Totenkopf*) assembled in the Pettend area. *Kampfgruppe Kleffner* attacked to the north. Flank protection was provided by *SS-Panzer-Artillerie-Abteilung 3* and *SS-Panzerjäger-Abteilung 3*. Attacking in the direction of Pazmand, in support from *1. Panzer Division*, was *Kampfgruppe Phillipp*.

After the fighting in Baracska, *Kampfgruppe Pitschellis* marched north via Psz Pettend, where it came under Russian antitank gunfire. This caused some damage to several of the tanks. As the *Kampfgruppe* moved farther toward Vereb, *SS-Sturmbannführer* Pitschellis's *Befehlspanther* was hit. He dismounted and tried to change *Panthers*. During the process he was badly wounded by shrapnel and died twenty minutes later. He was buried in Veszprem on the thirty-first. *SS-Panzer-Regiment 3* was now temporarily led by *SS-Obersturmbannführer* Dr. Gerhard Adam, who at the time was serving in the headquarters of *IV. SS-Panzer-Korps*. Adam had led *II/SS-Panzer-Regiment 3* from 1 November to 15 January before being assigned to the headquarters of the corps.

A bridgehead was formed over the Vali Canal between Val and Kajoszoszentpeter. Elements of *Kampfgruppe Phillipp* began to cross and push east about one kilometer before being recalled to assist in a new threat north of Pazmand as the Russian had brought new reinforcements and were soon committing large numbers of tanks. Here *General* Balck and *SS-Obergruppenführer* Gille got into a serious discussion about whether to continue the relief attack on Budapest or cancel it. In the end, *General* Balck ordered that the new threat of strong Russian forces to the north in the area of Lovasbereny posed a serious threat—hence the recall of *Kampfgruppe*

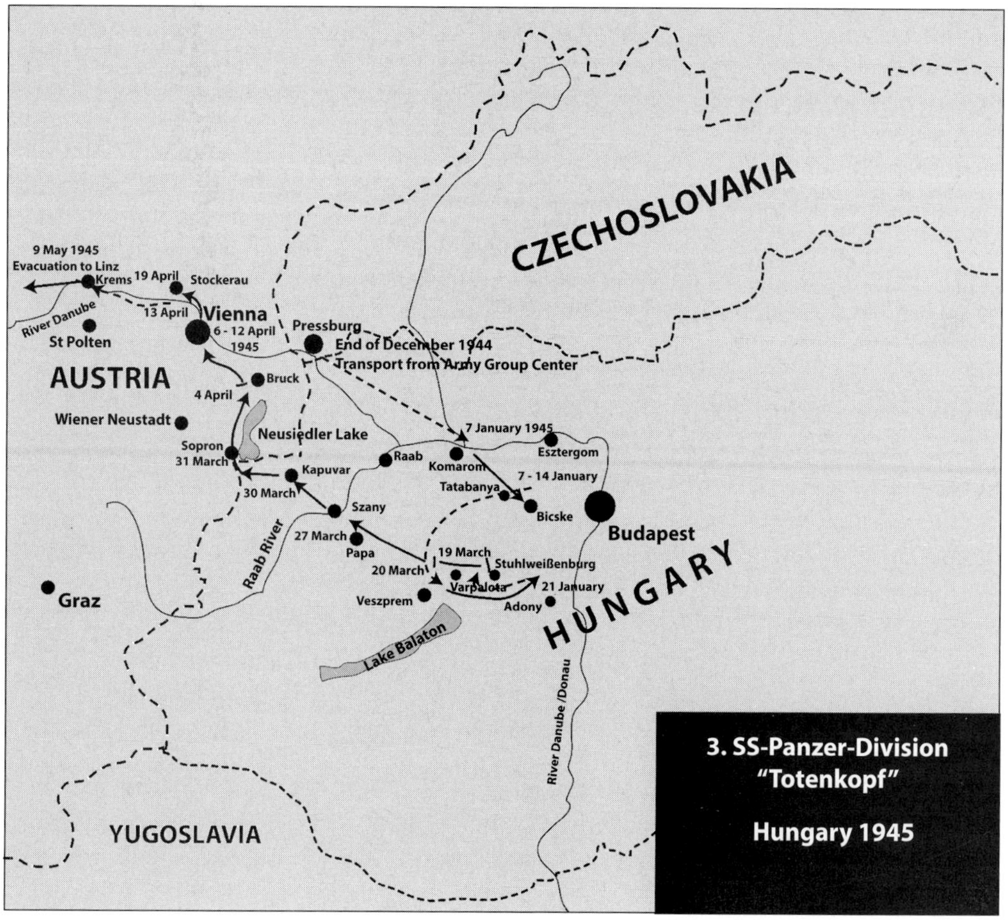

3. SS-Panzer-Division "Totenkopf"

Hungary 1945

Phillipp. During the night, the Russians tried to attack Vereb with about forty tanks, but the attack was repelled. During the day, *SS-Panzer-Regiment 3* and *SS-Panzerjäger-Abteilung 3* had lost one *Tiger* and one *Jagdpanzer IV*; *schwere Panzer-Abteilung 509* lost two *Tiger II's* (one was hit nine times, with four the crew dead; the other was hit four times, with three of the crew dead).

On the twenty-seventh, it was decided that *Totenkopf* would go over to the defense and start pulling back to a line of Baracska–Pettend–Kaplosnasnyek. Three *Panthers* and one *Tiger* from *9. Kompanie* provided support to the withdrawing units of *Kampfgruppe Kleffner* who were moving along the Vereb-Pazmand road. The Russian XXIII Tank Corps committed one of its brigades, which attacked Psz Pettend. Here four *Tigers II's* from *509*, supported by *I/SS-Panzer-Grenadier-Regiment Norge*, defended against the Russian attack. The *Tigers II's* managed to knock out forty-one Russian tanks—fifteen by *Oberfeldwebel* Neuhaus, who was nominated for the Knight's Cross.

The Russians committed more forces, which forced the Germans to go over to defense later that evening. A new defensive line was formed running from Kaplosnasnyek to Puszta Aggszentpeter. *SS-Panzer-Regiment 3* attempted a counterattack to the south of Baracska, reaching the southern edge of the village, but during the action, the regiment lost one *Panzer IV*, one *Befehlspanther*, and five *StuG's*, along with a *Tiger II* from *509*, which had been hit twice by large-caliber rounds.

The maintenance officer for Army Group Balck submitted a status report on the condition of the *Werkstatt* companies under the command of Army Group Balck. For *SS-Panzer-Regiment 3*, he reported that the *Werkstatt* company was one of the best he had visited and was especially pleased that the company had an officer assigned to inspect all damaged tanks before and after repairs. He stated that the regiment needed a new allocation of spare parts and at least eleven new engines for the *Panther* battalion. For *schwere Panzer-Abteilung 509*, he reported:

> Some of the repairs to *Tiger II's* have been carried out in Szekesfehervar; the forward operating workshop is located in Puszta Szabolcs. In Hajmasker one *Tiger II* requires rail transport and is ready for loading. The *Werkstatt* company has conducted eighty-two repairs due to mechanical damage and forty-one due to battle damage. Five *Tiger II's* required major repairs due to hull penetration. Two need new gears. Most of the battle damage has been to the tracks, running gear, and main gun.

Toward the end of January 1945, *SS-Unterscharführer* Dieter Thomas returned to the company after completing an *SS-Junkerschule* course in Germany. *SS-Rottenführer* Ruediger Berndhardt would return to *9. Kompanie* in March 1945.

On the twenty-eighth, *schwere Panzer-Abteilung 509* was regrouped in Szekesfehervar and attached to *III. Panzer-Korps*. On the thirty-first, twelve *Tiger II's* under the command of *Hauptmann* Tischendorf were sent along with a *Kampfgruppe* from *1. Panzer-Division* to relieve the trapped *Kampfgruppe Medicus* of *3. Panzer-Division* in the area of Dunapentele. The battalion lost three *Tiger II's* during this action. One was hit by three bombs near Hill 188, northwest of Nagy Perkata. Ten kilometers northwest of Dunapentele during a Russian air strike, another *Tiger II* was knocked out after being struck by T-34/85 rounds, killing three of the crew. A *Berge-Panther* was lost in the same location after being knocked out by 76mm antitank rounds. The third *Tiger II* was knocked out by bombs dropped during another Russian air strike along the Nagy Perkata-Dunapentele road, 500 meters southeast of Galambos.

On the twenty-eighth, the Russians launched air strikes on Kaplosnasnyek and Gardonny using Il-2 Sturmoviks and A-20 bombers. *Kampfgruppe Kleffner* completd its withdrawal from Vereb as *Totenkopf* defended along the Pettend-Baracska road. The Russians were now attacking the German positions to the south of Baracska. By midday, the front line now ran from Kaplosnasnyek to Psz Pettend. An order to pull back from the Vali Canal was issued; the new boundary was Baracska between *Totenkopf* and *Wiking*. *Totenkopf's* new front was to face northwest of Baracska.

On 29 January, to the north of Kaplosnasnyek, *9. Kompanie*, along with some *Panthers* from *I/SS-Panzer-Regiment 3*, engaged in defensive actions. In Gardonny, a *Tiger* and a *Panther* from *1. Kompanie* were assigned to help *I/SS-Panzer-Grenadier-Regiment 6 Eicke*. On the thirtieth, *SS-Hauptsturmführer* Berlin was promoted to *Sturmbannführer*. In Veszprem, *SS-Obersturmbannführer* Ernst assembled 210 men for a collection commando which was to return to Germany and collect new tanks for *SS-Panzer-Regiment 3*. The collection commando left Veszprem on 15 February and arrived at Sennelager on the eighteenth. This commando would not return and found itself incorporated into *Panzer-Brigade Westfalen*. The remnants of the group surrendered on 21 April in Suderode, near Wulperode in the Harz region in Germany.

On the thirtieth, elements of *9. Kompanie* and *I/SS-Panzer-Regiment 3* were still fighting in Kaplosnasnyek supporting *II/SS-Panzer-Grenadier-Regiment 5 Totenkopf*, under the command of *SS-Hauptsturmführer* Bachmann. Seven American Lend-Lease Shermans were knocked out during the fighting. To the south the Russians broke through the German lines between Nagyhalom and Puszta Szabolcs. Attacks on Kaplosnasnyek were repeated on the thirty-first, but this time in company strength. A *Panther* from *3. Kompanie* was struck by several bombs during an air strike on Kaplosnasnyek. One of the crew was killed; the rest escaped unharmed. Throughout the day, all Russian attacks against *Totenkopf* were repelled. On 1 February, Kaplosnasnyek was given up, with two *Tigers*. *9. Kompanie*, along with three *Panthers* from *I/SS-Panzer-Regiment 3*, pulled back into a new assembly area of Falubattyan.

February to March 1945

On 1 February, *SS-Kampfgruppe Kleffner* left the area around Falubattyan for redeployment and took up positions on the northern edge of Szekesfehervar. Attached to the battle group was *I/Panzer-Regiment 24* and two *Tigers* from *9. Kompanie*. To thc north of Szekesfehervar in Sarkeresztur were elements of *23.Panzer-Division*, with the attached *schwere Panzer-Abteilung 503*. *SS-Rottenführer* Willy Birke from *9. Kompanie* was wounded during the day. *Kampfgruppe Kleffner* advanced along the road to Zamoly. Still attached to *IV. SS-Panzer-Korps* was *1. Panzer-Division* and the elements of *509*.

Kampfgruppe Kleffner continued to attack along the Zamoly road until the third. On the fourth, *Kampfgruppe Kleffner*, with two *Tigers* from *9. Kompanie*, was to advance as far as the western edge of Patka. The attack continued until the afternoon of the fourth. The *Kampfgruppe's* front line ran from the northern edge of Szekesfehervar to Zamoly. On the fourth, *IV. SS-Panzer-Korps* released *1. Panzer-Division* and those assigned elements from *509*. *Kampfgruppe Kleffner* fended off several Russian attacks. Also still on hand were two *Tigers*.

On the southern side of Szekesfehervar on the fourth, three *Panthers* from *I/SS-Panzer-Regiment 3* were attached to *SS-Panzer-Grenadier-Regiment 9 Germania*, supporting the defenses around Csirib Puszta. On the fifth, the three *Panthers* from *I/SS-Panzer-Regiment 3* left the control of *SS-Panzer-Grenadier-Regiment 9 Germania* and were attached to *SS-Panzer-Regiment 5* and helped repel five Russian attacks along *5. SS-Panzer-Division Wiking's* front line. Returning to the company after completing the fourth *SS-Panzer-Sonder-Lehrgang* was *SS-Untersturmführer* Wolfgang Barth, who was placed in charge of the company's *Nachschub* platoon.

On the sixth, four *Tigers* were attached to *I/SS-Panzer-Regiment 5* under *Kampfgruppe Flieder*, which consisted of four *Tigers*, two *Panzer IV's*, and one *Panther*, commanded by *SS-Obersturmbannführer* Bauer. Also on the sixth, *SS-Oberscharführer* Wimmer and his crew, along with company engine specialist *SS-Oberscharführer* Karl Frank, left Szekesfehervar for Vienna to collect a repaired *Tiger* from the arsenal. The *Tiger* was loaded on 4 March and returned on the fifth; the reason for the long delay was that rail transports passing through Vienna for Operation Spring Awakening (the last major German offensive in the East) had priority.

On the seventh, the three *Panthers* were next dispatched to *1. Panzer-Division* and were fighting around Hill 130 and Janos Major. The Russian 521st Antitank Artillery Regiment lost all their 76mm guns in this area. The few remaining tanks from *SS-Panzer-Regiment 3* remained in the area southwest of Dinnyes between the eighth and ninth in readiness for further Russian attacks. On the tenth, these tanks were used in local counterattacks around Janos Major and Hill 151.

On the twelfth, *SS-Hauptsturmführer* Ther assumed command of *9. Kompanie* after taking over from *SS-Obersturmbannführer* Neff. Ther had entered the SS on 6 August 1937 and attended *SS-Junkerschule Braunschweig* for officer training from April to October 1939. He then served as a platoon leader at Braunschweig until being posted to the *7. Totenkopf Standarte Brunn* on 4 January 1940. On 16 May, he was transferred to *16. Totenkopf Standarte* as a platoon leader. On 3 March 1941, he was serving with *SS-Infanterie-Regiment 3* in *Totenkopf.* He was wounded on 16 July 1941 during the opening phases of Operation Barbarossa. From July 1941 to May 1942, he served in various roles within the *SS-FHA* in Berlin, with a brief spell attached to *Pz.A.O.K 1* from 10 October to 30 November 1942, after which he returned to Berlin to serve in the *SS-FHA*. He served as *2. Kompanie* commander in *schwere SS-Panzer-Abteilung 103* from 15 April to 19 November 1944, when he was transferred to *SS-Panzer-Regiment 1*. Ther's time with *Leibstandarte* was not happy, and on 22 December, he was placed in the officer reserve with the *SS-FHA*. On 12 January, he was again transferred, this time to *IV. SS-Panzer-Korps*, serving there until 12 February, when he took over *9. Kompanie*.

Within *SS-Panzer-Regiment 3*, several command changes took place. After being promoted to *Sturmbannführer* on 30 January, Anton Berlin assumed command of the tank regiment from *SS-Obersturmbannführer* Dr. Adam on 13 February. Adam returned to the headquarters of *IV. SS-Panzer-Korps*. *I/SS-Panzer-Regiment 3* was now commanded by *SS-Hauptsturmführer* Martin, who had transferred from the *Wehrmacht* to the *Waffen-SS*. *II/SS-Panzer-Regiment 3* was commanded by *SS-Hauptsturmführer* Lubich after *SS-Hauptsturmführer* Leibel was wounded; Leibel resumed command of his battalion on 11 March, and Lubich was transferred to *SS-Panzer-Grenadier-Regiment 5 Totenkopf.* Leibel was killed on 18 March during a Russian attack on Moha. The remnants of *II/SS-Panzer-Regiment 3* were led until the war's end by *SS-Obersturmbannführer* Molleken, former adjutant for the battalion.

On 12 February, *SS-Obersturmbannführer* Neff was supposed to take command of *1. Kompanie* of *SS-Panzer-Regiment 3* after *SS-Hauptsturmführer* Balzer was transferred to the headquarters company, but it seems that Neff remained with *9. Kompanie*. By the twenty-second, the bulk of *Totenkopf* had redeployed to the north of Szekesfehervar. The regiment's headquarters had set up a command post in Mor, while *I/SS-Panzer-Regiment 3*, *5. Kompanie* (*Panzer IV's*), and *9. Kompanie* were quartered in Magyaralmas. A rest area was set up in Fehervarcsurgo. The company's *Berge* platoon and maintenance section were located in Mor. The *Nachschub* platoon was based in Magyaralmas. The *Werkstatt* company had set up a forward workshop in Sored. The twenty-fourth was spent quietly, but on the twenty-fifth, the Russians launched an attack in regimental strength, made up of tanks and infantry, in the direction of Magyaralmas, but the attack was beaten back. Another Russian attack in the direction of Csakbereny was turned back by defensive fire from the 2nd Hungarian Tank Division.

On 1 March 1945, the *Tiger* company had the following vehicle inventory:

Kompanie Trupp—1 *Kübelwagen* for the company commander
Instand-Staffel—2 *Zgkw*
Nachschub Zug—1 *Kübelwagen* and 2 *Maultier LKW*
Waffenmeister—1 *LKW* (light truck)
Schirrmeister—1 *LKW*
Cook—1 *LKW* with trailer
Kradmelder—1 motorcycle

On 1 March, *SS-Panzer-Regiment 3* received 120 new recruits who had further training and instruction in Fehervarcsurgo until the sixteenth.

On the sixth, Operation Spring Awakening started south of Lake Balaton. *IV. SS-Panzer-Korps* had the task of straightening out its front line opposite Zamoly and Lovasbereny, and the main forces involved were *3. SS-Panzer-Division Totenkopf*, *5. SS-Panzer-Division Wiking*, *6. Panzer-Division*, and an armored group from the 2nd Hungarian Tank Division. *Totenkopf* had the task of advancing from the direction of Sarkeresztes toward Lovasbereny; the division was to shield the northern flank near Patka and the woods three killometers west of Patka. The Hungarian VIII Corps, along with the 2nd Hungarian Tank Division, was to cover the Vertis Hills and allow the *Totenkopf* to utilize most of its fighting components. *9. Kompanie* posted two *Tigers* at Felso Puszta on security duty.

On the sixth as well, elements of *3. SS-Panzer-Division Totenkopf*, along with elements of the 2nd Hungarian Tank Division, made limited attacks in the area of Csakbereny. The Russians reported some thirty tanks during this operation. On the seventh, another limited attack took place, this time with sixteen tanks and 120 grenadiers. They assembled near Felso Puszta and again attacked in the direction of Csakbereny. At least three *Panthers* from *3. Kompanie* escorted the grenadiers. The two *Tigers* at Felso Puszta remained in position. On the eighth, crews without tanks were formed into infantry battle groups. A scheduled attack in the direction of Lovasbereny failed to materialize.

On the ninth, the day was very quiet, but three *Panthers* from *3. Kompanie* were attached to *9. Kompanie* for a limited advance in the direction of Csakbereny, which was soon shelled by Russian artillery. On the tenth, *Totenkopf* began another advance, but it had to repel a Russian counterattack along its front line. The Russian infantry were provided with covering fire from artillery. The three *Panthers* from *3. Kompanie* positioned themselves along with the two *Tigers*.

On the eleventh, the two *Tigers* at Felso-Puszta remained on security duty. *SS-Untersturmführer* Barth visited the *Tigers* most days to make sure they had sufficient ammunition and fuel. In Mor, a rail transport brought replacement steel wheels for the *Tigers* and eleven new engine packs for *I/SS-Panzer-Regiment 3*. These engines had been requested on 27 January. But along the divisional front lines between Magyaralmas and Sarkeresztes, the Russians shelled the whole area with artillery fire from Sarkeresztes to Magyaralmas. During the night of the fourteenth and fifteenth, Russian scout troops conducted close reconnaissance on the positions around Magyaralmas and reported that the trench system in place was made up of slit trenches four deep. They also reported the presence of *Panthers* and *Tigers* in Magyaralmas.

Magyaralmas–Fehervarcsurgo, 16 March 1945

On 16 March 1945, the Red Army began its Vienna offensive. The 9th Guards Army began its assault on the front line of *3. SS-Panzer-Division Totenkopf* in the late afternoon after a thirty-minute artillery barrage. *9. Kompanie* was positioned as follows: two *Tigers* at Felso Puszta under the command of *SS-Obersturmbannführer* Neff and *SS-Oberscharführer* Bernhardt, two kilometers northeast of Magyaralmas. The remaining five *Tigers* were located in Magyaralmas under the command of the company commander, *SS-Hauptsturmführer* Ther. One other *Tiger* was still in long-term repair with the *Werkstatt* company in Hajmasker, and another was still at the arsenal in Vienna undergoing long-term repairs. The *Nachschub* platoon was stationed in Magyaralmas while the maintenance section and *Berge* platoon were placed in Mor.

Also located in Magyaralmas were *I/SS-Panzer-Regiment 3* with ten *Panthers*, *5. Kompanie* with seven *Panzer IV's*, and *I (gep)/SS-Panzer-Grenadier-Regiment 5 Totenkopf*.

SS-Hauptsturmführer Ther had just sat down for lunch with the commander of *I/SS-Panzer-Regiment 3* (*Panther's*), *SS-Hauptsturmführer* Martin. The *9. Kompanie* cook had just completed cooking the meal when the Russians opened fire with artillery. Ther remembered: "I looked down at my dinner, specially prepared by the company cook, and sighed. I looked at Martin and sighed again. I said, 'Time to go to work.' We both got up and left. That was the last time I saw Martin. I later learned that he was killed on the seventeenth during another Russian artillery barrage in Magyaralmas."

The two *Tigers* located at Felso Puszta were quickly knocked out in the afternoon by SU-76 self-propelled guns from the 1523rd Self-Propelled Artillery Regiment (trophy numbers 205 and 208). *SS-Oberscharführer* Bernhardt did manage to knock out a Russian antitank, but his *Tiger* was hit. The other *Tiger* was commanded by *SS-Obersturmbannführer* Neff. Both crews bailed out and safely made it back to German lines. At the same time, the whole event was witnessed by *SS-Untersturmführer* Barth, observing from Hill 153, just to the north of Magyaralmas. *SS-Sturmbannführer* Berlin (*SS-Panzer-Regiment 3* commander) ordered Ther to send two *Tigers* north in the direction of Mor. "When I received the order," Ther recalled, "I was not happy. I said I needed all available *Tigers* in Magyaralmas, but *SS-Sturmbannführer* Berlin stated this was a clear order."

Both *Tigers* set off toward Mor. This left three *Tigers* in Magyaralmas. One *Tiger* was positioned on the northern edge of Magyaralmas while two others were located in the southeastern part of the village, firing in the direction of Borbala Major at Russian infantry. Ther knocked out two Russian antitank guns. Later in the day, he ordered Barth to supervise the evacuation of the support units in Mor and return them to Magyaralmas.

In the afternoon, elements of *I/SS-Panzer-Regiment 3*, with four *Panthers* and three *Panzer IV's* from *5. Kompanie*, launched a counterattack in the direction of Borbala Puszta. The attack ground to a halt because of heavy Russian defensive fire. All seven tanks were lost about 1.5 kilometers southeast of Magyaralmas. According to Ther, "For some reason the Russians were concentrating on the *Panthers* and seemed to go after them really hard. The Russians left our *Tigers* alone, which seemed odd." Somehow Ther managed to call back the two *Tigers* in Mor, which drove back to Magyaralmas, bringing the number of *Tigers* in Magyaralmas to five.

17 March 1945

During the early-morning hours, the Russians launch a huge air strike on Magyaralmas. The 9th Guards Army's orders were clear: they had twenty-four hours to clear the German concentration in the village. The 98th Guards Rifle Division launched an assault with the 296th Guards Rifle Regiment. Inside Magyaralmas, five *Panthers* and *I (gep)/SS-Panzer-Grenadier-Regiment 5 Totenkopf* formed up and launched a counterattack, which aimed at the right flank of the 296th Guard Rifle Regiment. Like the previous day, the attack was beaten back by heavy defensive Russian fire. *9. Kompanie* had one *Tiger* based at the northern edge of the village which came under assault from a Russian infantry squad carrying antitank mines.

The crew inside the *Tiger* heard a large explosion outside the vehicle. They pulled back into cover, and the crew got out to inspect for any damage. Instead, they found body parts from a Russian soldier who had been killed by his own mine because of its premature detonation. The *Tiger* crew had to clear up the mess and quickly return to their original position at the northern edge of the village. The other *Tigers* were positioned alongside three *Panzer IV's* from *5. Kompanie*. On the eastern edge of Magyaralmas, *SS-Hauptsturmführer* Ther advanced about 800 meters to engage the Russian infantry with high-explosive shells when his *Tiger* became bogged down. The rear of the hull was stuck in thick mud. Ther sent the driver to find a *Berge-Panther*. The driver quickly returned with the vehicle, but all efforts were in vain. The Russian infantry were almost upon the *Berge-Panther* and *Tiger*. This was when Ther gave the order to bail out. His *Tiger* would later be recovered by the Russians and left on the main road between Mor and Szekesfehervar, just near the turnoff leading to Magyaralmas, until 1950.

The crew of the *Berge-Panther* had to leave their vehicle behind as well. When Ther got to the northern edge of Magyaralmas, he instructed the *Tiger* positioned there to fire one round into the stricken tank. The *Tiger* fired one round, which, to everyone's surprise, bounced off the *Tiger*. On the eastern edge of Magyaralmas, a *Panzer IV* was knocked out. Ther recalled: "I reported this event to the regimental commander, *SS-Sturmbannführer* Berlin, and his response was not a positive one, to say the least."

By 1230 hours, the Russians were fighting at the eastern edge of Magyaralmas. The *Tigers* and *Panzer IV's* were fighting in the central and northern part of the village. At noon, the *Tigers* had assembled under the command of *SS-Obersturmbannführer* Neff near the Catholic church. The few remaining *Panthers* were fighting in the southern half of the village. By 1238, the Russians had captured the northern section of the village, forcing five *Tigers* and three *Panzer IV's* to withdraw back onto the main road between Szekesfehervar and Mor. The *Tigers*, along with *Panzer IV's*, withdrew in the direction of Bodajk. The *Panthers* and *I (gep)/SS-Panzer-Grenadier-Regiment 5 Totenkopf* finally gave up the southern part of the village at 1800 hours that evening and withdrew back into Fehervarcsurgo. The remaining *Tigers* pulled back to Bodajk and were defending the crossroads and the rail station. The *Nachschub* platoon under *SS-Untersturmführer* Barth had also withdrawn from Magyaralmas into Fehervarcsurgo. These *Tigers* took up defensive positions on the outskirts of Bodajk; one *Tiger* was positioned next to the rail station.

In Mor, the maintenance section and the *Berge* platoon managed to evacuate their location, but as they pulled back to Bodajk, they came under heavy Russian fire from the direction of Sored. In Fehervarcsurgo, the *Nachschub* platoon's vehicles were pressed into service by the divisional military police to transport the wounded from the divisional command post to a medical clearing station. Barth rejoined his platoon later that day. His *Nachschub* platoon had a *Kübelwagen*, two *Maultier* half-track trucks, and a motorcycle for the dispatch rider.

The fighting for Magyaralmas was costly for both sides. *Totenkopf* lost ten *Panthers*, three *Tigers*, four *Panzer IV's*, thirteen *SPW's*, and 239 men taken prisoner by the Russians. The 98th Guards Rifle Division had suffered 228 killed and 618 wounded.

18–31 March 1945

On 18 March, Fehervarcsurgo had to be given up after intense fighting. The Russians captured the village at 1520 hours. *Totenkopf* units in Fehervarcsurgo pulled back to Guttamasi and then eventually Isztimer. The village of Fehervarcsurgo originally had 298 houses. By the time the fighting was over, 208 houses had been totally destroyed or partially damaged. In Guttamasi, *Totenkopf* divisional headquarters had some of its sub-units based there. As the Russians pressed on with their advance, large parts of the divisional headquarters were captured by the attacking Russian forces. The Russians reported the following: 39 POWs, 384 killed German soldiers, 93 motor vehicles, 62 trucks, 7 field cars, 3 *SPW's*, and 6 towed artillery pieces.

In Isztimer, *9. Kompanie's Nachschub* platoon's *Maultier* vehicles were being used to tow six *SPW's* from *I (gep)/SS-Panzer-Grenadier-Regiment 5 Totenkopf* that had become stuck while trying to move along the back country lanes heading north toward Balinka. During the day, *SS-Sturmmann* Karl Rettinger was killed along the Mor-Kisber road. *SS-Rottenführer* Paul Hoffmann was killed in Mor, and *SS-Oberscharführer* Karl Bauer, commander of the *Berge* platoon, was killed near Sarkeresztes.

During March 1945, *SS-Schütze* Walter Sablonty returned to the company and fought in an infantry *Kampfgruppe*. With *SS-Hauptsturmführer* Martin dead, *SS-Obersturmbannführer* Lummitsch took command of the remnants of *I/SS-Panzer-Regiment 3*.

To the north of Isztimer in Bodajk, the *Tigers* defending near the rail station had to pull back as the Russians had finally captured Sored and Mor. The *Tigers* withdrew from Bodajk and reached Balinka. During the move, some *Panzer IV's* from *II/SS-Panzer-Regiment 3* were knocked out between Bodajk and Balinka, losing a total of six *Panzer IV's*.

On the twentieth, one *Tiger* was reported defending Mecser Puzta. The *Tigers* of *9. Kompanie* basically withdrew along the road heading west to Zirc. During the twenty-first, elements of *Totenkopf* were fighting on the southern outskirts of Bakonycsernye. On the twenty-second, one *Tiger* from *9. Kompanie* was defending the road east in the direction of Bakonycsernye in support of *SS-Panzer-Pionier-Bataillon 3* and knocked out a Russian tank before pulling back in the direction of Bakonycsernye. In Hajmasker, the *Tiger* in long-term repair (awaiting new engine parts) with *SS-Panzer-Werkstatt-Kompanie 3* had to be towed from Hajmasker via Papa and Marczalto, over the border between Hungary and Austria, between Kophaza and Deutsch Kreutz on the thirtieth. On the twenty-third, the same *Tiger*, still in support of the *Pionier* battalion, was reported by the Russians as defending the main road between Szapar and Csteny. Later, the same *Tiger* and a *Panzer IV* were defending the road 500 meters east of Nagyesztergar before pulling back and withdrawing to Zirc. The *Tigers* drove through Zirc and headed toward Penzeskut. The bulk of *Totenkopf* was located around Penzeskut and Lokut.

On the twenty-fourth, the Russians received intelligence that four *Tigers* from *9. Kompanie* were in Bakonybel along with a large number of soldiers from *Totenkopf*. Bakonybel was the first assembly point for units of the division; the Russians had gained this information after the capture of a Hungarian officer from the 2nd Hungarian Tank Division. *Totenkopf* and elements of *12. SS-Panzer-Division Hitlerjugend* were defending strongpoints southeast of Bakonybel and the high ground west of Borzavar. The company was by this time split into two parts—the combat elements and the support elements. The support units withdrew along the road from Papa to Marczalto-Beled and then north to Fertoszentmiklos, crossing the border between Sopron (Odenburg) and Klingenbach in Austria. The combat elements followed the infantry *Kampfgruppen* belonging to *I* and *II/SS-Panzer-Regiment 3*. Also following were the *Werkstatt* company and the *Versorgungs-Kompanie* for *II/SS-Panzer-Regiment 3*. On the twenty-fifth, *Totenkopf* had to withdraw from the area southwest of Marczalto under heavy Russian pressure. On the twenty-sixth, the division was forced back to the Marczal Canal, forming defensive points along the west bank.

On the twenty-sixth, one *Tiger* was in action in the village of Luka, but it was hit by Russian artillery fire, which caused damage to the running gear. The *Tiger* was successfully towed away. On the twenty-eighth, *Totenkopf* and elements of *Hitlerjugend* were fighting on the north bank of the Raab River and repelled several Russian attacks. The *Tigers* followed a secondary road to the border after Beled, which led to Cirak and then onto Csapod-Rojtokmuzsaj-Pinnye-

Pereszteg-Nagycenk-Kophaza and crossing the border into Austria at Deutsch Kreutz on the thirtieth. During that same day, *Totenkopf* was tasked with defending the border near Lake Neusiedl See.

On the thirtieth, the *Werkstatt* company had set up a forward operating workshop in Ritzing, and a repaired *Tiger* drove from Ritzing and engaged the Russians near Neutal. Another *Tiger* was in action near Weppersdorf. Later the same day, the *Tiger* sustained mechanical damage again and had to be returned to the *Werkstatt* company. On the thirty-first, two *Tigers* were used in a counterattack on Horitschon in order to relieve the encircled *Grenadier-Regiment 587*. Infantry support was provided to *III/SS-Panzer-Grenadier-Regiment 26* under the command of *SS-Hauptsturmführer* Reide. During the encounter, *587* was freed from Horitschon, and the Russians lost some seventeen tanks.

After the battle, the German forces, including the *Tigers*, withdrew to the north. The *Tigers* followed the road through Kirchschlag, Krumbach and headed toward Edlitz through the Pitten Valley. On 1 April, they entered Erlach. The *Tiger* that had fought in Neutal came to a halt in Ofenbach after sustaining more engine trouble. The *Tiger*—under Privatski—had to be abandoned after Russian forces descended on Ofenbach, forcing the crew to escape across the fields toward Frohsdorf. The tank was left on the side of the road leading to Lanzen Kirchen. The other two *Tigers* drove on toward Lanzen Kirchen. The *Tiger* in Ofenbach was later inspected by the local children, who managed to unload around twenty-five rounds of 88mm ammunition. When the Russians left the village, they tried to set the shells on fire, fortunately, without success.

The *Totenkopf* battle groups that passed through Lanzen Kirchen included the infantry groups from *I* and *II/SS-Panzer-Regiment 3*, the *Versorgs-Kompanie* from *SS-Panzer-Regiment 3*, and *Werkstatt* company, which, after leaving Ritzing, had moved through Schwarzenbach and followed the other units through the Pitten Valley. After Lanzen Kirchen, the *Werkstatt* company headed north to Wiener Neustadt. On the second, *Totenkopf* was assigned to *II. SS-Panzer-Korps*. The following day, the *Werkstatt* company got into a short firefight in St. Egyden in which two T-34 tanks were knocked out; one soldier from *SS-Panzer-Regiment 3* was killed, and another four German soldiers died. The *Werkstatt* company then moved toward Baden and set up a temporary work place in Judenau. The *9. Kompanie's* support units moved to the west of Sankt Polten and set up quarters in Krems an der Donau. Official records for *9. Kompanie* were no longer kept as of 4 April.

The two remaining *Tigers* (Wimmer's and Tassler's) also headed in the direction of Judenau via Wiener Neustadt, Bad Fischau, Baden, and Helenental, where both saw some limited action. After Helenental, both withdrew toward Mayerling, Alland, Klausen Leopoldsdorf, Pressbaum, Sieghartskirchen, and Judenau on the sixth; maintenance was carried out. On the seventh, both *Tigers* took up defensive positions around Judenau. One *Tiger* was situated on Burgstallberg Strasse on the road leading toward Gollarn, and the other was positioned on the northeastern edge of Judenau. In support were some *Luftwaffe Flak* units with 88mm *Flak* guns. On the eighth, both *Tigers* engaged SU-100s from the 912th Self-Propelled Artillery Regiment. The *Tigers* knocked out one SU-100 and disabled a second. The *Flak* guns destroyed four more Russian tanks. The *Tigers* withdrew toward Langenrohr in the afternoon and eventually drove into Tulln, crossed over the rail bridge, and headed toward Dross near Krems an der Donau. The bridge in Tulln was blown up later that evening. The *Werkstatt* company was ordered into Vienna to set up a facility in the area of Pressburg Gasse in the Floridsdorf District of the city.

Tigers in Vienna

The *Tiger* that had been in long-term repair and required new engine parts was finally returned to service on 7 April. It took up a position near the

Vienna Arsenal, opposite the freight yards. Under the command of *SS-Oberscharführer* Tonges, it fought in the area of the Sud Bahnhof and the Schweizergarten, next to the Schloss Belvedere on the eighth. The next day, the *Tiger* had withdrawn in the direction of the Ring Strasse and the Inner City. On the tenth, the single *Tiger* was defending the area around the Marien Brucke in the Leopold Stadt district. On the eleventh, as the Russians approached the Reichs Bridge, Tonges's *Tiger* was positioned next to the present-day Heiliger Franz Kirche in Mexiko Platz and fired at the advancing Russian forces that decided to give this area a wide berth. On the twelfth, the *Tiger* crossed the Reichs Brucke later in the day, and in the evening, it took up a position on the north bank.

The *Tiger II* collected from the arsenal on 2 April was commanded by *SS-Unterscharführer* van Kerkhom, but still required repairs. It was a rebuilt tank with a Porsche turret. It had a new two-piece gun mantlet, new tracks for the eighteen-tooth front sprocket, and track guards. On the thirteenth, the *Tiger II* was returned to service and joined Tonges's *Tiger*. Both fired some rounds at the Russian XXth Guards Corps as it crossed the Danube and then withdrew from the northern suburbs of Vienna toward Stockerau and Korneuburg along with the last two remaining *Panthers* from *I/SS-Panzer-Regiment 3*.

On the thirteenth, *Kampfgruppe Neff* was formed. This included the three remaining *Tiger I's* and two *Panthers*. Attached to *SS-Panzer-Regiment 3* on the same date was *Kampfgruppe Langanke*; Langanke commanded *2. Kompanie* (*Panther's*) from *SS-Panzer-Regiment 2. Kampfgruppe Langanke* was composed of thirteen *Panther's,* nine *Panzer IV's,* four *Berge-Panthers*, and three *Tiger II's*. A single *Berge-Panther* had to be given up on the twenty-seventh for redeployment to the *Panzergruppe* being sent into the area of Dresden, Germany. *Kampfgruppe Langanke* was located in Kirchberg am Wagram.

On the last day of the war, *Totenkopf's* divisional Ia, *SS-Obersturmbannführer* Eberhardt, arrived by car and presented Langanke with a written order to blow up all his tanks. The *Kampfgruppe* then moved to Engelmanns Brunn and positioned itself in three different locations in the village, where they blew up their tanks.

Infantry Battle Group in Vienna

The twenty men collected by the company's *Spieß*, Beneke, for infantry duty in Vienna arrived on the tenth and saw action in the area of Schwarzenberg Square, Mariahilfer Street, Schweden Platz, and Augarten Brucke.

Ludwig Lachner recalled the last days of *9. Kompanie*:

> Two years had passed since I had been home on leave, and we were struggling with the retreat through Hungary back into Austria. We crossed the border near Odenburg (Sopron). I saw my company commander, *SS-Obersturmbannführer* Neff, and I asked him if I could see my family as they did not live far from our present location. Neff said this was fine, but on my word of honor, I was to return to the company after twenty-four hours. I gave my guarantee. This was done on 31 March.
>
> I hitched a ride to Klausen Leopoldsdorf, Helenental, and from there on to Sankt Polten. When I reached Sankt Polten, I immediately experienced a U.S. bombing raid. I had to take cover under a bridge. After the raid I walked through the town in the direction of the rail station. Everything was totally unrecognizable, and people were still taking cover inside their air raid shelters. I managed to hitch a ride to my family farm southwest of Sankt Polten. I stayed with my family until 2 April. On the third, I managed to get all the way to Krems, where the company support units were stationed.
>
> I had been at the company no more than two hours when the *Spieß*, *Hauptscharführer* Beneke, came around and collected

twenty of us (mostly crews without *Tigers*) for infantry duty in Vienna. We were loaded onto a truck and driven through Langenlois, Tulln, and then over the Donau Brucke, St. Andra-Woerden, Klosterneuburg, and then unloaded at the Vienna west rail station. Once there, we were placed into the front line.

The *Kampfgruppe* saw action in the following places: Schwarzenberg Square, Mariahilfer Street, St. Stephens Church near Schweden Platz, Maria Brucke, and then along Augarten Street and Augarten Brucke. I was fighting along the Augarten Street near the Rossauer Barracks when I was wounded. A Russian hand grenade went off nearby, wounding me in the arm and foot. I was recovered by my comrades and taken by motorcycle to a medical clearing station in Stammersdorf, which came under air attack by Russian fighter-bombers. The next day, the eleventh, I was taken to Pisek am der Moldau. I spent six weeks in the hospital recovering. This hospital was under the control of the International Red Cross. On 3 May, U.S. troops and Czech paramilitary forces took over the hospital.

By the end of May, I was able to walk again and was discharged from the hospital. The Americans handed me over to the Russians, along with 300,000 other soldiers from Army Group Schorner.

I later learned that the battered company had been officially disbanded in Perg. This was done at the start of May. Parts ended up in Russian or American captivity. Luckily, some comrades managed to escape and make it home without being caught. Thus ended three years of our tank company's operational life.

Sepp Glockl was taken prisoner in Perg and spent ten years in a camp in Siberia. Karl Kuster was captured in Enns by the Russians and spent eleven years in a Russian camp in the Ural Mountains. Eric Lehmkuhl was recovering from wounds in Linz when the Americans took him prisoner; he eventually recovered in a POW camp outside Wegscheicht near Linz. Gustl Krippl was being treated for his wounds in Salzburg. Barth was taken prisoner by the Americans and interned in Regensburg Camp in Germany. Tassler and Wimmer both tried to escape through the forests to Geiersburg near Reid but were caught and placed in a prison camp normally reserved for government officials in Glasenbach near Salzburg.

Fifteen men from the company were taken prisoner near Friestadt. Van Kerkhom's crew was taken prisoner in Krems an der Donau. Privatski and his crew were caught along the road to Linz. Besides van Kerkhom's crew, another five men were also captured in Kems by the Russians on the ninth. Tonges and his crew were taken prisoner near Pregarten.

Kuno Ther's remembered of the last days of the war: "Morale was always very high until toward the end. Then the rumor was going around that *Totenkopf* was going to be turned around and sent to join the Americans and fight the Russians again." On 13 April, Ther assumed command of *II/SS-Panzer-Grenadier-Regiment 6 Eicke* after the battalion commander, *SS-Hauptsturmführer* Endress, was wounded on the same day. Ther remained in command until 6 May and returned command of the battalion to Endress.

The last three *Tigers* remained in Krems an der Donau along with two *Panthers* until the last day of the war. The *II. SS-Panzer-Korps* instructed *Totenkopf* that it would cover the withdrawal of the corps to the West. *Kampfgruppe Neff* was to cover the approaches slightly to the north of Krems and hold their positions until 1700 hours. The two *Panthers* drove to Noehagen bei Krems. The *Tigers* drove to Gneixendorf and then headed north to Stratzing, where an *Sd.Kfz. 7/1* was blown up. The *Tigers* turned west in the direction of Senftenberg and then along the road to Stixendorf. As the *Tigers* approached Weinzierl am Walde, one broke down next to a roadside shrine just short of Weinzierl am Walde; the other two made it into the center of the village before breaking down. Following behind them was an *SPW*, which was blown up next to the residence of the local vicar, nearly setting his house on fire; the local fire brigade was called out. The two *Panthers* were abandoned in and around Noehagen bei Krems. The *Tiger II* with the Porsche turret was abandoned on the southern edge of the Krems freight rail station; the crew, under the command of *SS-Unterscharführer* van Kerkhom, was taken prisoner the next day by the Russians after having one last night on the town.

The company personnel and support units left Krems an der Donau and headed along the Donau embankment road heading in the direction of Klein Pochlarn to assemble in Perg, where the company held a disbandment parade. The personnel then followed what was left of the tank regiment and tank destroyer battalion to the area around Mistlberg, where the divisional personnel assembled before proceeding into the area southeast of Pregarten. The *Tiger* crews from *Kampfgruppe Neff* made it to Freistadt, while the *Panther* crews, the *Panther* battalion support units, and *SS-Obersturmbannführer* Neff arrived in Neumarkt im Muhl Kries during the night of 8–9 May. They were taken into captivity on the ninth by the U.S. 11th Armored Division.

On the tenth, U.S. forces ordered *Totenkopf* to move to the area of Gallneukirchen. During the night of 12–13 May, the Americans turned over *Totenkopf* to the Russian forces. On the fourteenth, the U.S. 11th Armored Division reported that in a two-day period, it had turned over 34,125 soldiers of the *II. SS-Panzer-Korps* to the Russians, including moer than 18,000 in one day alone. Out of all this chaos, one of the former company officers, *SS-Hauptsturmführer* Ther, managed to escape and head north. He laid low for more than three years before returning home and slipping back into society to gain a place at a university and complete his law degree, which he had started before the war. He went on to practice law for forty-five years.

Ludwig Buss recalled the end of the war:

> On 30 April, we still had some tanks. We received the news that Hitler had killed himself. Between 6 and 8 May, the *Tigers* belonging to Wimmer and Tassler were blown up. The fate of Tassler's crew is not known to me, but Wimmer's was composed of Wimmer, Horst Bottcher (gunner), Walter Rohr (loader, ex-*Luftwaffe*), Helmut Brieger (driver), and Ludwig Buss (radio operator). After blowing up our *Tiger*, we drove on toward Freistadt with a motorcycle with sidecar and an *SPW*. There we destroyed our pay books and insignia. At the end, we had three *Tigers* and fifteen men when we disbanded our company.
>
> About Helmut Brieger—when he was setting the charges inside the *Tiger* in order to blow it up, he forgot to unscrew the detonation cap, so he went back and climbed up onto the *Tiger* and threw hand grenades inside the turret, but as he was climbing down, there was an almighty blast that threw Helmut in the air. Bottcher and I ran up to him and quickly put him in a *Schwimmwagen* with an *Untersturmführer* who drove to a military hospital in Melk.

Infantry *Kampfgruppe Barth*

Kampfgruppe Barth was formed on 28 March near Fertoszenmiklos after *SS-Brigadeführer* Becker (*Totenkopf* commander) ordered him to collect stragglers from the *Tiger* company and the *Panzer* regiment. *SS-Untersturmführer* Barth managed to assemble eighty-four men, who were then organized into three platoons. He had one *SS-Unterscharführer* and two *SS-Rottenführer's* as platoon leaders. The vehicles of the *Nachschub* platoon from *9. Kompanie* were placed under the leadership of *SS-Hauptscharführer* Beneke and proceeded in the direction of Sopron. The *Kampfgruppe* withdrew along the main road heading in the direction of Sopron. It was somewhere near Fertoszentmiklos that Barth saw the *Tiger* of *SS-Unterscharführer* Sperner. They exchanged waves. Sperner's *Tiger* would later be knocked out just outside Pereszteg on the thirtieth.

On the thirty-first, *Kampfgruppe Barth* reached Eisenstadt. The *Kampfgruppe* was positioned next to a *Wehrmacht* 88mm *Flak* battery, which knocked out a Russian tank.

On 1 April, *Kampfgruppe Barth* left Eisenstadt and, on the second, took up positions in Oggau, where they were reinforced by eighty *Volksturm* (inadequately trained civilians) from Tulln. The *Kampfgruppe* at this time was lightly armed with pistols, rifles, and about sixty *Panzerfaust.* In Oggau, the *Kampfgruppe* engaged Russian tanks, knocking out two of them with *Panzerfaust*, but were forced to withdraw in the direction of Donners Kirchen. The *Volkssturm* suffered five killed in action.

In Donners Kirchen, the *Kampfgruppe* fought a limited action before retreating north in the direction of Hof an Leithabirge on 3 April. The next day, the *Kampfgruppe* reached Mannersdorf am Leithagebirge and again fought a limited action and withdrew north toward Gotzendorf, meeting up with *SS-Kampfgruppe Kuhn*. In Gotzendorf, *SS-Kampfgruppe Kuhn* was supported by two *Panthers* from *SS-Panzer-Regiment 3*, *SS-Flak-Abteilung 3*, and elements of *SS-Panzer-Artillerie-Abteilung 3*.

On the fifth, *Kampfgruppe Barth* was fighting in the area of Schwadorf and Schwechat airfield. On the sixth, it withdrew along the Simmering Road. At Lehmgasse, Barth found part of the divisional command and reported to an *SS-Obersturmführer*. Barth received orders to move to the Vienna Arsenal and collect a new issue of weapons and equipment and then take positions near the Vienna south rail station. On the seventh, *Kampfgruppe Barth* took up positions alongside a small *Kampfgruppe* from *1. SS-Panzer-Division Leibstandrte Adolf Hitler,* which was commanded by an *SS-Obersturmführer*. On the seventh, *SS-Untersturmführer* Barth was wounded and evacuated to a general hospital in Linz, where he was eventually taken prisoner by U.S. forces. Between 28 March to 6 April, the *Kampfgruppe* suffered no casualties. The fate of the eighty-four other men is not known.

There were no *Tigers* from *SS-Panzer-Regiment 3* in the area of Gotzendorf and Pischelsdorf. In the area west of Rauchenwarth-Himberg, there were *Tigers* from *SS-Panzer-Regiment 2*. On 1 April, six *Tiger I's* were collected from the Vienna arsenal after being repaired and returned to service. On the fourth, two of these *Tigers* were deployed alongside the positions of the local *Flak* units dug in on the Koenigskogel near Rauchenwarth. Both fought a fighting withdrawal back to Himberg. After Himberg was captured, the Russians found two burnt-out *Tigers* on the northern edge of the village.

On the fifth, another *Tiger I* was knocked out near the brick factory just north of Oberlaa, and on the eighth, the two other *Tiger I's* were knocked out in the freight yard opposite the Vienna arsenal. The sole surviving *Tiger*, under the command of *SS-Hauptscharführer* Warnick, was blown up in Melk on 8 May; this *Tiger* had the old-style commander's cupola. Of the three *Tiger II's* assigned to *SS-Panzer-Regiment 2* and *Kampfgruppe Langanke* (*2. Kompanie/SS-Panzer-Regiment 2*). One *Tiger II* was taken over from *schwere SS-Panzer-Abteilung 501* at the Vienna arsenal after completing repairs on 1 April. This vehicle stayed with *Kampfgruppe Langanke* until the war's end and was blown up on 8 May in Engelmanns Brunn near Kirchberg am Wagram. The two other *Tiger's* came from *schwere Panzer-Abteilung 503 FHH* and had been at the arsenal undergoing repairs since February 1945. The crews collected them on 2 April, and they saw action with *Panzer-Ersatz-Abteilung 4* (tank replacement unit) in the area of Modling.

After serving with *Panzer-Ersatz-Abteilung 4*, they were assigned to *SS-Panzer-Regiment 2* on 4 April. They saw service in the area of Laxenburg and Unterlaa. On the seventh, both *Tigers* were towed over the Floridsdorf Bridge to

Stammersdorf for repairs. After completing repairs, both moved to Klosterneuburg and then Stockerau. Further repairs were carried out at Schloss Burg Kreuzenstein near Harmannsdorf. On the twentieth, both were assigned security duty on the edge of Krems an der Donau. On the twenty-first, both were ordered to move to Melk in readiness for a counterattack on St. Polten, but the forthcoming counterattack never materialized. The tanks drove to Pochlarn to await loading under the supervision of *SS-Panzer-Regiment 2* on the twenty-seventh, but were left near the station at war's end. Both crews were driven back to Kirchberg am Wagram and rejoined *Kampfgruppe Langanke*, which surrendered to American forces on 9 May.

Lachner pictured with his family southwest of Sankt Polten on 1 April 1945. Lachner had received permission from *SS-Obersturmführer* Neff to visit his family with a twenty-four-hour pass. Permission was given on 31 March 1945, and Lachner returned in Langenlois on 2 April 1945.

A *Tiger I* from *9. Kompanie* receives serious repairs near Acs. Also undergoing repairs are some *Panzer IV's* and *StuG's*. The turret of the *Tiger* is mounted on a makeshift rig made of oil barrels and wooden beams. MIRKO BAYERL / HM-HIM

A *Tiger* crossing a small stream on 2 January 1945 near Lábatlan, with grenadiers from *II/SS-Panzer-Grenadier-Regiment 6 Eicke* in support. MIRKO BAYERL

Officer-cadet Wolfgang Barth. BARTH

SS-Untersturmführer.d.Res. Barth awaiting rail transport for the return journey back to Hungary on 3 February 1945. BARTH

The rear of *Tiger 934* photographed by the Russian trophy team northwest of Many-Zsambek road junction. *Tiger 934* was commanded by *SS-Unterscharführer* Privatski. All the crew escaped to safety. TSAMO

The same *Tiger* but from the front. The photograph clearly shows where the *Tiger* was hit by a 76mm antitank round. TSAMO

This *Tiger* (trophy number 60) was lost on 24 January 1945, west of Pettend. It was commanded by *SS-Unterscharführer* Becker and was examined on 11 February 1945 by the Russian trophy team. ASKM

A collection site for German *Panzer* wrecks. All these vehicles came from *3. SS-Panzer-Division Totenkopf*. The *Panther* is a *Befehls.Wg.* from the *Stabs.Kp. / SS-Panzer-Regiment 3*. In the background are a *Panzer IV*, *StuG III*, and the *Tiger* from Pettend. ASKM

Another photograph of the same collection site, but with a clearer view of the *Tiger* knocked out west of Pettend. ASKM

A *Tiger* knocked out on 27 January 1945 on the northern edge of Baracska. Two of the crew were killed in action: the radio operator, Etmayer (transferred from the *Luftwaffe*); and the driver, *SS-Sturmmann* Karl Dietz. The turret crew managed to escape to safety. The *Tiger* was commanded by *SS-Hauptscharführer* Berger. The Russians gave this vehicle trophy number 135, and it was examined by their trophy team on 23 February 1945. ASKM

A close-up of the same *Tiger* (trophy number 135) showing the entry hole of the 76mm round that penetrated the turret. The shell also caused damage to the engine deck. ASKM

SS-Hauptsturmführer Ther giving his first address during a *Kompanie* parade on 12 February 1945 near Fehervarcsurgo. BARTH

Another view of *SS-Hauptsturmführer* Ther at the same parade. Ther had been transferred on 22 December 1944 from *SS-Panzer-Regiment 1*, where he had served as the transport officer during the Ardennes offensive. Before being put in command of *9. Kompanie*, Ther had served in the *Stabs.Kp.* of *IV-SS-Panzer-Korps*.
BARTH

SS-Obersturmführer Helmut Neff at the same parade.

Tiger I from *9. Kompanie* (trophy number 308a). Extensive research shows that this *Tiger* was lost on 17 March 1945. It had large amounts of mud on the wheels and tracks, suggesting that it was bogged down and the Russians pulled the vehicle out of the mud. The right side of the *Tiger* had been hit during an attempt to destroy it. It was commanded by *SS-Hauptsturmführer* Ther. ASKM

A *9. Kompanie Tiger I* (trophy number 208) lost on 16 March 1945. This time the Russians moved the *Tiger* to a collection site on the southern edge of Szekefehervar.

Tiger I (trophy number 205) in the same collection site. This Tiger was one of two *Tigers* lost near Felso Major on 16 March 1945.

A series of modern photographs of the Ofenbach/LanzenKirchen, through which the *Panzer Werkstatt Kompanie* of *SS-Panzer-Regiment 3* retreated on 1 April 1945.

Looking east from Ofenbach. MARKUS REISNER

Entrance to Ofenbach. The red car is parked where a *Tiger I* was abandoned due to engine trouble on 1 April 1945. MARKUS REISNER

Looking west from Ofenbach toward Lanzenkirchen. It was down this road that elements of *SS-Panzer-Regiment 3* retreated—mainly the infantry battle groups from *I* and *II/SS-Panzer-Regiment 3* and the *Pz.WerkSt.Kp.* from *SS-Panzer-Regiment 3*. MARKUS REISNER

The terrain facing north. Lanzenkirchen is on the left, Ofenbach on the right.
MARKUS REISNER

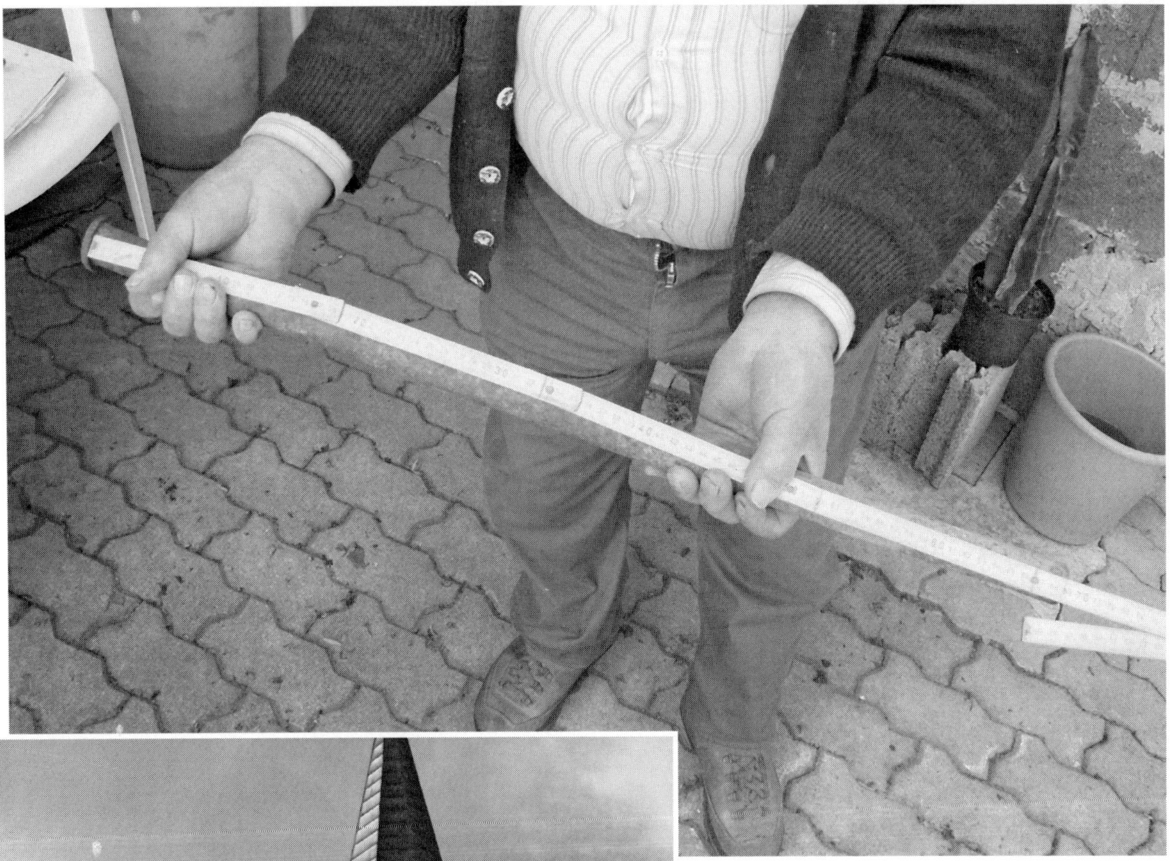

A track link from an abandoned *Tiger I* belonging to *9. Kompanie*, in Wienzierl am Walde. A local farmer holds the link pin.
DIETRICH WOLF

The estate car shows the position of the first *Tiger I* to break down in Wienzierl am Walde, next to the church.
DIETRICH WOLF

The second Tiger also broke down due to technical damage and was abandoned by the crew on a side street in Wienzierl am Walde. DIETRICH WOLF

This building is located on the south side of the Krems freight rail yard. It was here that *SS-Unterscharfürer* van Kerkhom and his crew abandoned the *Tiger II* and proceeded back into Krems on foot, 8 May 1945. DIETRICH WOLF

This series shows *3. SS-Panzer-Division Totenkopf* assembling on the last day of the war in the area between Burbach and Greisinghof, about four kilometers southeast of Pregarten. These stunning shots were taken by a member of the Pfahnl family, which owns the mill that can be seen in some of the photographs. The photos were kindly provided by Margarette Pfahnl via Herr Hollwirth, Pregarten.

EPILOGUE

After the capitulation, Wolfgang Barth spent two years in an American POW camp in Regensburg. He had to rebuild his life and start all over again, but over the following years, he began to search out and find former members of *9. Kompanie*. In fact, he found his first three former comrades in the Regensburg camp. He formed the company's veterans association, which had its first meeting in 1959; sixteen veterans attended. The association met every two years until 1990, when it started meeting every year until 1995, when the last association meeting occurred. After that, many veterans had died, but the circle of friends still kept in touch with Barth, who remained at the center of contact. Barth had also assembled a vast collection of personal accounts and reports, which he kept in a sort of *9. Kompanie* archive. It represents the sum total experience of over 250 men who fought in a war which caused much devastation.

APPENDIX A

Killed in Action

SS-Sturmmann Koshik (first name not known), *Werkstatt* platoon, crushed to death on 20 February 1943 by a maintenance vehicle with a mounted portal crane in Poltawa.

Driver of *SS-Untersturmführer* Rinner's *Tiger*, drowned during a river crossing near Pereschtschepino on 22 February 1943.

SS-Unterscharführer Fritz Hackl, tank commander, killed by Russian partisans near Olschani, 10 March 1943.

SS-Hauptsturmführer Alois Mooslechner, company commander and tank commander, killed by faulty ammunition inside his *Tiger*, 19 March 1943.

SS-Untersturmführer August Rinner, former platoon leader and tank regiment adjutant, 21 March 1943.

SS-Unterscharführer Richard Muller, tank commander, Kosliki, 7 July 1943.

SS-Scharführer Zimmermann (first name not known), loader, Kosliki, 7 July 1943.

SS-Unterscharführer Josef Gockl, tank commander, Wisloje-Ternowka, 8 July 1943.

SS-Rottenführer Ludwig Muller, gunner, Wisloje-Ternowka, 8 July 1943.

SS-Obersturmführer Wilhelm Schroder, company commander and tank commander, Wassiloje, 8 July 1943.

SS-Untersturmführer Walter Kohler, company commander and tank Commander, 12 July 1943.

SS-Sturmmann Mathai (first name not known), driver, Hill 213.9, Mius Front, 30 July 1943.

SS-Sturmmann Gunter Groner, radio operator, Hill 213.9, Mius Front, 30 July 1943.

SS-Scharführer Schweitzer (first name not known), radio operator, Hill 213.9, Mius Front, 31 July 1943.

SS-Oberscharführer Lampert (first name not known), tank commander, Hill 213.9, Mius Front, 31 July 1943.

SS-Sturmmann Norbert Kochesser, gunner, Hill 213.9, Mius Front, 31 July 1943.

SS-Sturmmann Gunther Schreyer, loader, Mius Front, 1 August 1943.

SS-Untersturmführer Heinz Schussler, company commander and platoon leader, Mius Front, 2 August 1943.

SS-Unterscharführer Fein (first name not known), tank commander, Walki, 12 August 1943.

SS-Oberscharführer Franz Hofer, loader, Walki, 12 August 1943.

SS-Sturmmann Olitzka (first name not known), gunner, Walki, 12 August 1943.

Blockert (rank and first name not known), radio operator, Walki, 12 August 1943.

SS-Scharführer Rudolf Liepack, post not known, Kolontajew, 25 August 1943.

SS-Untersturmführer Heinz Quade, company commander/platoon leader/tank commander, Hill 308, 30 August 1943.

SS-Sturmmann Ernst Vogler, radio operator, Kolontajew, 30 August 1943.

Hans Ludwig Bachmann (rank not known), driver, Kolontajew, 30 August 1943.

SS-Oberscharführer Willi Muller, tank commander, Stepanowka, 3 September 1943.

SS-Sturmmann Ferdinand Boxleitner, loader, Stepanowka, 3 September 1943.

SS-Scharführer Karl Rechlin, driver, Charkow, 4 September 1943.

Karl Eberl (rank not known), Charkow, 8 September 1943.

SS-Hauptsturmführer Waldemar Baedke, company commander/tank commander, Iwanowka, 11 March 1944.

SS-Sturmmann Alois Mucke, radio operator, Iwanowka, 11 March 1944.

SS-Rottenführer Herman Mocnik, gunner, Balta, 27 March 1944.

SS-Rottenführer Gunther (first name not known), radio operator, Balta, 27 March 1944.

SS-Untersturmführer Walter Wenzel, platoon leader/tank commander, executed by Russian forces, Adamowicze, 17 July 1944.

SS-Unterscharführer Adolf Siebnhaler, tank driver, executed by Russian forces, Adamowicze, 17 July 1944.

SS-Sturmmann Fritz Lau, tank gunner, executed by Russian forces, Adamowicze, 17 July 1944.

SS-Sturmmann Theodor Metzger, loader, executed by Russian forces, Adamowicze, 17 July 1944.

SS-Sturmmann Heinz Bartl, vehicle driver, killed during a Russian air strike near Sopockinie, 19 July 1944.

SS-Hauptsturmführer Hans Fischer, company commander, died from wounds in Lojku, 20 July 1944.

SS-Sturmmann Walter Steinau, radio operator, Warsaw, 1 August 1944.

SS-Oberscharführer Emil Weitner, tank commander, Krusze, 19 August 1944.

SS-Sturmmann Christian Schmidt, tank radio operator, Krusze, 19 August 1944.

SS-Sturmmann Hermann Meier, tank driver, Krusze, 19 August 1944.

SS-Unterscharführer Willy Kronmuller, tank commander, near Klembow, eight kilometers east of Radzymin, 26 August 1944.

SS-Rottenführer Franz von Berg, radio operator, near Klembow, eight kilometers east of Radzymin, 26 August 1944.

SS-Hauptsturmführer Rolf Neidhardt, former company commander, 1 September 1944.

SS-Unterscharführer Willi Probst, tank commander, Hill 104, one kilometer west of Slupno, 13 September 1944.

SS-Sturmmann Hubert Laux, radio operator, Hill 103, two kilometers west of Rembelszczyzna, 16 September 1944.

SS-Sturmmann Walter Lucht, tank driver, Hill 103, two kilometers west of Rembelszczyzna, 16 September 1944.

SS-Rottenführer Walter Kowalski, gunner, Hill 103, two kilometers west of Rembelszczyzna, 16 September 1944.

SS-Sturmmann Walter Weber, Hill 104, 16 September 1944.

SS-Sturmmann Hans Kautz, cook, Jablonna, 10 October 1944.

SS-Oberscharführer Harry Wendt, tank commander, Jablonna, 10 October 1944.

SS-Rottenführer Otto Koppen, tank gunner, Jablonna, 10 October 1944.

SS-Sturmbannführer Fritz Beiermeier, former company commander, near Modlin, 11 October 1944.

SS-Rottenführer Josef Hodap, maintenance section, Legionowo, 12 October 1944.

SS-Sturmmann Richard Priess, maintenance section, Jablonna, 12 October 1944.

SS-Rottenführer Georg Preisendanz, truck driver, died of wounds, 24 October 1944.

SS-Oberjunker Rudiger Blau, platoon leader and tank commander, Bajna, 3 January 1945.

SS-Scharführer Hugo Rose, truck driver, near Agard, 22 January 1945.

SS-Sturmmann Etmayer (first name not known), radio operator, Baracska, 26 January 1945.

SS-Sturmmann Karl Dietz, driver, Baracska, 26 January 1945.

SS-Oberscharführer Karl Bauer, commander of the recovery platoon, near Sarkeresztes, 18 March 1945.

SS-Rottenführer Paul Hoffmann, maintenance section, Mor, 18 March 1945.

SS-Sturmmann Karl Rettinger, loader, along the Mor–Kisber road, 20 March 1945.

SS-Sturmmann Herbert Gocht, Pereszteg, 30 March 1945.

SS-Unterscharführer Adolf Sperner, tank commander, Pereszteg, 30 March 1945.

SS-Rottenführer Johannan Weber, radio operator, Vienna, 10 April 1945.

SS-Scharführer Josef Ritschl, truck driver, Stockerau, 13 April 1945.

APPENDIX B

Tank Deliveries

10 *Panzer III* (*lang*—5.0cm L/60 main gun). Delivered 1 January 1943 in Fallingbostal.

9 *Tigers*. Collected on 30 January 1943; delivered on 7 February 1943, in Fallingbostal.

5 *Tigers*. Sent 13 May 1943; arrived on 20 May 1943.

3 issued via *Panzer-Ausbildungs-Abteilung 500* in Paderborn, F.Nr. 494670 Panzer.K 845.

2 issued via *Panzer.Ausbildungs-Abteilung 500* in Paderborn, F.Nr. 494670 Panzer.K 846.

1 *Befehls Tiger*. Sent on 11 May 1943 from HZA Magdeburg/Konigsborn to Paderborn, F.Nr 430064 Panzer.K 844.

8 *Tigers*. Taken over from *SS-Panzer-Regiment 1* on 29 July 1943 in Artemowsk.

5 *Tigers*. Sent 20 September 1943 (Zug.Nr. 334). Arrived on 3 October 1943 in Protopopowka. Included in this shipment is 1 *Befehlstiger*, issued via *Nachschub Ost*, *Heeresgruppe Süd*.

9 *Tigers*. Arrive in Bacau on 6 May 1944 (Zug.Nr. 958 with 3 Tigers and Zug.Nr. 525 with 6 Tigers).

4 to *III/Panzer-Regiment Großdeutschland*

4 to *9. Kompanie/SS-Panzer-Regiment 3*

1 reissued to *schwere Panzer-Abteilung 505*, but the transport is diverted to Roman

4 *Tigers*. Arrived in Bacau on 19 May 1944 (Zug.Nr. 613), but the transport is forwarded to Roman and unloaded on 20 May. Transport had left Germany on 3 May and became stuck near Siebenburgen for about fourteen days due to an RAF bombing raid.

6 *Tigers*. Sent 17 May 1944 (Zug.Nr. 612). Arrived in Bacau on 31 May. These Tigers had originally belonged to *schwere SS-Panzer-Abteilung 103*. The tanks are collected at HZA Magdeburg by a collection party consisting of thirty men who had left Romania on 15 May 1944.

6 *Tigers*. Sent on 18 May 1944 and arrive in Bacau on the 7 June 1944 (Zug.Nr. 615). Of these, 2 are collected by crews from *9. Kompanie*. The Tigers are part of a shipment meant for *III/Panzer-Regiment Großdeutschland*. By order of *Heeresgruppe Süd*, *SS-Panzer-Regiment 3* is instructed to hand them over on 11 June. *SS-Panzer-Regiment 3* informs *Heeresgruppe Süd* that a collection party from *Panzer-Regiment Großdeutschland* had collected the 2 tanks the same day.

5 *Tigers*. Sent 26 July 44 (Panzer.K 1007), Transport Nr. 594-142. Arrived in Lochow on 31 July. These tanks form a 4th Platoon within the company. A collection party of twenty-five men left Romania on the 7 July 1944.

1 *Tiger II* collected from the Vienna arsenal on 3 April 1945. The tank is commanded by *SS-Unterscharführer* van Kerkhom. It had a Porsche turret with a new main gun and a two-piece gun mantlet. It also had new tracks and track guards.

APPENDIX C

Tiger Losses, 1943–45

4. (s) Kompanie

During the fighting between February and March 1943, *4(s) Kompanie* lost three Tigers. All three were recovered and sent to Dnepropetrovsk for major long-term repairs and returned to service on 10 May 1943. The first *Tiger*, commanded by *SS-Untersturmführer* Rinner, broke through the ice on a frozen river near Pereschtschepino on 22 February 1943 and was recovered on 27 February. Two *Tigers* were lost on 8 March 1943: *SS-Untersturmführer* Kohler's, which sank in the river, and *SS-Untersturmführer* Rathsack's, which bogged down in the river embankment; the tanks were eventually recovered in April 1943.

9. Kompanie

7 July 1943 One *Tiger* (*SS-Oberscharführer* Muller) destroyed after being hit by Russian artillery fire east of the main road between Belgorod and Kursk near the Village of Smorordino.

31 July 1943 Two *Tigers* (*SS-Oberscharführer* Lampert, *SS-Unterscharführer* Bieber) knocked out by Russian antitank gunfire near Hill 213.9. Both blown up on 7 August 1943 by a demolition team.

12 August 1943 One *Tiger* (*SS-Unterscharführer* Fein) knocked out near Kosliki by Russian antitank gunfire.

30 August 1943 One *Tiger* (*SS-Unterscharführer* Privatski) is destroyed by a direct hit from Russian artillery near Kolontajew.

12 December 1943 Seven *Tigers* returned to Germany for factory maintenance.

16 January 1944 Four *Tigers* (*SS-Untersturmführer* Neff, *SS-Unterscharführer* Pavlu, and *SS-Unterscharführer* Heurich) knocked out by U.S. Lend-Lease antitank guns (probably 90mm) in Russian service during an attack from the direction of Petrowka in the open terrain. The *Tigers* were attacking toward Hill 215.6 just north of Owskanikowka.

23 March 1944 One *Tiger* being transported by rail back to Germany from Odessa for factory maintenance is captured along with two other *Tigers* from *schwere Panzer-Abteilung 503* in the rail station of Kopychinsty.

26 March 1944 One *Tiger* (*SS-Oberscharführer* Tonges) captured intact by the 81st Guards Rifle Regiment just north of Balta during a local counterattack. The *Tiger* had to be abandoned by the crew.

27 March 1944 One *Tiger* (*SS-Untersturmführer* Neff) attached to *Kampfgruppe Pitschellis* is knocked out by Russian antitank gunfire just of south of Balta.

30 March 1944 One *Tiger* (*SS-Oberscharführer* Weitner) is abandoned by the crew after running out of fuel on the southern edge of Balta. The *Tiger* is later found intact by the Russian 73rd Rifle Regiment.

2 April 1944 Seven *Tigers* blown up at the rail station of Rozdil'na (Rasdelnaja) on the orders of *SS-Untersturmführer* Neff. The rail transport carrying these tanks had come to a halt in Rozdil'na along with thirty other rail transports. A *Wehrmacht* officer of the General Staff approached Neff next to the main station building and ordered him to blow up his *Tigers* since the Russians were not far away and further travel in the direction of Tiraspol was now considered very difficult. The *Tigers* are blown up, and Neff and the remaining crews gather their belongings and begin a fifty-kilometer march in the direction of Tiraspol. One other transport that had departed Rozdil'na earlier reached Tiraspol carrying one *Tiger*, one *Panzer-Beobachters-Wagen III*, and one *Befehlswagen Panzer III*. Rozdil'na is captured by the Red Army on 4 April 1944.

11 June 1944 Six *Tigers* delivered on 7 June 1944. Two are collected by soldiers from *9. Kompanie*. On 11 June 1944, *Heeres-Gruppe Süd* orders *Totenkopf* to hand them over to *III/Panzer-Regiment Großdeutschland*. *Totenkopf* reports that a collection team from *III/Panzer-Regiment Großdeutschland* had taken over the two *Tigers* on 11 June 1944 and that they had been loaded on the same day.

17 July 1944 One *Tiger* (*SS-Untersturmführer* Wenzel) is hit multiple times by Russian antitank gunfire, immobilizing the tank in Adamowicze. Russian troops rush forward and drag the crew out of the tank. Four members of the crew are executed; the radio operator (Rudolf) is taken prisoner. The *Tiger* remains in Adamowicze for three days. On 20 July 1944, German forces stage a local counterattack and retake the stricken Tiger; per orders, it is soaked in petrol inside and out and set on fire. Radio operator Rudolf is not seen again until the 1968 company veterans meeting in Fallingbostal.

19 August 1944 Three *Tigers* (*SS-Untersturmführer* Weitner, *SS-Unterscharführer* Sandler, and *SS-Untersturmführer* Neff) are knocked out or immobilized by JS-2 heavy tanks from the 62nd Guards Heavy Tank Regiment during the fighting 1.5 kilometers southeast of Krusze. One *Tiger* is hit on the left side of the hull, and another round hits the turret at a range of 1,000 meters. Another *Tiger* is hit twice; both rounds hit the front of the hull. The third *Tiger* is immobilized and abandoned by the crew. The two *Tigers* knocked out by JS-2 tank fire are given trophy numbers 123 and 124. All three losses are recorded on the same day by *A.O.K. 9*.

26 August 1944 One *Tiger* (*SS-Oberscharführer* Kronmuller) is knocked out by Russian antitank gunfire near Klembow, eight kilometers east of Radzymin. This loss is recorded by *A.O.K. 9* on 30 August.

13 September 1944 One *Tiger* (*SS-Unterscharführer* Probst) is destroyed by a direct hit from Russian artillery fire near Hill 104, one kilometer west of Slupno.

16 September 1944 One *Tiger* (*SS-Untersturmführer* Neff) is hit and knocked out by Russian artillery fire near Hill 103, two kilometers west of Rembelszczyzna, while in support of *III/SS-Panzer-Grenadier-Regiment 6 Eicke* and *2./SS-Panzer-Jäger-Abteilung 3*.

6 January 1945 A *Tiger* is knocked out by Russian antitank fire in the open terrain just west of Hill 289, next to the Szomor and Zsambek road at a range of fifty meters. Another (*SS-Obersturmführer* Wenke) receives multiple hits to the front and turret sides. Another advances past the two stricken *Tigers* and provides covering fire. *Tiger 901* (Wenke) is recovered and sent to Vienna for long-term repairs. This *Tiger* is captured on 9 April 1945 while still at the arsenal. *SS-Unterscharführer* Privatski's *Tiger* is knocked out by Russian anti-tank gun fire just to the north of the Many-Zsambek road junction, the *Tiger* took several direct hits to the right side of the hull and chassis and at least one hit to the front of the Tiger.

24 January 1945 One *Tiger* (*SS-Unterscharführer* Becker) is knocked out 1.5 kilometer west of Pettend. It is struck by an 85mm round on the front bow plate; another 85mm round hits the right side track. The crew is forced to bail out. The Russians give this *Tiger* trophy number 60 and examined it on 11 February 1945.

26 January 1945 One *Tiger* (*SS-Hauptscharführer* Berger) is knocked out on the northern edge of Baracska by a direct hit from a 76mm antitank round, which hits the left side of the turret and causes damage to the engine deck; one other round hits the front bow plate but does not penetrate the interior. The *Tiger* is examined on 23 February 1945 by Russian forces and given trophy number 135.

16 March 1945 Two *Tigers* (*SS-Untersturmführer* Neff, *SS-Oberscharführer* Bernhardt) are knocked out by multiple hits from SU-76 self-propelled guns from the 1523rd Self-Propelled Artillery Regiment next to Felso Puszta, which is about 1.5 kilometers northeast of Magyaralmas. Both had been posted there on security duty on the 6 March 1945.

17 March 1945 One *Tiger* (*SS-Hauptsturmführer* Ther) becomes bogged down in a field 1,000 meters northeast of Magyaralmas, and about 200 meters from Felso Puszta, Ther sends the radio operator back to Magyaralmas to find a *Berge-Panther* to aid in the recovery of the sunken *Tiger*. During the attempted recovery, Ther is forced to abandon the tank as the attacking Russian infantry close in. Ther made it back to Magyaralmas, found another *Tiger*, and ordered the commander to destroy the immobilized *Tiger*. One round is fired into the rear of the stuck tank, but much to the surprise of all, the round bounces off the rear. Ther reported the event to *SS-Sturmbannführer* Berlin, regimental commander. Ther recalled that Berlin's reaction was not positive. The three *Tigers* found near Magyaralmas were given trophy numbers 205, 208, and 308a.

30 March 1945 One *Tiger* (*SS-Unterscharführer* Sperner) destroyed during the withdrawal from Pereszteg on a back road leading to Nagycenk by SU-100 self-propelled guns from the 912th Self Propelled Artillery Regiment. The *Tiger* is hit several times, causing it to burst into flames.

1 April 1945 One *Tiger* (*SS-Unterscharführer* Privatski) is abandoned in Ofenbach on the road leading to Lanzenkirchen after sustaining mechanical damage. The crew is forced to make an escape across the fields in the direction of Frohsdorf as Russian forces suddenly appear in Ofenbach, catching the Germans by surprise. The crew's personal effects are left inside the tank. Later, local children empty the *Tiger* of about twenty-five 88mm shells and attempt to set fire to the ammunition in the hope they would go off—nothing happened, but the local children did find several *Panzerfaust*, which they started firing in the woods, causing Russians to return and investigate. During the recovery of this tank for scrap, the Russians towed it through Lanzenkirchen, where a local resident was knocked down and killed after losing a leg.

9 April 1945 One *Tiger* captured at the Vienna arsenal while still undergoing long-term repair. (See entry for 6 January 1945.)

8 May 1945 Three *Tigers* (*SS-Oberscharführer* Tassler, *SS-Oberscharführer* Wimmer, and *SS-Oberscharführer* Tonges) abandoned: one on the road from Stixendorf to Wienzierl am Walde next to a road side shrine just outside Wienzierl am Walde, the other two (plus an *SPW*) in the center of Wienzierl am Walde. The Germans had attempted to blow up the *SPW*, which caught fire. During this attempt, Wimmer's driver, Helmut Brieger, was seriously wounded and rushed to the hospital in Melk after Ludwig Buss and Horst Bottcher pulled Brieger from the danger zone. The local fire brigade had to be called out as the *SPW* (which was blown up next to the parish vicar's house) was by now a raging fire. The remaining crews travel in the direction of Friestadt. After the war, the locals recounted that the Russians had huge problems trying to tow the two *Tigers* in the center of Wienzierl am Walde. One was abandoned next to the local church on a narrow side road, blocking road traffic for some time.

8 May 1945 One *Tiger II* with Porsche turret (*SS-Unterscharführer* van Kerkhom) abandoned on the southern side of the Frachten Bahnhof Krems. Van Kerkhom and his crew left the tank and walked back into Krems and spent the night before being captured the next morning by the Russians. In July of the same year, a Russian cutting crew began work on scrapping the tank. As they began doing so, one of the Russians cut through the fuel tank with his cutting torch, not realizing that tank still had fuel in it. He blew himself up along with two others.

APPENDIX D

Operational Figures

1943 (*4. (s) Panzer-Kompanie* and *9. Panzer-Kompanie*)

February
10 Loading on rail transport s takes place in Fallingbostal
16 First transport arrives in Poltawa
17 Second transport arrives in Poltawa
19 9
21 9
23 9
27 9
28 9

March
1 9
2 6 (3 *Tigers* in short term repair; 6 new engines arrive)
3 6
4 6
5 6
6 6
10 5 (6 *Tigers* reported ready for action in the morning)
11 6 (3 *Tigers* in long-term repair)
13 3
14 3
15 3
16 3
17 4
18 3
19 1
20 1 (3 *Tigers* later reported as operational)
21 1
22 1
23 0
24 2
25 2
26 1
27 2

April
1 2
2 2
3 2
4 1
5 0
6 2
7 2
8 1
9 1
10 1
11 1
12 1
13 0
14 0
15 0
16 0
17 1
18 1
19 1
20 4
30 4

May
1 4 (2 *Tigers* in long-term repair)
4 4
10 10
20 11(12 *Tigers* reported later as being operational)

June
1 10 (2 *Tigers* in short-term repair, 3 *Tigers* in long-term repair)
2 10
3 10
4 10
5 10
10 10 (2 *Tigers* in short-term repair, 3 *Tigers* in long-term repair)
20 10 (2 *Tigers* in short-term repair, 3 *Tigers* in long-term repair)

29 10
30 10 (2 *Tigers* in short-term repair, 3 *Tigers* in long-term repair)

July

1 10 (2 *Tigers* in short-term repair, 3 *Tigers* in long-term repair)
2 11 (2 *Tigers* in short-term repair, 3 *Tigers* in long-term repair)
3 11
4 12
5 10
6 6
7 6
8 5
9 2
10 11 (1 *Tiger* in short-term repair, 2 *Tigers* in long-term repair)
11 10 (2 *Tigers* in short-term repair, 2 *Tigers* in long-term repair)
12 10 (3 *Tigers* in short-term repair, 1 *Tiger* in long-term repair)
13 0
14 5
15 7
16 9
17 7 (A new delivery of spare parts arrives by air transport in Charkow-Woltschanka. The parts had been sent from HZA Magdeburg and sent to *Pz.Inst.Abt.* (Panzer Replacement Battalion) *555* for storage. *9. Kompanie* organizes a collection party so the parts can be collected)
18 7
19 4
20 5
22 Loading in Charkow for redeployment on the Mius Front. Departure on 24th
28 Unloading takes place.
28 5
29 9
30 8
31 1

August

1 10
2 3
3 0
4 0
5 0
6 0
7 Loading on rail transports commences for redeployment back to the Charkow Front.
8 Departure movement by rail.
9 Unloading in Charkow and road march toward Walki
10 2
11 6
12 6
15 3
17 6
20 5
21 5
22 5
24 5
26 3
27 0
28 0
29 2
30 2
31 2 (another report states only 1 *Tiger* operational)

September

1 2 (9 *Tigers* in short-term repair)
2 2
3 0
4 1
10 4
19 3
20 3
21–30 All *Tigers* in for repair

October

1 5 (3 *Tigers* in short-term repair)
3 0
4 5
5 5 (17 *Tigers* in short-term repair, 1 *Tiger* in long-term repair)
6 6
7 6
8 4
9 4
10 2

11 2
12 2
13 2
14 2
15 2
16 2
17 2
18 2
19 3
20 4
21 6
22 4
23 4
24 5
25 3
26 3
27 8
28 8
29 4
30 4
31. 4

November

1 4 (7 *Tigers* in short-term repair)
2 4
3 4
5 5
6 5
7 4
8 3
9 3
10 3
11 4
14 5 (6 *Tigers* are reported operational later in the day)
15 0 (at 1750 hrs, 1 *Tiger* reported operational)
16 1 (another 3 *Tigers* returned to service, making a total of 4 *Tigers* operational)
17 0
18 0
19 1
20 1
21 1
22 1
23 1
24 1
25 1
26 1
27 1
28 1
29 1
30 1

December

1 1 (11 *Tigers* in short-term repair, 11 *Tigers* in long-term repair)
2 1
3 1
4 1
5 2
6 2
7 2
8 2
9 2
10 2
11–18 All *Tigers* are in for repairs
19 2
20 2
21 2
22 1
23 1
24 1
25 1
26 2
27 2
28 2
29 0
30 0
31 2 (8 *Tigers* in short-term repair, 6 *Tigers* in long-term repair) New delivery of engines for *9. Kompanie*

1944 (*9. Kompanie*)

January

1 2 (8 *Tigers* in short-term repair, 6 *Tigers* in long-term repair)
2 3
3 3
4 3 (4 *Tigers* in short-term repair, 4 *Tigers* in long-term repair with division, 4 *Tigers* in long-term repair with Army Group South maintenance units)
5 3

6 2 (4 *Tigers* in short-term repair, 5 *Tigers* in long-term with division, 5 *Tigers* in long-term repair with Army Group South maintenance units)
7 3
8 2 (5 *Tigers* in short-term repair, 4 *Tigers* in long-term repair with division, 5 *Tigers* in long-term repair with Army Group South maintenance units)
9 3 (6 new engines arrive for *9. Kompanie*)
10 2 (5 *Tigers* in short-term repair, 4 *Tigers* in long-term repair with division, 5 *Tigers* in long-term repair with Army Group South maintenance units)
16 5
17 5
18 5
19 5
20 1
21 1
26 1
27 1
28 1
29 4
30 4
31 4

February
1 4 (3 *Tigers* in short-term repair)
2 4
3 6
5 6
21 4
26 4
27 4
28 3
29 4

March
1 4 (5 *Tigers* in short-term repair)
2 4
3 4
4 4
5 4
7 4
9 4
10 4
11 4
12 4
13 4 (loading for redeployment on rail transports in Nowo Ukrainka and Kapistino in the direction of Balta)
16 4 (*9. Kompanie* unloaded in Balta)
17 4
18 4
19 4
23 3
24 2
25 1
26 3
24 3
28 0
30 1
31 1

April
1 1
2 1 (*9. Kompanie* moves from Dubossary by road; 1 rail transport leaves Wessely Kut for Rasdelnaja at 1435 hrs with 1 *Tiger*, 1 *Pz.Bef.Wg III* and a *Pz.Beo.Wg III*. The second transports with 7 *Tigers*, including 1 command *Tiger*, moves from Iwanowka via Wessely Kut to Rasdelnaja, where it is stopped.)
3 The company moves to Kishinew, where it spends about 6 days
6 1
7 1
8 1
9 1
10 1 (March to Lapusna)
11 0 (Move into the area of Negresti)
12 Assembly in the area of Husi/Krassna and Vaslui in readiness for rail transport
13 Rail transport to Roman
14 Arrival in Bacau
15 1
16 1
17 1
18 1
19 1
20 0

May

1 0
2 1
3 1
6 0
7 0
8 0
9 0
10 0
31 2

June

1 2 (5 *Tigers* in short-term repair)
5 2
6 2
7 8
8 8
9 8
10 8
11 8
12 8
13 8
14 8
15 8
16 9
17 9
18 9
19 9
20 9
21 9
22 9
23 9
24 9
25 9
26 9
27 9
28 9
29 9
30 9

July

1 9 (1 *Tiger* in short-term repair)
2 9
3 9
4 9
5 9
6 9
7 9
8 9 (*9. Kompanie* is loaded onto rail transports in Roman)
15 Elements of *9. Kompanie* unloaded (*Zug.Nr 614108*) in Orlowicze
15 6
16 10
17 10
18 10
19 9
20 4
21 2
22 4
23 3
24 4
25 6 (With *A.O.K. 4*)
26 1 (With *A.O.K. 2*)
5 (With *A.O.K. 4*)
27 6 (With *A.O.K. 4*)
28 6 (With *A.O.K. 4*)
29 6 (With *A.O.K. 2*)

Move from *A.O.K. 4* to *A.O.K. 2*; 4 *Tigers* arrive in Osowiec on the 25th for rail transport to Sokolow; 3 *Tigers* are loaded and 1 *Tiger* is left behind at the rail station in Osowiec; the 3 *Tigers* arrive on 26th in Sokolow; 1 *Tiger* enters Siedlce at 1950 hrs; 2 other *Tigers* leave Sokolow at 2205 hrs for Siedlce; the remaining *Tiger* is forced on 3 August to conduct a road march in order to rejoin *9. Kompanie*

On the 26th, 5 other *Tigers* are still in action 5 km east of Dabrowa supporting *III/SS.Pz.Gr.Rgt. 6 "Eicke"* at 0540 am; these *Tigers* were due to be loaded in Osowiec on the 27th. On the 28th, the *Panzer WerkStatt.Kp.* is loaded in Osowiec at 1515 hrs with 2 damaged *Tigers* and is unloaded in Sokolow on the 3th. On the 29th, 5 more *Tigers* are loaded in Osowiec at 0530.hrs and arrive in Sokolow and are unloaded at 1725 hrs; another rail transport with 3 *Tigers* leaves Osowiec at 2230 hrs and is diverted to Warsaw due to the combat situation and arrives in Warsaw at 2325 hrs but is not unloaded until the 31st.

30 1
31 1 (2 *Tigers* in Warsaw, 6 *Tigers* west of Siedlce)

August
1 1 (7 *Tigers* in Warsaw)
2 1 (7 *Tigers* in Warsaw, 4 *Tigers* at the Stauffer barracks, 1 *Tiger* in Osowiec)
3 2 (7 *Tigers* in Warsaw; orders issued that all *Tigers* from *9. Kompanie* under repair are to be evacuated from Warsaw by the 6th)
4 3 (7 *Tigers* in Warsaw)
5 1 (7 *Tigers* in Warsaw)
6 3 (7 *Tigers* in Warsaw)
7 4 (7 *Tigers* in Warsaw)
8 4 (7 *Tigers* in Warsaw, 3 *Tigers* in short-term repair, 3 *Tigers* on the road returning to the *Panzer* regiment)
9 2 (3 *Tigers* reported in short-term repair)
10 2 (3 *Tigers* reported in short-term repair)
11 2 (3 *Tigers* reported in short-term repair)
12 4 (6 *Tigers* in Warsaw, 1 *Tiger* on the road returning to the *Panzer* regiment)
13 4 (1 *Tiger* reported in short-term repair)
14 4 (2 *Tigers* remaining in Warsaw)
15 4 (1 *Tiger* reported in short-term repair)
16 4 (2 *Tigers* in Warsaw, 6 *Tigers* in short-term repair, 1 *Tiger* in long-term repair)
17 4 (6 *Tigers* in short-term repair, 1 *Tiger* in long-term repair)
18 4 (6 *Tigers* in short-term repair, 1 *Tiger* in long-term repair)
19 3
20 3
21 3
22 4
23 4
24 7
26 6
27 6
29 7
30 6
31 3

September
1 6 (6 *Tigers* in long-term repair)
2 3
3 6
4 3
6 4
7 4
9 6
10 6
11 6
12 5
13 3
14 3
15 4
16 2
17 3
18 2
19 2
20 4
21 4
22 3
23 3
24 5
25 6
26 6
27 6
28 6
29 6
30 6

October
1 6
2 6
3 6
4 6
5 6
6 6
7 6
8 7
9 8
10 8
11 3
12 3
13 2
14 3
15 4
16 4
17 6
18 6
19 7
20 6
21 5

22 5
23 6
24 7
25 10
26 10
27 5
28 6
29 6
30 8
31 8

November

1 8 (2 *Tigers* in short-term repair)
2 8
3 8
4 8
5 8
6 10
7 8
8 8
9 8
10 9
11 10
12 10
13 10
14 10
15 10
16 10
17 10
18 11
19 11
20 11
21 10
22 10
23 10
24 9
25 9
26 9
27 9

December

1 10 (1 *Tiger* in short-term repair)
2 9
3 10
4 10
5 10
6 10
7 10
8 10
9 10
10 10
11 10
12 10
17 9
22 11
24 11
25 11
26 11 (Loading on rail transports for redeployment to Hungary; loading takes place in Nasielsk)
30 9 (*9. Kompanie* is unloaded in Komarom)
31 9

1945 (*9. Kompanie*)

January

1 9 (The divisional reports state 11 *Tigers* operational)
2 7
3 3
5 4
6 4
7 4
11 2
12 Relocation to Komarom for loading onto rail transport to Veszprem
13 4
15 2
16 4
17 4 (11 *Tigers* still in rail transit; they arrive late on the 17th; unloaded in Veszprem and move by road to the area of Berhida
18 4
19 4
20 2
21 2
22 1
23 1
24 1
25 2
26 1
27 1
28 1
29 1
30 1

February

1 2 (1 *Tiger* in short-term repair)
3 2
4 2
5 4
6 2
7 2
10 2
11 2
12 2
13 2 (5 *Tigers* in short-term repair, 2 *Tigers* on long-term repair at the Vienna Arsenal)
15 7
17 6
19 5 (2 *Tigers* in short-term repair, 2 *Tigers* in long-term repair at the Vienna Arsenal)
20 6
21 5
24 7
26 7

March

1 6 (1 *Tiger* in short-term repair)
2 6
3 6
4 6 (1 *Tiger* in short-term repair, 2 *Tigers* in long-term repair at the Vienna Arsenal)
5 7
6 6
7 7
10 7
11 7
15 7
16 5 (2 *Tigers* in short-term repair in Mor)
17 3 (2 *Tigers* in short-term in Mor evacuated from Mor)
18 2
21 2
22 1
23 1
24 2
25 2
26 1
27 2
30 2
31 2

April

1 2
2 1
3 1
4 1
5 2
6 3 (2 *Tigers* in the area of Judenau, 1 *Tiger* in Vienna)
7 2 (both defending Judenau)
8 2 (area of Langenrohr)
10 1 *Tiger II* in repair along with 2 *Tigers*
12 1 *Tiger* operational near the Reichs Bridge in Vienna
13 2
15 0
25 0

May

6 3 *Tigers* seen on the move in Stratzing
7 2 *Tiger I's* operational and 1 *Tiger II* operational
8 2 *Tigers* near Enns and 1 *Tiger II* in Krems

APPENDIX E

Soviet After-Action Report for 19–21 August 1944

During the three days the regiment fought against superior German tank forces during which Krusze was captured. By 19 August 1944, the regiment approached Krusze, and by 21 August 1944, the village had been captured, with the regiment operating from ambush positions. The regiment had to repel several enemy counterattacks, after which the enemy started operating in small groups in order to locate our positions and destroy our Josef Stalin tanks. Due to our constant moving of positions, the regiment managed to avoid significant losses and repel any German counterattacks and slowly advance toward Krusze.

German losses:
2 *Tigers* knocked out
20 *Panthers*
1 *Panther* captured intact

Our losses:
1 Josef Stalin tank destroyed, completely burnt out
2 Josef Stalin tanks severely damaged

Casualties:
2 dead and 12 wounded

To back up the Russian claims, listed below are the official total losses for the 9th German Army for the same period:

SS-Totenkopf—19 August 1944—3 *Tigers*
SS-Totenkopf—20 August 1944—4 *Panthers*
SS-Wiking—20 August 1944—18 *Panthers*

APPENDIX F

Rank Comparisons

U.S. ARMY	RUSSIAN ARMY	WAFFEN-SS	GERMAN ARMY
Enlisted Men			
Private	*Krasnoarmeyets*	*SS-Schütze*	*Schütze*
Private First Class		*SS-Oberschütze*	*Oberschütze*
Corporal	*Mladshiy Serzhant*	*SS-Sturmmann*	*Gefreiter*
Senior Corporal		*SS-Rottenführer*	*Obergefreiter*
Staff Corporal		*SS-Stabsrottenführer*	*Stabsgefreiter*
Noncommissioned Officers			
Sergeant	*Serzhant*	*SS-Unterscharführer*	*Unteroffizier*
		SS-Scharführer	*Unterfeldwebel*
Staff Sergeant		*SS-Oberscharführer*	*Feldwebel*
Sergeant First Class	*Starshiy Serzhant*	*SS-Hauptcharführer*	*Oberfeldwebel*
Master Sergeant		*SS-Sturmscharführer*	*Hauptfeldwebel*
Sergeant Major	*Starshina*		*Stabsfeldwebel*
Officers			
Second Lieutenant	*Mladshiy Leytenant*	*SS-Untersturmführer*	*Leutnant*
First Lieutenant	*Leytenant*	*SS-Obersturmführer*	*Oberleutnant*
Captain	*Kapitan*	*SS-Hauptsturmführer*	*Hauptman*
Major	*Major*	*SS-Sturmbannführer*	*Major*
Lieutenant Colonel	*Podpolkovnik*	*SS-Obersturmbannführer*	*Oberstleutnant*
Colonel	*Polkovnik*	*SS-Standartenführer*	*Oberst*
Brigadier General		*SS-Brigadeführer*	*Generalmajor*
Major General	*General Major*	*SS-Gruppenführer*	*Generalleutnant*
Lieutenant General	*General Leytenant*	*SS-Obergruppenführer*	*General der Fallschirmjäger, etc.*
General	*General Armii*	*SS-Oberstgruppenführer*	*Generaloberst*
General of the Army	*Marshal Sovetskogo Souza*	*Reichsführer-SS*	*Feldmarschall*

BIBLIOGRAPHY

Bacyk, Norbert. *Warsaw 2: The Battle for Praga: July–September 1944*. Stockholm, Sweden: Leandoer & Eckholm, 2009.

Brettner, Friedrich. *Die letzten Kämpfe des II. Weltkrieges im südlichen Niederösterreich*. Self-published, 1999.

Buchinger, Josef. *Das Ende des 1000 jährigen Reiches*. Vienna: Self-published, 1972.

Domanski, Jacek, and Janusz Ledwoch. *Wien 1945*. Wydawnictwo Militaria 243. Warsaw, Poland: Wydawnictwo Militaria, 2006.

Ebeling, Kurt. *Bis zur letzten Patrone*. Privately published.

Hinze, Rolf. *East Front Drama 1944*. Winnipeg, Canada: J. J. Fedorowicz, 1997.

Jentz, Thomas L., ed. *Panzertruppen: The Complete Guide to the Creation and Combat Employment of Germany's Tank Force*. Vol. 2. Atglen, PA: Schiffer, 1996.

Jentz, Thomas L., and Hilary Doyle. *Germany's Tiger Tanks: D.W. to Tiger I*. Atglen, PA: Schiffer, 2000.

Kleine, Egon, and Volkmar Kühn. *Tiger: The History of a Legendary Weapon, 1942–45*. Winnipeg, Canada: J. J. Fedorowicz, 2004.

Maier, Georg. *Drama between Budapest and Vienna: The Final Fighting of the 6th Panzer-Armee in the East, 1945*. Winnipeg, Canada: J. J. Fedorowicz, 2004.

Niepold, Gerd. *Battle for White Russia: The Destruction of Army Group Centre, June 1944*. Washington, DC: Brassey's Defece, 1987.

Nipe, George M. *Blood, Steel, and Myth: The II. SS-Panzer-Korps and the Road to Prochorowka, July 1943*. Stamford, CT: RZM Publishing, 2011.

———. *Decision in the Ukraine, Summer 1943: II. SS and III. Panzerkorps*. Winnipeg, Canada: J. J. Fedorowicz, 1996.

———. *Last Victory in Russia: The SS-Panzerkorps and Manstein's Kharkov Counteroffensive, February–March 1943*. Atglen, PA: Schiffer, 2000.

Rauchensteiner, Manfried. *Der Krieg in Österreich, 1945*. Vienna: Österreichischer Bundesverlag, 1984.

Solarz, Jacek. *Totenkopf, 1939–1943*. Wydawnictwo Militaria 290. Warsaw, Poland: Wydawnictwo Militaria, 2006.

Swirin, M., et al. *Budapest-Balaton 1945*. Wydawnictwo Militaria 246. Warsaw, Poland: Wydawictwo Militaria, 2006.

Sydnor, Charles W. *Soldiers of Destruction: The SS Death's Head Division, 1933–1945*. Princeton, NJ: Princeton University Press, 1977.

Trang, Charles. *Totenkopf*. Bayeux: Heimdal, 2006.

———. *Totenkopf Archives*. Bayeux: Heimdal, 2011.

Ullrich, Karl. *Like a Cliff in the Ocean: A History of the 3rd SS-Panzer-Division Totenkopf*. Winnipeg, Canada: J. J. Fedorowicz, 2003.

Ungváry, Krisztián. *Battle for Budapest: One Hundred Days in World War II*. London: I. B. Tauris, 2004.

Volkner, Werner. *Many Rivers I Crossed*. Self-published, 2004.

Vopersal, Wolfgang. *Soldaten-Kämpfer-Kameraden*. Osnabrück: Biblio Verlag.

Warnick, Rüdiger, and Stephan Cazenave. *Tiger! Von schwere Kompanie/SS-Pz.Rgt.2 bis s.SS-Panzerabteilung 102/502*. Bayeux: Heimdal, 2009.

Wroblewski, Robert, and Krzysztof Mucha. "Totenkopf Tigers in Poland." *Militaria XX* Wieku Nr. 1(5) (2008).

Zährl, Hugo. *Vier Jahre in vorderster Front: Kriegstagebuch eines Trägers der Ehrenblattspange der SS-Panzerdivision "Totenkopf"*. Osnabrück: Munin-Verlag, 2007.

Zetterling, Niklas, and Anders Frankson. *Kursk 1943: A Statistical Analysis*. London: Frank Cass, 2000.

Other Sources

BAMA

RH 14 Chef Heeresrustung und Bef.Ers.Heer
RH 11 Waffengenerale im OKH
RH 12-6 Inspektion der Panzer Truppen
RH-2 OKH/Gen.Std H
RH-2/1314 Starkeberechung SS.Pz.Gr.Div Totenkopf 1943
RH-2/1465 Zustandberichter der Waffen-SS 1.1.45–1.3.45
Org Sceme 3 SS.Pz.Div Totenkopf 1.2.45
Org Sceme 3 SS.Pz.Div Totenkopf 1.3.45

RH-10 Gen.Ins.d.Pz.Tr
RH 10/20
RH-10/22
RH-10/23
RH-10/25
RH-10/60
RH-10/61
RH-10/62
RH-10/63
RH-10/64
RH-10/69
RH-10/70
RH-10/71
RH-1072
RH-10/89
RH-10/90
RH-10/103
RH-10/109
RH-10/118
RH-10/314
RH-10/349
RH-10/350
I SS.Pz.Korps-Anhang zu KTB Nr 5, 10.4.43 bis 28.5.43

HGp Mitte (Part a)
RH 09 II/098
RH 09 II/099

HGp Sud Ukraine
RH 19-V25/HGp A 1.3.44–31.3.44
RH 19-V26/ HGp Sud Ukraine 1.4.44–30.4.44

Pz.A.O.K 1
RH 21-1/359
RH 21-1/361
RH 21-1/362
RH 21-1 363
RH 21-1/364
RH 21-1/365
RH 21-1/366
RH 21-1/368
RH 21-1/371

A.O.K 6
RH 20-6/507
RH 20-6/830
RH 20-6/831
RH 20-6/833
RH 20-6/836
RH 20-6/837
RH 20-6/907

A.O.K 8
RH 20-8/223
RH 20-8/225
RH 20-8/226
RH 20-8/227
RH 20-8/230

HGp Mitte (Part b)
RH 19II/198 Parts 1, 2, 3, and 4
RH 19II/199 Parts 1, 2, and 3
RH 19II/203
RH 19II/213
RH 19II/214
RH 19II/215
RH 19II/221
RH 19II/222
RH 19II/232
RH 19II/327

XXXX Pz.Korps
RH 24-40/69
RH 24-40/70
RH 24-40/97
RH 24-40/98
RH 24-40/99
RH 24-40/101
RH 24-40/175
RH 24-40/177
RH 24-40/178
RH 24-40/179

XXXXVII Pz.Korps
RH 24-47/98
RH 24-47/98
RH 24-47/99

A.O.K 2
RH 20-2/931
RH 20-2/932
RH 20-2/933
RH 20-2/934
RH 20-2/935
RH 20-2/936
RH 20-2/937
RH 20-2/938
RH 20-2/939
RH 20-2/940
RH 20-2/941
RH 20-2/942
RH 20-2/943
RH 20-2/944
RH 20-2/945
RH 20-2/946
RH 20-2/947
RH 20-2/988
RH 20-2/1582

A.O.K 4
RH-20-4/560
RH 20-4/561
RH 20-4/562
RH 20-4/563
RH 20-4/564
RH 20-4/570
RH 20-4/571

XVII A.K
RH 24-17/ 1.4.44–30.4.44 Ia KTB Nr 12
RH 24-17/ 1.4.44–20.4.44 Ia KTB Nr 12

A.O.K 9
RH 20-9/595 BVTO TB 20.7.44–31.12.44
RH 20-9/230 Ia Anl KTB Nr 11 Bd 23, 11.7.44–31.12.44
RH 20-9/231 Ia Anl KTB Nr 11 Bd 24, 11.7.44–31.12.44
RH 20-9/233 Ia Anl KTB Nr 11 Bd 26, 11.7.44–31.12.44

A.O.K 1
RH 20-1/116
RH 20-1/117
RH 20-1/118
RH 20-1/119
RH 20-1/137
RH 20-1/175
RH 20-1/231 TB OQu Nr 4
RH 20-1/232 TB OQu Nr 4 Bd 1

RH 20-1/233 TB OQu Nr 4 Bd 2
RH 20-1/234 TB OQu Nr IV, BVTO
RH 20-1/235 TB OQu Nr 4 Bd 3
RH 20-1/236 KTB OQu Nr 5
RH 20-1/237 KTB OQu NR 5 Bd 1
RH 20-1/238 KTB OQu Nr 5 Bd 2
RH 20-1/239 KTB OQu IV b, BVTO
RH 20-1/240 KTB OQu Nr 5 Bd 3
RH 20-1/241 KTB OQu TB
RH 20-1/242 TB OQu Bd 1
RH 20-1/243 TB OQu IVb
RH 20-1/244 OQu IVb
RH 20-1/245 OQu Bd 3

II-SS.Pz.Korps
RS2-2/3 KTB Nr 3 1.11.42-81.1.43
RS4-/1460. Nachschub.Tr II-SS.Pz.Korps

LXVI Res.Korps, September 1942
RH 24-66/2 Ia KTB 21.9.42-28.2.43
RH 24-66/3 Ia KTB 21.9.42-28.2.43

LXXXIII A.K
RH 24-83

A.O.K 15
RH 20-15/16 Ia KTB Nr 2
RH 20-15/17 Ia KTB Nr 2
RH 20-15/18 Ia KTB Nr 2
RH 20-15/19 Ia KTB Nr 2
RH 20-15/20 Ia KTB Nr 2
RH 20-15/21 Ia KTB Nr 2
RH 20-15/22 Ia KTB Nr 2
RH 20-15/23 Ia KTB Nr 2
RH 20-15/25 Ia KTB Nr 2
RH 20-15/39 Ia KTB Nr 3
RH 20-15/40 Ia KTB Nr 3
RH 20-15/41 Ia KTB Nr 3
RH 20-15/43 Ia KTB Nr 3
RH 20-15/44 Ia KTB Nr 3
RH 20-15/45 Ia KTB Nr 2
RH 20-15/46 Ia KTB Nr 2
RH 20-15/21 Ia KTB Nr 2 Bd 5
RH 20-15/106 OQu KTB
RH 20-15/108 OQu KTB
RH 20-15/109 OQu KTB
RH 20-15/110 OQu KTB
RH 20-15/111 OQu KTB
RH 20-15/112 OQu KTB
RH 20-15/113 OQu KTB
RH 20-15/114 OQu KTB
RH 20-15/146 OQu KTB
RH 20-15/147 OQu KTB
RH 20-15/151 OQu KTB
RH 20-15/167 OQu KTB
RH 20-15/168 OQu KTB

LXXX A.K October 1942-January 1943
RH 24-80/43 Ia KTB Nr 7 1.10.42–31.1.43
RH 24-80/44 Ia KTB Nr 7 1.10.42–31.1.43
RH 24-80/45 Ia KTB Nr 7 1.10.42–31.1.43
RH 24-80/46 Ia KTB Nr 7 1.10.42–31.1.43
RH 24-80/47 Ia KTB Nr 7 1.10.42–31.1.43
RH 24-80/48 Ia KTB Nr 7 1.10.42–31.1.43
RH 24-80/162 Ia KTB Nr 7 1.10.42–31.1.43

Pz.A.O.K 4
Armee Kraftfahr Offizier
RH 21-4/403 Abt V Kraftfahrwesen 1.1.43–23.3.43
RH 21-4/449 Abt V Kraftfahrwesen 15.4.43–30.6.43
RH 21-4/450 Abt V Kraftfahrwesen 1.7.43–31.12.43

RH2 Kartlage West, September 1942–January 1945
RH2-W/120-11.9.42
RH2-W/121-11.9.42
RH2-W/123-22.10.42
RH2-W/125-10.11.42
RH2-W/136-25.9.42
RH2-W/145-11.12.42
RH2-W/154-31.12.42
RH2-W/158-15.1.43

RH2 Kartlage Ost
RH2/5532- 3.3.43
RH2/5533- 4.3.43
RH2/5534- 5.3.43
RH2/5535- 6.3.43
RH2/5545- 4.4.43
RH2/5546- 5.4.43
RH2/5547- 6.4.43
RH2/5548- 7.4.43
RH2/5549- 8.4.43
RH2/5550- 9.4.43
RH2/5551- 10.4.43
RH2/5552- 11.4.43
RH2/5553- 12.4.43
RH2/5554- 13.4.43
RH2/5555- 14.4.43
RH2/5556- 15.4.43
RH2/5557- 1.6.43
RH2/5575- 2.6.43
RH2/5576- 3.6.43
RH2/5577- 4.6.43
RH2/5583- 27.6.43
RH2/5584- 28.6.43
RH2/5585- 29.6.43
RH2/5586- 30.6.43
RH2/5587- 1.7.43
RH2/5588- 2.7.43
RH2/5589- 3.7.43
RH2/5594- 8.7.43
RH2/5596- 10.7.43
RH2/5597- 11.7.43
RH2/5598- 12.7.43
RH2/5599- 13.7.43
RH2/5600- 14.7.43
RH2/5601- 15.7.43
RH2/5602- 16.7.43
RH2/5603- 17.7.43
RH2/5604- 18.7.43
RH2/5605- 19.7.43
RH2/5606- 20.7.43
RH2/5607- 21.7.43
RH2/5608- 22.7.43
RH2/5609- 23.7.43
RH2/5610- 24.7.43
RH2/5611- 25.7.43
RH2/5612- 26.7.43
RH2/5613- 27.7.43
RH2/5614- 28.7.43
RH2/5615- 29.7.43
RH2/5616- 30.7.43
RH2/5617- 31.7.43
RH2/5618- 1.8.43
RH2/5619- 2.8.43
RH2/5620- 3.8.43
RH2/5621- 4.8.43
RH2/5622- 5.8.43
RH2/5623- 6.8.43
RH2/5624- 7.8.43
RH2/5643- 26.8.43
RH2/5644- 27.8.43
RH2/5645- 28.8.43
RH2/5646- 29.8.43
RH2/5647- 30.8.43
RH2/5648- 31.8.43
RH2/5649- 1.9.43
RH2/5650- 2.9.43
RH2/5651- 3.9.43
RH2/5652- 4.9.43
RH2/5667- 19.9.43
RH2/5668- 20.9.43

RH2/5669- 21.9.43
RH2/5670- 22.9.43
RH2/5671- 23.9.43
RH2/5672- 24.9.43
RH2/5673- 25.9.43
RH2/5674 26.9.43
RH2/5675- 27.9.43
RH2/5676- 28.9.43
RH2/5677- 29.9.43
RH2/5678- 29.9.43
RH2/5679- 30.9.43
RH2/5681- 3.10.43
RH2/5682- 4.10.43
RH2/5683- 5.10.43
RH2/5684- 6.10.43
RH2/5685- 7.10.43
RH2/5686- 8.10.43
RH2/5687- 9.10.43
RH2/5688- 10.10.43
RH2/5689- 11.10.43
RH2/5690- 12.10.43
RH2/5691- 13.10.43
RH2/5692- 14.10.43
RH2/5693- 15.10.43
RH2/5695- 17.10.43
RH2/5696- 18.10.43
RH2/5697- 19.10.43
RH2/5698- 20.10.43
RH2/5699- 21.10.43
RH2/5700- 22.10.43
RH2/5701- 23.10.43
RH2/5702- 24.10.43
RH2/5703- 25.10.43
RH2/5704- 26.10.43
RH2/5705- 27.10.43
RH2/5706- 28.10.43
RH2/5707- 29.10.43
RH2/5708- 30.10.43
RH2/5709- 31.10.43
RH2/5710- 1.11.43
RH2/5711- 2.11.43
RH2/5712- 3.11.43
RH2/5713- 4.11.43
RH2/5714- 5.11.43
RH2/5715- 6.11.43
RH2/5716- 7.11.43
RH2/5717- 8.11.43
RH2/5718- 9.11.43
RH2/5719- 10.11.43
RH2/5728- 21.11.43
RH2/5729- 22.11.43
RH2/5730- 23.11.43
RH2/5731- 24.11.43
RH2/5732- 25.11.43
RH2/5743- 6.12.43
RH2/5744- 7.12.43
RH2/5745- 8.12.43
RH2/5746- 9.12.43
RH2/5747- 10.12.43
RH2/5748- 11.12.43
RH2/5749- 12.12.43
RH2/5750- 13.12.43
RH2/5751- 14.12.43
RH2/5752- 15.12.43
RH2/5755- 17.12.43
RH2/5756- 18.12.43
RH2/5757- 19.12.43
RH2/5758- 20.12.43
RH2/5760- 23.12.43
RH2/5761- 24.12.43
RH2/5762- 25.12.43
RH2/5763- 26.12.43
RH2/5764- 27.12.43
RH2/5765- 28.12.43
RH2/5768- 30.12.43
RH2/5831- 1.3.44
RH2/5835- 5.3.44
RH2/5853- 23.3.44
RH2/5856- 26.3.44
RH2/4837- 1.4.44
RH2/4840- 4.4.44
RH2/4842- 6.4.44
RH2/4843- 7.4.44
RH2/4844- 8.4.44
RH2/4845- 9.4.44
RH2/4846- 10.4.44
RH2/4853- 17.4.44
RH2/4854- 18.4.44
RH2/4855- 19.4.44
RH2/4856- 20.4.44
RH2/4858- 22.4.44
RH2/4867- 1.5.44
RH2/4868- 2.5.44
RH2/4869- 3.5.44
RH2/4872- 6.5.44
RH2/4873- 7.5.44
RH2/4874- 8.5.44
RH2/4875- 9.5.44
RH2/4876- 10.5.44
RH2/4887- 26.5.44
RH2/4897- 6.6.44
RH2/4898- 7.6.44
RH2/4899- 8.6.44
RH2/4900- 9.6.44
RH2/4901- 10.6.44
RH2/4802- 11.6.44
RH2/4907- 16.6.44
RH2/4908- 17.6.44
RH2/4909- 18.6.44
RH2/4910- 19.6.44
RH2/4911- 20.6.44
RH2/4912- 21.6.44
RH2/4913- 22.6.44
RH2/4914- 23.6.44
RH2/4915- 24.6.44
RH2/4916- 25.6.44
RH2/4917- 26.6.44
RH2/4918- 27.6.44
RH2/4919- 28.6.44
RH2/4920- 29.6.44
RH2/4921- 30.6.44
RH2/4922- 1.7.44
RH2/4923- 2.7.44
RH2/4924- 3.7.44
RH2/4925- 4.7.44
RH2/4926- 5.7.44
RH2/4927- 6.7.44
RH2/4928- 7.7.44
RH2/4929- 8.7.44
RH2/4930- 9.7.44
RH2/4931- 10.7.44
RH2/4932- 11.7.44
RH2/4933- 12.7.44
RH2/2739- 17.7.44
RH2/2740- 18.7.44
RH2/2741- 19.7.44
RH2/2742- 20.7.44
RH2/2743- 21.7.44
RH2/2744- 22.7.44
RH2/2745- 23.7.44
RH2/2746- 24.7.44
RH2/2747- 25.7.44
RH2/2748- 26.7.44
RH2/2749- 27.7.44
RH2/2750- 28.7.44
RH2/2751- 28.7.44
RH2/2752- 29.7.44
RH2/2753- 30.7.44
RH2/2754- 31.7.44
RH2/2755- 2.8.44
RH2/2771- 18.8.44
RH2/2785- 1.9.44
RH2/2787- 3.9.44
RH2/2805- 21.9.44
RH2/2807- 23.9.44
RH2/2815- 1.10.44
RH2/2820- 6.10.44
RH2/2823- 9.10.44
RH2/2837- 23.10.44
RH2/2846- 1.11.44
RH2/2853- 8.11.44
RH2/2870- 25.11.44
RH2/2872- 27.11.44
RH2/2876- 1.12.44
RH2/2877- 2.12.44

RH2/2878- 3.12.44
RH2/2879- 4.12.44
RH2/2880- 5.12.44
RH2/2881- 6.12.44
RH2/2882- 7.12.44
RH2/2883- 8.12.44
RH2/2884- 9.12.44
RH2/2886- 11.12.44
RH2/2902- 20.12.44
RH2/2904- 21.12.44
RH2/2907- 23.12.44
RH2/5263- 5.1.45
RH2/5257- 11.1.45
RH2/5280- 13.1.45
RH2/5298- 20.1.45
RH2/5316- 25.1.45
RH2/5336- 31.1.45
RH2/5339- 1.2.45
RH2/5349- 3.2.45
RH2/5355- 5.2.45
RH2/5367- 8.2.45
RH2/5385- 13.2.45
RH2/5312- 15.2.45
RH2/5391- 15.2.45
RH2/5403- 18.2.45
RH2/5408- 20.2.45
RH2/5421- 24.2.45
RH2/5423- 25.2.45
RH2/5433- 1.3.45
RH2/5435- 2.3.45
RH2/5448- 8.3.45
RH2/5455- 11.3.45
RH2/5457- 12.3.45
RH2/5473- 17.3.45
RH2/5486- 22.3.45
RH2/5491- 24.3.45
RH2/5519- 25.3.45
RH2/5508- 30.3.45
RH2/5512- 1.4.45
RH2/6909- 17.4.45

SS-FHA.Abt.Org 1942/1943 and OKH.Abt.Org 1942
NS 19-2569
NS 33-232
NS 33-233
H37- 83 Index 1, 2 and 3
H37-85 Index 1, 2 and 3
Private via email

SS-T Vermissten Bildliste DRK

A.O.K 8
KTB Nr 3, 1.3.44-31.3.44
KTB Nr 3, 1.4.44-30.4.44
KTB Nr 3, 1.5.44-31.5.44
KTB Nr 3, 1.6.44-30.6.44

NARA

A.O.K 8
T312-64
T312-65
T312-67
T312-68
T312-69
T312-70

A.O.K 4
T312-239
T312-243
T312-246
T312-247

A.O.K 2
T312-1316
T312-1317
T312-1318
T312-1319
T312-1324

A.O.K 9
T312-339
T312-343
T312-344
T312-345
T312-347
T312-348

Pz.A.O.K 4
T313-387
T313-390
T313-391

HGp Mitte
T311-216
T311-217
T311-218
T311-227
T311-228
T311-233

HGp Sud
T311-160
T311-161
T311-162
T311-163

II-SS.Pz.Korps
T354-605
T354-606
T354-607
T354-118
T354-119
T354-120

SS-FHA
T175-108
T175-109
T175-110
T175-111
T175-127
T175-140
T175-141
T175-174
T175-178
T175-179

Other microfilm used
T314-1495 LVII Pz.Korps QM records
T314-658, XX A.K
T314-659, XX A.K
T78-418, Gen.St.d.H/Org.Abt
T78-525
T78-719, Waffen-SS
T733-7, Waffen-SS Guide Roll
T78-622
T78-623
T78-624
T78-619
T77-1422

TsAMO, Russia

79th Guards Rifle Corps
49th Guards Rifle Corps
26 Guards Rifle Corps
25th Guards Rifle Division
94th Guards Rifle Division
110th Guards Rifle Division
1st Guards Airborne Division
9th Guards Army
6th Guards Army
6th Guards Tank Army
1st Guards Mechanised Corps
30th Guards Mechanised Corps
18th Guards Mechanised Corps
9th Guards Mechanised Corps
5th Guards Tank Corps
37th Guards Rifle Corps
38th Guards Rifle Corps
39th Guards Rifle Corps
18th Tank Corps

23rd Tank Corps
100th Guards Rifle Division
103 Guards Rifle Division
104th Guards Rifle Division
105th Guards Rifle Division
107th Guards Rifle Division
113th Rifle Division
114th Rifle Division
98th Guards Rifle Division
99th Guards Rifle Division
252nd Rifle Division
63rd Cavalry Division
12th Cavalry Division
220th Cavalry Division
47th Cavalry Regiment
1st Guards Mechanised Brigade
2nd Guards Mechanised Brigade
3rd Guards Mechanised Brigade
54th Guards Artillery Brigade
90th Guards Cannon Brigade
170th Tank Brigade
20th Tank Brigade
22nd Tank Brigade
46th Guards Tank Brigade
18th Guards Mechanised Brigade
30th Guards Mechanised Brigade
31st Guards Mechanised Brigade
18th Guards Tank Regiment
33rd Guards Tank Regiment
83rd Guards Tank Regiment
85th Guards Tank Regiment
62nd Guards Heavy Tank Regiment (with JS-2)
484TH Artillery Anti-Tank regiment
1438th Self Propelled Artillery regiment
382nd Self Propelled Artillery regiment
49th Artillery Anti-Tank Brigade
1008th Artillery Anti-Tank Regiment
1249th Artillery Anti-tank Regiment
9th Guards Tank Brigade
74th Guards Artillery Anti-Tank Regiment
300th Guards Rifle Regiment
302nd Guards Rifle Regiment
317th Guards Rifle Regiment
322nd Guards Rifle Regiment
324th Guards Rifle Regiment
328th Guards Rifle Regiment
332nd Guards Rifle Regiment
296th Guards Rifle Regiment
297th Guards Rifle Regiment
299th Guards Rifle Regiment
346th Guards Rifle Regiment
172nd Guards Motor Regiment
106th Guards Motorised Rifle Battalion
3rd Guards Motorised Rifle Battalion
17th Air Army
10th Air Assault Corps
47th Army
2nd Guards Cavalry Corps
11th Tank Corps
77th Rifle Corps
125th Rifle Corps
60th Rifle Division
306th Air Assault Division
912th Self Propelled Artillery Regiment (with SU-100)
1523 and 1513 Self Propelled Artillery Regiments (with SU-76)
Site visits

Hungary 2011
Magyaralmas
Sored
Bodajk
Csilaki Psz
Szekesfehervar
Szomor
Dunaalmas
Zsambek
Many
Neszmely
Bajot
Gyermely
Kapolsnasnyek
Pettend
Baracska
Gardony
Agard
Dinnyes
Szabadbattyn
Falubattyan

Austria, C/O Dietrich Wolf, Markus Reisner and Hr Kalt the local historian for Krems.

LanzenKirchen
Ofenbach
Krems an der Donau
Nohagen
Stratzing
Rehberg
Senftenberg
Wienzierl an Walde
Gfohl
Jaidhof
Langenlois

Photographs

All photographs courtesy of the following archives and institutions unless stated otherwise:

Wolfgang Barth
Ruediger Warnick
Stephan Cazenave
ASKM
TsAMO
Jon Koser
Paul Turner
Leopold Hollwirth (Pregarten)
Fr Margarette Pfahnl (Pregarten)

ACKNOWLEDGMENTS

This book came about after an introduction to Wolfgang Barth and the surviving veterans of *9. Kompanie/SS-Panzer-Regiment 3*. Before the current work came into being, I had decided to write a book covering the operational life of *IV. SS-Panzer-Korps*. This very quickly became a very lengthy process as I tried to find research material on the *3. SS-Panzer-Division Totenkopf*.

After eight years, I had amassed a great deal of material covering the tank regiment and *9. Kompanie*. Herr Barth allowed me the use of his personal collection of photographs, and I was fortunate enough to have the assistance of three fellow researchers Dietrich Wolf and Markus Reisner in Austria and Rüdiger Warnick in Germany. Dietrich Wolf drove all over the countryside north of Krems an der Donau and interviewed one of the last surviving company commanders. Dietrich was able to locate and photgraph the last wreck sites of the *Tigers* from *9. Kompanie*. Markus Reisner kindly provided me with his own research notes on the fighting around Ofenbach–Lanzen Kirchen and took photographs of the of the site where a *Tiger I* was abandoned on 1 April 1945. Rüdiger Warnick took time out from his busy schedule to interview the last veterans of *9. Kompanie* during the latter half of 2011 and the early part of 2013.

I would like to thank especially Kamen Nevenkin, who put me in contact with Mike Olive, who agreed to take on the project on behalf of Stackpole Books. Kamen also provided the necessary guidance and knowledge when it came to searching Russian archives and contacting private archives in Moscow. I also owe much to Oliver van Hettinga, who managed to find out that *Totenkopf* veterans still meet every year.

I would also like to thank the following: Mirko Bayerl (Sweden), Stephan Cazenave (France), Robert Wroblewski (Poland), Wojciech Grzegorz Stanczyk (Poland), Sebastian Remus (Germany), Otto Josza (Hungary), Sigrid Kleinschmidt (Germany), Peit Duits (Holland), Charles Trang (France), Hans Weber (Switzerland), Jeff Dugdale (United Kingdom), Jon Koser (United Kingdom), Paul Turner (United Kingdom), Herr Kalt (Krems), Herr Hollwirth (Austria), Margarette Pfahnl (Austria), Simon Vosters (Belgium), Frau Ebeling, widow of Kurt Ebeling (Germany), Kuno Ther (former *9. Kompanie* commander), Ludwig Buss (*9. Kompanie*), and Erich Lehmkuhl (*9. Kompanie*).

All interviews with former veterans were conducted between September 2011 and March 2013. Unfortunately, Gustav Krippl died before an introduction could be made; he died in late 2011.